U.S. NATIONAL
SECURITY

Selected Titles in ABC-CLIO's
CONTEMPORARY
WORLD ISSUES
Series

For a complete list of titles in this series, please visit
www.abc-clio.com.

Books in the Contemporary World Issues series address vital issues in today's society such as genetic engineering, pollution, and biodiversity. Written by professional writers, scholars, and nonacademic experts, these books are authoritative, clearly written, up-to-date, and objective. They provide a good starting point for research by high school and college students, scholars, and general readers as well as by legislators, businesspeople, activists, and others.

Each book, carefully organized and easy to use, contains an overview of the subject, a detailed chronology, biographical sketches, facts and data and/or documents and other primary-source material, a directory of organizations and agencies, annotated lists of print and nonprint resources, and an index.

Readers of books in the Contemporary World Issues series will find the information they need in order to have a better understanding of the social, political, environmental, and economic issues facing the world today.

U.S. NATIONAL SECURITY

A Reference Handbook,
Second Edition

Cynthia A. Watson

**CONTEMPORARY
WORLD ISSUES**

A B C CLIO

Santa Barbara, California
Denver, Colorado
Oxford, England

Library of Congress Cataloging-in-Publication Data
Watson, Cynthia Ann.
    U.S. national security : a reference handbook / Cynthia A. Watson.
        p. cm. — (Contemporary world issues)
    Includes bibliographical references and index.
    ISBN 978-1-59884-041-4 (hard copy : alk. paper)—
    ISBN 978-1-59884-042-1 (ebook)
    1. National security—United States.   2. United States—Military
    policy.   3. World politics—1945–   4. United States—Foreign
    relations—1945–1989. 5. United States—Foreign relations—1989–
    I. Title.
    UA23.W36397 2008
    355'.033073—dc22

13   12   11   10   09   08   1   2   3   4   5   6   7   8   9   10

ABC-CLIO, Inc.
130 Cremona Drive, P.O. Box 1911
Santa Barbara, California 93116-1911

This book is also available on the World Wide Web as an ebook. Visit
www.abc-clio.com for details.

This book is printed on acid-free paper ∞

Manufactured in the United States of America

*To the most famous carpool (inaugurated in 1992) ever at the National
War College, the members of which honored me with their teaching
about national security and much else:*

*Colonel Jim "Jimmy" Dixon, USAR and the Defense Intelligence
Agency (retired)*

Colonel John "Cipster" Cipparone, USMC (retired)

Captain/Dr. Bud Cole, USN

Vice Admiral Tom Kilcline, USN

Captain Bill "Wild Man" Tyson, USN (retired)

Colonel/Dr. Roy Stafford, USAF

Captain George Murphy, USN (retired)

Colonel Mark Pizzo, USMC (retired)

Contents

Preface

I greatly appreciate the opportunity to update the 2001 edition of this book. Encouraging public debate about national security *because it is our security* is my goal because I would like to see people understand what their government is asking them to do if they send daughters and sons overseas to fight for us. I have been lucky enough to be a student of national security for most of my life, looking at the field from various angles. I readily acknowledge that I do not have all of the right answers; I don't think in terms of "right" or "wrong" answers. But I desperately want my fellow citizens to understand that each answer has consequences (some intended, others completely unintended) with which all of us will live. I write about national security because I want people to think about whether they are willing to bear the burden or pay the price of those consequences. While I believe I have the most interesting job in the world, no one should ever confuse enthusiasm on the part of those involved in national security to grasp our work with a desire to go to war; they are not the same thing. No one understands the costs of war better than those who wage it; make no mistake.

Mim Vasan has privileged me as my friend and editor for more than two decades. Dayle Dermatis is patient and gently encouraging. Both were exceedingly frustrated with my unorthodox approach to writing this volume, but I believe we have managed to produce an excellent understanding of national security, keeping our eyes on the prize. Cami Cacciatore was a sensational editor. The staff at ABC-CLIO, no matter what role, is incredibly helpful. I thank each and every one of them.

Bonnie and Scott Nordstrom are the two most patient, supportive children in the world. In our few hours together weekly, they ask wonderful questions and are tolerant of my disappearances into the study to type. Thank you.

My colleagues at the National War College are simply the best, professionals and friends, past and present. Our new commandant, Major General (Promotable) Robert Steel, USAF, shows enthusiasm about our work, which makes it a grand place to work. The commandant who served while I wrote most of this volume, Major General Marné Peterson, USAF (ret.), brought us a freshness and class that made one want to come in the doors of Roosevelt Hall daily. Susan Sherwood is a dear friend and valued colleague. Captain Steve Camacho, USN, has reminded me about priorities: I hope I continue to listen to his wise suggestions. I dread the day that Dr. Roy Stafford finally retires because his counsel and his commitment to what we do have been so valuable over the past fifteen years. Additionally, Roy was generous to read this volume and offer substantive comments, which I hope to have adequately incorporated, as did Dr. Alan Gropman of our sister institution, the Industrial College of the Armed Forces. Dr. Paul Godwin invariably finds a way to ask a superb question that makes me rethink. Ms. Lisa Bronson's enthusiasm and commitment to our curriculum has reinvigorated me and others, while bringing a crispness to what we do. While that does not sound important to outsiders, the need to infuse new techniques and excitement into the teaching of what can be deadly serious discussion is a key to keeping us going. Retired Colonel Mark Pizzo, USMC, does his best to make life so much easier. Dr. Bud Cole is my best friend and I cherish that. His support, encouragement, and gentle redirection at times keep me going.

The views expressed in this book are my own, not those of the U.S. government or the National War College. Any mistakes are mine alone.

1

Background and History

The concept of national security changed dramatically for some analysts on the morning of September 11, 2001. Others believe the disaster that occurred that morning was a manifestation of the national security concerns that have faced the country for all of its history. Some saw September 11 as merely one more form of threat against the nation, while many others thought it was an existential threat to the fabric of the United States. These different viewpoints within the community of analysts and practitioners reflect the difficulty of achieving consensus in how to approach the issue of national security. For the George W. Bush administration, there is no question that the events of that day were an end to complacency and the beginning of a sense of mission that outweighs all other priorities.

The purpose of this volume is to discuss the field of national security to help society consider its options. National security, although it is practiced by professional military men and women and ordered by civilian politicians, is in the end a public policy decision for the entire nation, not merely for the professional community. Increasingly, national security requires civilian professionals, the government, and the private sector to cooperate with, support, and often supplant the traditional military instrument of war in the United States.

September 11 may be too close an event for us to take stock of its true nature because we were largely participants, albeit mostly from afar. But the power of the images and the magnitude of the shock may have paralyzed our ability to grasp the nature of the threat.

National security is a fundamental responsibility of any government. Without security, people cannot trust their government or their neighbors, nor can they focus on loftier goals because they are worried about their ability to provide for their families or to prepare adequately for the future. Without basic security, people operate in a highly volatile environment that does not support traditional functioning in a society and leads to severe mistrust of all institutions and individuals in a position of power. Many societies around the world confront this daily challenge in trying to provide the most fundamental elements of security in their citizens' lives daily; Iraq and Colombia come to mind immediately as states where the struggle goes on, while Somalia seems a place where everyone has given up.

This basic reality of the desire for sanctuary proved true on September 11 when millions in the United States waited in confusion for definitive information on the number and locations of the attacks against the nation; it also proved true for hundreds of thousands living along the Gulf Coast in August 2005 where a natural element—water—terrorized them equally as they sought to understand why help did not appear on the horizon in a relatively short time. An inability to provide the basic human sense of safety characterizes both examples and illustrates why national security is a difficult concept for many of us to agree upon today, indeed throughout the period since the Berlin Wall fell in 1989, heralding the end of the Cold War.

The United States has always literally had a unique position in the world because of the two massive oceans on the East and West coasts, along with two relatively benign neighbors in Canada and Mexico. Before World War II, U.S. interventions did occur, largely around the Caribbean Basin. The United States intervened ostensibly for national security reasons, but often in fact to promote the national expansion known as Manifest Destiny or the Monroe Doctrine.

World War I was a relatively novel experience for the nation—deploying U.S. forces in a ground war far away from the nation's heartland. The United States Navy had operated in far seas since the founding of the republic, but the nation had prided itself on not intervening overseas—just as President George Washington had advised at the end of the eighteenth century: "[S]o likewise, a passionate attachment of one nation for another produces a variety of evils . . . [T]he great rule of conduct for us, in regard to foreign nations, is, in extending our commercial relations, is to have with them as little political connexion [sic] as possible" (Washington 1796). During World War II, there were some critics of the war effort, such as Jeannette Rankin of Wyoming (she voted against both world wars), but most citizens embraced the war effort after the shock of the Japanese attack at Pearl Harbor on December 7, 1941. That "bolt from the blue" attack colored U.S. concerns from World War II to the Cold War that followed.

The U.S. response to the international community during the Cold War is arguably an aberration in U.S. history. The Soviet Union (as it was known) had the capability to physically end the United States and the United States had the capability to do the same to the Soviet Union. The armed forces were the buttress against that happening, but these men and women were playing a different role, in some ways, than ever before. For the overwhelming majority of the nation's experience, the military had remained small and the general population demilitarized. The exceptions were nation-building efforts in the West or when the navy was used to protect U.S. assets abroad, such as the shipping trade with Europe. In the Cold War era (1947–1989), however, the United States maintained a large standing military that was frequently deployed well beyond U.S. shores to help "contain" a Soviet threat against the world. Spending on defense and security was virtually unchallenged because the stakes were so high. While many debates remain about what actually led to the Soviet demise, the deployment of U.S. military forces abroad in significant numbers with high-technology armaments and the possibility of a nuclear conflict between the two states certainly provided some measure of a deterrent.

With the end of the Soviet empire, the United States seemed to be entering a period of ensured safety, thus considerably less financial commitment to national security would be required. Early in 1990, Congress and the executive branch debated the range of possible uses for the anticipated "peace dividend" that would result from the lack of a threat against the nation because national security would no longer be focused exclusively on the Soviet-based problem, which was in the process of disappearing.

Instead, the August 1990 invasion of Kuwait by Iraqi dictator Saddam Hussein, and the subsequent buildup and use of a multinational coalition force in operations Desert Shield and Desert Storm, indicated that peace might not be exactly at hand. The Iraq problem coincided with a greater series of requests by the United Nations, under Secretary General Boutros Boutros-Ghali, for international peacekeepers under the Agenda for Peace, a program to encourage preventive actions to keep conflicts within states from becoming civil wars. The 1990s became a series of actions by the international community to end domestic traumas in Somalia, Bosnia and Herzegovina, Kosovo, Liberia, and East Timor, althouh these did not represent the globalized thermo-nuclear war many feared during the Cold War. At the dawn of the new millennium, many experts concluded that the post–Cold War era would be characterized by a series of smaller, manageable problems probably best handled not by traditional combat forces but by the nation builders who could help create institutions.

The Effects of Jihadists

The shock of the September 11 attacks was a wake-up call paralleled only by the Pearl Harbor attack. The nation had shared a history of relative peace and security with Mexico to the south and Canada to the north. Terrorism did not seem to happen here, although the April 1996 bombing of the Alfred P. Murrah Federal Building in Oklahoma City had partially washed away that belief. The attack by jihadists or al Qaeda or Osama bin Laden himself showed that the world was indeed more interconnected by technology and by hatred than had been understood before.

Along with a fear that we are no longer absolutely safe from terrorists on our shores or nature altering our safety, over the past several years the United States has found that superpower status is not a guarantee of any ability to rebuild the world in a manner that supports our view of how to provide national security. By any empirical measure, the United States had the military prowess to defeat the Taliban regime in Afghanistan and the brutal dictatorship of Saddam Hussein in Iraq. Yet the hard lesson that empirical might does not guarantee the ultimate, quick victory over a system opposing our will has been and continues to be a painful one. As long as we believe the international system must align with our analysis of the requirements for a nonthreatening world, this frustrating state of affairs seems irreversible.

What Does National Security Mean?

How do we generally define national security? The nation has long had a national security strategy, developed by various parts of the government security community. The most recent one appeared in March 2006 (U.S. GPO 2006). The introduction by President George W. Bush does not define the concept but notes that it relies on two pillars: "promoting freedom, justice, and human dignity" and "confronting the challenges of our time by leading a growing community of democracies."

Various organizations, many of which are discussed elsewhere in this book, have a focus on national security, even if that focus is not reflected in their titles. However, each group has a definition of national security that is specific to the group and its goals.

Former Secretary of Defense Harold Brown's definition of national security seems most basic: "National security, then, is the ability to preserve the nation's physical integrity and territory; to maintain its economic relations with the rest of the world on reasonable terms; to protect its nature, institutions, and governance from disruption from outside; and to control its borders" (Brown 1983, 4).

National security today, in the George W. Bush period, is no longer concerned with defending national borders alone. National security includes protecting U.S. citizens abroad, guaranteeing access to the assets we need to maintain our standard of living, and protecting the type of government we find important to sustaining the nations with which we interact in the world. This is a dramatic shift from the views long held by many in the United States who might have preferred democratic governance but deferred to the will of the peoples of other states. If asked in an essay exam to define national security, the answers of President George W. Bush's administration would be significantly different and broader in scope than those of the Coolidge or either of the Harrison administrations. This is not to say that President Bush is wrong, nor is he entirely unique; President Harry S. Truman's decisions in the late 1940s similarly upset a number of citizens who believed national security required only protecting the property and limb of citizens of the United States. But President Bush's decision to enforce democratic governance *is* a shift from the self-determination so long advocated by the United States.

National Security Encompasses New Issues

The number of issues and concepts included in national security have increased. Since the Cold War ended, national security increasingly has an economic and environmental, even informational, component instead of merely defining our borders.

During the Cold War, the fear of a physical attack on the United States with nuclear weapons was overwhelming. In the 1980s, as reports began to circulate about parents beginning to doubt whether their children would have a better lifestyle than they had, questions of economic security began to surface. The petroleum embargo and attendant gas price increases of the 1970s were thought an aberration in our national security. The effects, until the twenty-first century, appeared an anomaly on the screen and disappeared not long after they appeared. However, the flight of steel and auto manufacturing jobs from the massive factories of the Midwest to Japan and Korea, the "Asian Tigers," illustrated a vulnerability that had never been recognized before. In the 1990s, economic security assumed a position comparable to political and military security.

Similarly, environmental concerns arose in the 1990s and accelerated in the following decade. Worries had earlier focused on problems such as the desertification of northern Africa or the disappearance of the Aral Sea in central Asia, but those problems were "over there," far away from the continental United States. Concern over the growth of environmental pollution in the northeast United States was joined by concern over water shortages in the West, as year after year of drought in northern California or the Pacific Northwest seemed to spawn more damaging fires that got closer to expensive neighborhoods. The 2005 catastrophe resulting from Hurricane Katrina in New Orleans and the Gulf Coast region, however, proved that nature could still throw a major city into prolonged chaos—with profound national security implications.

Fears of a growing plague or medical disaster also raised questions of security. In 2003, severe acute respiratory syndrome (SARS) caused no direct deaths in the United States but alerted the population to the real issues that a global pandemic would cause. National security concern revolved around the inevitability of a global pandemic, possibly avian flu. Scenarios considered up to 62 million deaths worldwide and quarantine of the United States should it become necessary. This abstract medical concern adds a dramatically different view of national security than was true a decade or century ago.

These new fears raise interesting questions of whether international communications and transportation, that is, globalization, caused the national security definitions to change or whether they are simply making us aware of a vulnerability that has always been there. One of the ways this globalization has occurred is through growing access to the Internet and the information the World Wide Web provides. Many of us simply take the access to information for granted, a necessity for commerce and a luxury for day-to-day activities, but others fear its infiltration by outsiders, such as Chinese or Russian hackers, or its generalized use by Islamists seeking to galvanize international jihad.

A mere generation ago, these additional definitions of national security would have seemed ludicrous because the intensity of a single threat—Soviet nuclear-carrying missiles—overwhelmed the sense that anything else could overcome us.

The U.S. Experience since the September 11 Attacks

The Preemption versus Prevention Debate

The debate about the nature of the post-9/11 world includes more than merely a broader definition of national security. Today, the president has defined national security in a broader way that includes the responsibility to prevent attacks on the United States. While this has a certain common-sense appeal, the controversy surrounding the commander-in-chief's 2002 speech enunciating this policy at the U.S. Military Academy at West Point still elicits comments and questions from our friends and foes abroad. President Bush's argument that "For much of the last century, America's defense relied on the Cold War doctrines of deterrence and containment. In some cases, those strategies still apply . . . If we wait for threats to fully materialize, we have waited too long" concerned many who feared the United States would engage in preemption and preventative war instead of traditional defensive actions. As the most powerful military on the planet, the U.S. armed forces' ability to exercise such preventative steps is worrisome to many who fear it will be used too easily without adequate proof of a serious threat. Debate continues as to whether President Bush has expanded the definition of what a defense of the nation would entail or whether, as many of his supporters believe, his policy is merely continuing the long-existent defense of the nation required by the U.S. Constitution.

Iraq and Afghanistan: Superpowers Sometimes Don't Find it Easy

Within less than four weeks after the 2001 terrorist attacks, the United States launched a major attack against the Taliban-led government of Afghanistan, which Washington believed was providing safe haven to al Qaeda mastermind Osama bin Laden. The action was swift and decisive, and the Taliban fled Kabul within a few weeks. The United States helped broker a government, which ultimately led to an Afghani named Hamid Karzai becoming interim president and later elected president of Afghanistan. Karzai had been educated in the United States and was a long-time resident.

In late 2001 and early 2002, U.S. forces launched a massive attack on the southeastern mountains along the Pakistani border, known as the Tora Bora. Bin Laden successfully eluded the massive operation and remains at large as of 2007. Similarly, the Taliban melted into the mountains of Tora Bora and into northwestern Pakistan. Some six years later, the Taliban has proven not finished.

President George W. Bush began contemplating the removal of Iraqi dictator Saddam Hussein as early as 2001 in the days after the September 11 attacks. Many accounts indicate that some of the president's top advisers feared that Saddam had to be linked to the attacks. A number of books, including Ron Suskind's book on Paul O'Neill (2003), Michael Gordon and Bernard Trainor's *Cobra II* (2006), and Tom Ricks' *Fiasco* (2006), have discussed the doubts, fears, and concerns about this view. President Bush's national security advisers largely argued, once the momentum developed for the attack to progress, that invading Iraq would not only be necessary to prevent a devastating attack with weapons of mass destruction upon the U.S. homeland but it would also be a relatively easy task in which Iraqis would welcome the U.S. forces as liberators.

The invasion began on March 20, 2003, and by April 9, U.S. troops were helping the Iraqis topple Saddam's statue. Indeed, the ground invasion proved relatively simple and moved with staggering speed as one would anticipate for a military superpower engaging a repressed, broken armed force that had been deprived since the international community began a serious embargo against Saddam's regime after the 1990–1991 Gulf War. On May 1, 2003, President George W. Bush made an appearance on the flight deck of the USS *Abraham Lincoln*, in front of a banner saying "Mission Accomplished," to announce that "major combat operations" were concluded. When the president made that speech, it did indeed appear that the United States and its allies had crushed Saddam's government with only minimal effort and few casualties: 139 U.S. forces by that date. Five years later, the situation appears somewhat less rosy.

Instead, both Afghanistan and Iraq, weakened by divisions and isolation, have proven extremely difficult challenges for the United States because they have evolved into longer, less-decisive, or clear-cut conflicts than originally believed. Conditions in Iraq have deteriorated dramatically since 2003, whether measured by political violence against the United States, common crime, sectarian violence, provision of such basic needs as electricity, and myriad other possible measures of success. In Afghanistan, the initial gains stalled and appear to have reversed as the Taliban attempts to reinstitute its power over portions of the country. By the end of July 2007, the United States saw the deaths of its armed forces in operations ENDURING FREEDOM and IRAQI FREEDOM go beyond the 4,000 milestone and casualties from improvised explosive devices detonated at roadsides have skyrocketed as medical care keeps people alive yet badly wounded. Iraqi casualties have been at least in the tens of thousands if not hundreds of thousands. As the conditions have led President Bush to move toward deploying a higher number of troops in Iraq, conditions for those Iraqis outside the diplomatic "Green Zone" have become significantly less tenable.

In Afghanistan, the apparent success of the 2001 invasion has also been called into question. In 2003, U.S. forces turned over the international security task in the mountainous country to the North Atlantic Treaty Organization (NATO), and Afghanistan became its first "out of area" (non-European) mission. Gradually, Taliban attacks have picked up in a country where the regional tensions remain exceedingly high. Attacks on government officials outside the capital have increased, and many question whether President Karzai actually controls anything outside his palace. The United States quietly moved to reinforce its portion of the NATO force in 2006.

The question for the United States from both of these conflicts has been why the United States has been unable to tame both adversaries. Neither the insurgents nor sectarian groups in Iraq match the resources or power of the U.S. military. Neither the

Afghani warlords nor al Qaeda has anywhere near the prowess of the United States or the NATO members seeking to help Afghanistan develop a democracy.

These situations illustrate that superpower status does not guarantee success in resolving conflicts or achieving global transformation. Indeed, perhaps the most apparent effect of six years' struggle in Afghanistan and five years' struggle in Iraq is that military superiority does not guarantee rapid, strategic victory. Fundamental, systemic transformation requires a sustained commitment to changes at all levels of the society with a mind to including all elements of that population.

Will Crafting Countries as Democracies Protect U.S. Security?

Over the months after Saddam Hussein's removal from office in Baghdad, U.S. goals there changed. The highly feared weapons of mass destruction that were thought to be in Iraqi hands never materialized. The devastation caused to Iraq by the more than ten years of sanctions imposed by the international community had left the country broken.

The U.S. concerns in Iraq and elsewhere around the world gradually began to address this phenomenon by pushing the quality of governance in all regimes. While the United States has always supported democracy as the most representative, equitable form of government, no administration in Washington has ever pushed for democracies as overtly and consciously as has that of President George W. Bush. This orientation often reminds many of the administration's close ties with the "neoconservatives" who have been so supportive of his move to oust Saddam Hussein. Former Vice President Dan Quayle's chief of staff, William Kristol, and Carnegie Endowment for International Peace scholar Robert Kagan have been aggressively arguing for the establishment of democratic governments around the world to promote the values so woven into the fabric of the U.S. political system. These analysts praise the unique qualities of the U.S. political system, arguing that these qualities allow the United States to promote democracy in a manner no other state could and with important effects for the world.

Even more importantly to many, former Deputy Secretary of Defense Paul D. Wolfowitz, seen by many as the prime architect of the war in Iraq, advocated rebuilding the states of the world in a democratic format, starting with Afghanistan and Iraq. Wolfowitz argued that people living under repressive regimes will welcome the opportunity to exercise their true desires in free societies. Wolfowitz illustrated his views when testifying before the Congress shortly before the ground invasion of Iraq: He scoffed at Army Chief of Staff Eric Shinseki's opinion that his service would require "several hundred thousand" troops in Iraq after the initial invasion. Much as Vice President Dick Cheney did, Wolfowitz dismissed Shinseki's estimates by arguing that Iraqis would welcome the U.S. forces. Yet virtually no one from the armed forces stood up to challenge the appraisals until well into the conflict, when a number of retired officers cast aspersions on the war effort in April 2006. In retrospect, strategists planning the war seemed to violate the first principle of good strategic analysis: question and requestion one's assumptions about any set of circumstances.

Reconstructing a political system is a daunting task. There is little evidence of success in rebuilding and reorienting a country like Iraq, which has serious geographic/ethnic/sectarian divides, or Somalia or Afghanistan, which have divides based on tribal distinctions. Yet President Bush made clear, through his own speeches and those of his senior administration officials, the need to do just that. The United States began subtly and not so subtly nudging states in the Middle East, among other places, to take a much more democratic path, allowing citizens to reach their fundamental goals as citizens. In many cases, particularly in the Middle East, these admonitions were greeted with skepticism on the part of long-standing rulers who were there because of their firm hands over the reins of power.

The United States also learned in Afghanistan and Iraq that institutionalizing democracy requires more than holding elections. Both of these societies in transition held elections, only to find that the citizenry either ignored the results or put more stock on tribal or religious connections than popularly voted support. In Iraq, the hopes that elections would lower or erase violence were dashed repeatedly when violence not only returned after brief respites but usually accelerated as if to signal a refusal on the part of whole sectors of the Iraqi polity to participate in this democratic experiment. In the years since the Taliban was removed from power, the circle of democratic governments in Afghanistan seems to contract over time rather than resulting in the hoped-for expansion across the mountainous country.

Many around the world, including those in states already fully ensconced in the democratic camp, believe this brazen intervention in states' fully sovereign decision making is antithetical to all the United States has historically held dear. Additionally, states with a hypersensitivity to sovereignty, such as China, believe the interventions in Kosovo and then in Iraq over the past decade violate the basic norms of statehood in the international system, harkening back to a period when the powerful states of the nineteenth century colonized and humiliated weaker states such as China.

While President Bush and his government talk less about this goal than they did for the first three years of the war in Iraq, it would appear the president's firm commitment to spreading democracy has not changed. The president's March 2007 trip through Latin America, where he praised those regimes that have taken steps to address their community needs versus those such as Venezuela's where popular dictates are ignored for the sake of the leadership, illustrates this point, as do trips by the secretaries of state and defense to allies and emerging states around the world.

The Changing National Security Community

Governments, like the populations they govern and represent, are dynamic and ever-changing organizations. Even without the horror of the September 11 attacks, the U.S. government evolves on a continuing basis. The experience of the 2001 attacks, however, has generated several blue-ribbon assessments and countless reappraisals within the government, including the Kean-Hamilton 9/11 Commission, in which a plethora of former government officials held extensive hearings to consider what had gone wrong to allow the attacks. The 9/11 Commission, as it has largely become known, is still working to get its recommendations accepted by the whole U.S. government (Roemer 2007; National Commission 2004). When the congressinally mandated Iraq Study Group released its findings in late 2006 (Baker and Hamilton 2006), many of its recommendations incorporated findings of previous studies that had been rejected as unnecessary or unworkable. In the intervening months, the Bush administration, to its credit, has reached out to many of those it had previously rejected in looking for an improved strategy.

The Legislative Institutions

For those who lived through the final decade of the twentieth century and first decade of the twenty-first, the memory of bipartisanship across the two houses of Congress in the hours and days immediately after the September 11 attacks was utterly remarkable. Washington has been a highly politicized place throughout its history but especially in the years of the administrations of Bill Clinton and George W. Bush. Congressional leaders as diverse in their beliefs as Barbara Boxer or Nancy Pelosi, both California Democrats, singing patriotic songs with House Speaker Dennis Hastert, the Illinois Republican, and Republican Senator Orin Hatch of Utah was a sight few anticipated ever seeing after the passionate meltdown of the Clinton impeachment of 1998 or the rhetoric on tax relief in early 2001.

The bipartisanship did not endure, however, and both houses returned to their respective party balances soon after the September 11 attacks. Both the House of Representatives and the Senate supported the president in his efforts to raise the standards of protecting the country, but partisan divisions were clearly seen. In general, Congress not only sought to fund the president's requests for national security projects but often increased the funding further. While the 106th through 109th congresses will carry a reputation of significant pork barrel spending through history, most of the additional funding these congresses offered was to help the troops.

President Bush won reelection in 2004 with national security as his basic platform. He argued successfully that the Republican White House and Congress had shown their willingness to protect the nation better than the Democratic opposition since 9/11 and would continue to do so in the future. The Republican-led Congress continued to support national security funding at high levels but grew increasingly concerned as war efforts floundered in Iraq and Afghanistan between 2003 and 2006.

The same campaign strategy did not work in the 2006 midterm elections when the Republicans lost their majorities in both chambers. The Democratic politicians capitalized on growing apprehension across the nation that progress was not occurring, especially in Iraq, as the number of deaths in the conflict escalated and overall instability in Baghdad appeared daily on the television screens across the country. In particular, many people cited the president's seeming lack of understanding that the deteriorating conditions in Iraq that were shown on television directly contradicted his optimism and constant proclamation that things were improving in Iraq. Similarly, public concerns about Secretary of Defense Donald Rumsfeld's running of the war led many voters to believe the United States was blindly committing young men and women to die in a seemingly rudderless war.

The 110th Congress, which is under Democratic leadership, appears extremely likely to continue many oversight hearings. Immediately upon assuming their majority on January 4, 2007, Democratic House Speaker Nancy Pelosi and Senate Majority Leader Harry Reid sent a joint letter to President Bush strongly encouraging him to begin the withdrawal of U.S. forces from Iraq, condemning the widely anticipated announcement that the president intended to send another 30,000 troops to the theater in an effort to "surge" forces to stabilize the violence of Baghdad itself (Baker and Wright 2007). Pelosi and Reid, along with Republican colleagues in both chambers, indicated serious concerns about the surge strategy yet, when asked whether Senator Reid anticipated that Congress would use its constitutional power of the purse, granted in Article 1, Section 8, to stop the U.S. involvement in Iraq, Reid responded that the U.S. Congress would never hurt the troops by cutting their funds but would like to send a message to the president about the limits on his authority.

Beyond Iraq: National Security across the Horizon

While a wry joke that appears regularly in Washington is that national security consists of three words today, "Iraq, Iraq, Iraq," the national concerns of the United States are considerably broader than this Middle Eastern country. Iraq is an important state at the crossroads of an important region of the world. The impact of the "surge" in U.S. troops, begun in January 2007, remains open to interpretation with President Bush retaining optimism about its ultimate success. But the future of a Middle East state still appears daunting because of the sectarian divisions confronting the Iraqi people. The violence that the surge aimed to address has shifted to other parts of the country while analyses differ on whether the violence has declined; but the political problems confronting the Shiite government remain bitter and seemingly intractable.

The United States also worries about the stability of some of its closest allies: Pakistan, Egypt, and the Kingdom of Saudi Arabia. In all three cases, although less-than-democratic regimes seek to retain power, they provide pro-Western stances that are crucial to U.S. support in the region. In the case of Saudi Arabia, the connection to the al-Saud family matches the U.S. dependence, or overdependence in fact, on petroleum at a reasonable price that the Saudis facilitate.

In Pakistan, President and General Pervez Musharraf provides a pro-U.S. government in the face of mounting Islamic supporters who appear willing to endorse the ways of Osama bin Laden and the Islamists who are seeking to hurt the United States and Western culture. Musharraf's anti-democratic coup d'état in 1999, before the September 11 attacks, has not resulted in a return to democracy, but he does allow some cooperation with the United States in seeking to destroy pro–al Qaeda elements in the Waziristan frontier with southeast Afghanistan. How long the Pakistani military can keep the Islamists at bay is an open but crucial question for U.S. efforts to stabilize Afghanistan as it is widely believed that the pro–al Qaeda Taliban get assistance there.

All of Pakistan's problems—which are many—are heightened by the reality of it being one of two known nuclear weapons states in south Asia, a prospect that was brought home to Washington in 2002 when it appeared Pakistan and India might wage nuclear war against each other. Whatever President Musharraf's limitations, national security strategists fear what would occur if he were forced from office by nondemocratic means, which could allow one of a number of groups to get control over those nuclear weapons.

Finally, Egypt under President Hosni Mubarak has also proven less than democratic, more than a quarter-century after he succeeded the assassinated Anwar Sadat. Mubarak's government has been repressive but without it the United States would likely see even greater problems for Israel, its strong ally in this region.

The Israeli-Palestinian problem remains an unresolved and thorny issue for the United States. As a democratic state of Jews in a region of growing Muslim populations seeking its end, Israel is vulnerable. While Washington has taken pro-Israeli positions, the Bush administration has been more strident in its support for Israel than any prior regimes. Early in his term, President Bush made clear his unwillingness to force Israel to move away from the Jewish state's best interests for the sake of negotiation with the Palestinians. President Bush was uncomfortable with advocates of negotiations with former Palestinian leader Yasir Arafat in November 2004. President Bush made clear his view that Israeli security, once guaranteed, would help the region and that other views were not likely to sway him.

Gradually, as the reality of the difficulties with Iraq have become apparent, the administration has begun to view the Palestinian-Israeli difficulties in a manner somewhat more consistent with that of many prior regimes. The recognition that much of the world is sympathetic to Palestinian demands for statehood and a better standard of living to deter attacks on Israel has ever so slowly begun to take root. Secretary of State Condoleezza Rice has gradually begun to take a position of negotiating with the two parties, as did prior governments in Washington. The need for a resolution to this simmering, sixty-year-old problem is an important issue for U.S. national security because it will demonstrate that the United States views all religions as equal and legitimate.

The Hamas takeover of Gaza in June 2007 galvanized the Israeli government in Jerusalem to begin opening more channels to rival Fatah's government in the West Bank in hoping to prop up its power with Palestinians. Hamas appears too radical and undesirable as a governing party to many around the world, making Fatah less-than-perfect but preferable as a partner in efforts to reduce violence.

Similarly, the Middle East plagues the United States in the form of Iran, as has been true for almost thirty years, and its nuclear potential. Since the Iranian Revolution of 1979, Washington has had limited contacts with the government in Teheran. Over the past five years, however, as the Iranian capacity to enrich uranium has grown, Washington's fears about the potential for an Iranian nuclear weapon have also grown. Washington's conviction that Iran must understand that a nuclear weapons capability would not be tolerated is a key aspect to Washington's message to this region. As Washington tries to convey this message to the leaders of the Iranian state, often with President Mahmoud Ahmadinejad brushing off the warnings, the United States tries to corral its allies in nonproliferation efforts in Western Europe, China, and Japan, all of whom may be seeking in better ties with Iran for their own reasons. At a time when Washington is stretched thin with commitments elsewhere, it hopes that others will help carry these messages of deterrence, but it is clear that all states pursue their national interests, not necessarily those espoused by the world's remaining superpower.

A Dramatically Evolving Asian Scenario for Security

The United States has also begun to examine security problems and reappraise its standing around the world. At the same time the United States had its eyes on the possibility of weapons of mass destruction in Iraq, for instance, U.S. intelligence agencies expressed their concerns about a North Korean nuclear weapons program. The Clinton administration had ostensibly wiped out that program in the 1990s with the "Agreed Framework" between the United States, South Korea, Japan, and the Democratic People's Republic of Korea (DPRK) only to find that intelligence estimates at the beginning of the Bush term indicated that the North Koreans were not abiding by their side of the agreement. At a time when North Korea was part of President Bush's so-called "axis of evil" (Bush 2002), the North Koreans felt their regime was under siege. Between 2002 and early 2007, the United States, in conjunction with five other states, engaged in the Six-Party Talks to end the North Korean nuclear program. That agreement was signed in 2007, but the DPRK's willingness to abide by the accord remains unclear.

Similarly, the United States had to recognize not a rising China but an emergent China. The People's Republic of China (PRC) in the first decade of the new millennium was modernizing its military and economy at a sustained rate. Advocated as early as the 1970s as one of Four Modernizations, the PRC sought to have an economy that would raise the standard of living for its population while improving its military to stand as a respected international player on the world scene. The Communist Party of China seeks to retain its power by proving to the 1.3 billion citizens that it alone can continue to raise China's prestige in the global system at the same time it dramatically improves their standard of living. The name China means "Middle Kingdom," which reflects its people's belief in the centrality of their culture to the world, so the idea that China might not be able to accomplish all of its goals with a weak military would not be acceptable. The financial wherewithal to do that modernization is now available as China continues touting its roughly 10 percent annual growth rates. For many in the United States, this evokes tremendous fears of a resurgent Communist power threatening the peace and stability of the world. For others, China's emergence as an economically dynamic partner that will hopefully accept the norms of the world system is a thrilling prospect to be welcomed.

Optimists and pessimists in the United States agree that the one cloud on the horizon in the Sino-U.S. relationship is Taiwan. The island, located a hundred miles off the Fujian coast, was a formal diplomatic ally of the United States between 1949 and 1979 during the Cold War. Washington shifted recognition from Taipei to Beijing in 1979, thus creating a peculiar vulnerability for Taiwan since it has formal diplomatic recognitions by no large states. While disappointment in that move shattered the close connections between Washington and Taipei almost thirty years ago, Taiwan still has a special place in the hearts of many in the United States because of its increasing democratic culture and its traditional "underdog" spirit. In 1979, Congress formalized the U.S. interest in Taiwan by passing the Taiwan Relations Act, which gave a hint of U.S. commitment to help the island with its defense if attacked. Like much congressional legislation, however, the specifics for implementation are rather vague, and this has left the United States in a somewhat ambiguous position with Taiwan and the PRC. With democracy on the island, however, have come a number of difficulties in the Sino-U.S.-Taiwan triangle.

In 1996, to no avail, Beijing fired missiles off the north and south tips of Taiwan in an attempt to influence domestic elections. But, Washington sent a strong signal to Beijing that it would not tolerate violence in trying to resolve the Taiwan "splittist" question, as the PRC refers to it. Four years later, a distinctly pro-independence leader, Chen Shui-bian, became the minority president in Taiwan, winning by a thin margin. His avowed position of formal independence for Taiwan is highly controversial because Beijing has declared it will not tolerate this action but will respond with military force to maintain the integrity of the "homeland." Oddly enough, rather than reinforcing its military capacity to make such an action more plausible, the Taiwan security community proved unable to approve budgets for needed military modernization to match that of the PRC military, known as the People's Liberation Army (PLA). Thus, Washington watched nervously as the democratic government on the island seemed to take more provocative steps bound to irritate the mainland at a time when Washington hoped to bring the PRC into the circle of "responsible stakeholders" in the world community. Statements by PLA officers in 2005 attracted much attention in the United States when it appeared that U.S. intervention on behalf of the island in a conflict could create a nuclear exchange between the U.S. and Chinese forces, not a happy prospect for anyone.

A great deal of the frustration Taipei feels results from its virtual lack of allies around the world. Only twenty-four states recognize Taiwan as a nation-state, but none of them is a particularly important player. The Taiwanese believe China is depriving them of "international space" and grasp at the most meager of prospects that other states, such as Japan, will provide help in a crisis. This appears highly unlikely.

Japan's generation-long demise in the international financial scene has also begun to slowly turn around, but Japan is still seeking to understand its role in the world. A cautious, traditional society by nature, Japan's evolution appears glacial by most standards. Touted by the George W. Bush administration as the primary partner in Asia, Japan found that Washington, regardless of its intentions, had developed strong ties with China that were not easily supplanted by a return to Japanese economic growth. President Bush had superb relations with Prime Minister Junichiro Koizumi during his tenure as head of the Democratic Liberal Party but the durability of these relations into the term of his successor, Shinzo Abe, is not as clear as July 2007 elections indicated that Japan's political future is open to the public's changing views.

Indonesia

Bombings between 2002 and 2005 indicated that Indonesia had taken on a new, somewhat menacing role for terrorism in Asia. The October 2002 attack at Bali, one of Asia's most popular vacation sites, targeted Western, particularly Australian, tourists, resulting in the death of more than 200. Two years later, the Indonesian capital, Jakarta, saw attacks at Western hotels. In October 2005, bombers returned to Bali with fewer deaths but a graphic, chilling reminder that militants recognized that Westerners patronized the island paradise and could be targets there. The largest Islamic nation in the world by population, Indonesia in the new millennium has a more strident Islamic orientation than had been previously true. Many critics argued that Washington's desire to oust the Taliban and then Saddam Hussein as well as the widely held perception that the United States was waging war against Islam only exacerbated the feelings of those who feared the West was waging war on the peoples of Indonesia. The bombings illustrate that even peaceful states could have tremendous tensions.

Nontraditional Threats

A number of threats on the international scene that do not fit the traditional mold exist and are not uniformly accepted as threats by all. Nevertheless, they are part of the national security calculation upon which military, informational, economic, and diplomatic forces are constructed. These are also relatively more important to some parts of the world than others, depending on the peculiar nature of the threat.

Medical Security

The world has begun to recognize that there are known medical threats that may affect national security and probable new threats ahead. For instance, the international community has had to confront the scourge of acquired immunodeficiency syndrome (AIDS) for more than a quarter of a century. For places like Uganda or South Africa, AIDS is killing off a generation as infection rates are well into the double digits and no relief is available at an affordable price.

Fears of a new pandemic along the lines of the 1918 Spanish influenza have also occupied the attention of the international medical world. Specialists believe that it is not a matter of "if" but "when" a similar flu develops and spreads, as these phenomena are a natural course of events. The Spanish flu of 1918 killed roughly the same number as did World War I: 20 million people. But technology, transportation, and all the benefits of the twenty-first century would allow the disease to move much farther and faster so a modern pandemic would likely kill 40 to 105 million people worldwide.

Fears of a pandemic first arose in late 2002 and early 2003, when a strange form of pneumonia began to appear in southern China and Hong Kong. Gradually, it spread from those regions into central and northern China, Vietnam, Singapore, the Philippines, Taiwan, Canada, and parts of Europe. SARS gripped the world with panic in the early months of 2003 as people tried to figure out what it was and how it was transmitted. Airplanes to Asia were virtually empty because Asia was the home of the virus. Gradually, modern science diagnosed the problem and steps were taken to quarantine the problems. Fear abated but did not completely disappear.

Then at the dawn of the twenty-first century, the advent of the bird flu virus seemed to indicate a pandemic might be upon us. Outbreaks of this avian flu appeared in Vietnam, Indonesia,

Thailand, and spread as far as Turkey. Birds were culled in Britain, Central Europe, and Russia to prevent its spread. The feared mutation of bird-to-bird contact into bird-to-human-human contact has not developed to date, but the inevitable questions of how the nations of the world, including the United States, will cope with a pandemic remain.

Drugs

Drugs have been a long-term issue for the United States but the chaos in Afghanistan and Iraq will likely exacerbate the problem. Colombia, a major source of coca from Latin America after it was driven north by antidrug campaigns in Bolivia and Peru in the 1980s, still receives a surprisingly large portion of U.S. foreign assistance (it is the third largest recipient behind Israel and Egypt when Iraq and Afghanistan are taken out of the equation) to reduce the drug scourge. Increasingly, the Drug Enforcement Administration appears to follow Colombian-grown drugs as they transfer north into the Mexican drug cartels but Mexico is also growing its own indigenous crops.

Afghanistan is a major producer of opium poppies as is Pakistan's northwestern frontier. Drugs tend to migrate to regions where government oversight is limited, thus Afghanistan has long been a problem area. With President Karzai's government focused first on survival, and then in expanding its reach, pressing Afghan farmers to decrease their opium production has already been a lower priority than it was under the Taliban regime of the late 1990s. With globalization, the movement of these drugs is considerably easier and thus the consumption of heroin will likely expand.

Myanmar remains a major source of opium poppies for similar reasons of government inattention, if not overt collaboration with the growers and traffickers. Along with the northern provinces of Thailand, Laos, and southwest China, the area known as the "Golden Triangle" remains an area where drug trafficking and associated criminal activity thrives.

Additionally, drugs have taken on new roles in the post-9/11 environment. Partially because of globalization efforts and partially because of innovation, new drugs are now an issue in national security. Methamphetamines are produced in virtually all parts of the world but particularly the United States, and the effects have been devastating in rural populations. As the trafficking of the chemicals needed to produce methamphetamines increasingly crosses national boundaries, U.S. drug enforcement officials will also have to contend with gun running, prostitution, and other illegal activities that seem to accompany the drug trade.

Drug trafficking also tends to be associated with political corruption, such as the corruption of the judiciary. This corruption undercuts efforts to curb immigration, can result indirectly in people trafficking as a form of payment, and undercuts the law in general terms, Corruption may also facilitate the practice of shipping substandard products in the international pharmaceutical trade, endangering not only intellectual property but human health. Massive press coverage in mid-2007 of tainted Chinese foodstuffs and animal products, among a long list of exports that cross oceans as a part of increased international trade, indicated the dangerous effects of corruption beyond pharmaceuticals.

Immigration

Immigration is also an increasingly relevant national security concern. The United States focuses on its long, exposed border with Mexico but that is hardly the only illegal migration concern. As tensions rise and fall with neighbors in the Caribbean Basin and Mexico, the immigration issue is likely to remain perpetually at the top of the list of national security concerns. The reality is that free trade has improved the lives of many in neighboring states but not to the point where the economic disparities in incomes of the United States and its neighbors have been eliminated. As Europeans are finding, illegal immigration is becoming a much more global phenomenon than ever.

Trade

Finally, trade is a nontraditional issue in national security but arguably the one that has grown the most over the past decade. Trade and economic prosperity are viewed as absolutely crucial to national security as the government aims to preserve the highest possible standard of living. Trade problems, by extension, are a threat to the nation's health. Concern about China or India not abiding by their obligations under a number of trade agreements, for example, has elevated the Office of the Trade Representative to a high status.

Similarly, states around the world desire access to the U.S. market. In the middle of this decade, the United States faces a number of interesting challenges that highlight the political options available to the security community. Colombia, as noted, is a major recipient of U.S. foreign assistance but, as a Latin American state, has not seen the U.S. Congress sign and ratify a free trade pact as occurred with Chile (2003) and the North American Free Trade Agreement for Mexico and Canada (1994). President George W. Bush has negotiated a free trade agreement with Colombia, which President Álvaro Uribe Vélez desperately needs to cement many of the changes to his society that will undercut violence and open opportunities. Yet the U.S. Congress, under either party, appears unlikely to ratify such a pact for fear of undercutting U.S. producers. The question remains, however, whether long-term trade access to the U.S. market isn't much cheaper than other forms of assistance, but it is a highly complex, controversial topic.

Government

Although much of the informed discussion on the topic of national security takes place in the private sector through think tanks, universities, and other institutions, not to mention public opinion as demonstrated at the ballot box, it is important to understand the government's role in national security. This section provides a brief discussion of arms of the government that are involved in national security.

Legislative Branch

While most people think of national security as an aspect of the executive branch, the Constitution begins with a discussion of the congressional role in national affairs, such as national security. The two houses of the Congress hold both appropriation and oversight hearings regularly. Congress has the power to provide or withdraw funding for various national security policy options. Congress also requires the executive branch to provide reports on myriad issues ranging from human rights conditions in Tibet to updates on progress in Afghanistan to drug cooperation certification in Burma.

Congressional Research Service and Government Accountability Office

Additionally, Congress has a small number, particularly compared with the executive branch, of analytical support bodies. The two most prominent are the Congressional Research Service of the Library of Congress, which has a staff of experts who answer congressional requests with studies of pressing policy questions. These relatively brief reports are done on a rapid-fire basis but with superb quality and nonpartisan basis. Similarly, the Government Accountability Office, founded in 1921, serves as the legislative branch's auditors, evaluating the expenditure of federal funds and the associated policy reviews of various government programs.

Executive Branch

The primary driver for national security strategy and policy is the executive branch in its many manifestations. This chapter examines the most important of those bodies.

The tensions between bureaucratic entities are well known around the world. The conflict between the state and defense departments in the current Bush administration stands in stark contrast to that of President George H. W. Bush's government between 1989 and 1993 and will remain the topic of considerable study for decades to come.

Within the executive branch reside the executive agencies, such as the Department of State, the Department of Defense, the Office of the Trade Representative, the myriad branches of the intelligence community, and other smaller organizations.

Department of State

For President George W. Bush's first term, Secretary of State Colin L. Powell ran the Department of State. Uniquely popular as the former chairman of the Joint Chiefs of Staff, Powell served for the period of the invasion of Iraq and the immediate aftermath. Under his tenure, the department fought for greater resources and sought to take an equal role to that of the Department of Defense. The State Department not only lacked money and forces on the ground but was simply too dispersed to fight Secretary of Defense Donald Rumsfeld's efforts to consolidate efforts in nation building, stability operations, and other activities. Under Powell, the State Department had developed its own views on various policy efforts and created the Future of Iraq Project to anticipate problems, but its role in the post-invasion conflict has proven virtually nonexistent. The lower visibility and lack of domestic consistency often dampens the power of the State Department to accomplish what it might otherwise do in national security affairs.

Secretary Powell's departure in early 2005 signaled a return to the State Department's logical power as representing foreign affairs to the presidential administration when National Security Advisor Condoleezza Rice assumed the secretary's position. With extraordinarily strong personal connections to the president himself, many believed Rice's move to this position indicated that President Bush wanted a more aggressive reaction to threats around the world and a greater public persona for the department. In Rice's tenure, she has visited the broader Middle East and has continued to promote diplomatic solutions, but the strategy has not proven a major success; conditions in Iraq are still bad and there is great frustration on the part of other traditional allies in the region, such as Egypt and Saudi Arabia.

Department of Defense

Easily the most expensive and largest arm of the U.S. government engaged in the nation's security is the Defense Department. This behemoth consists of the four services that constitute the active-duty force (the Marine Corps, Army, Navy, and Air Force) along with the National Guard, the Reserves for each service, and civilians who work for the department. The department continues to play the central role in national security and has actually increased its role with greater intelligence functions under former Secretary of Defense Donald Rumsfeld.

The Department of Defense was formed with the 1947 Defense Reorganization Act, in which the Air Force took on a separate role from the Army, the War Department became the Defense Department, and the Central Intelligence Agency (CIA) grew out of the wartime Office of Special Services. The Defense Department has its own capabilities in intelligence, first the Defense Intelligence Agency of the Robert McNamara period of the 1960s and the position of under secretary of defense for intelligence under Steven Cambone in the Rumsfeld period. The Defense Department also has its own criminal investigation services, public affairs, and an extensive list of activities.

During the post-9/11 period, the Pentagon has greatly increased its traditional position as it is at the center of reconstruction efforts in President Bush's project for promoting democracy around the world. In particular, the Defense Department has been the central coordinating point for reconstruction efforts in Iraq. This is a significant shift away from the Department of

State's traditional role as coordinator for these activities because of its links to foreign governments. These activities have both highlighted as well as shown difficulties with the Defense Department's role in activities beyond traditional war fighting. While the U.S. forces are extraordinarily capable, the missions of traditional war fighting and nation building differ substantially.

Similarly, in late 2005, the Defense Department issued DoD Directive 3000.5, expounding on the need to elevate security, stability, transition, and reconstruction efforts to the same position within the department's priorities. While President George W. Bush came into office criticizing his predecessor's decisions in this direction, Bush and his administration have reversed their positions dramatically.

The Intelligence Community

Arguably the greatest post-9/11 reforms have been within the intelligence community. The creation of the director of national intelligence position, first headed by former ambassador to Iraq John Negroponte, was one move to prevent the problems that the post-9/11 analyses pointed out in the overall intelligence community.

Before the mid-2000s, the highest-ranking person within the intelligence community was the director of central intelligence, coincidentally the head of the CIA. That position, however, also meant head of intelligence within the U.S. government. By creating the new position of director of national intelligence, the intelligence community has an oversight layer intended to assess the overall product of the field.

As many people feared, however, the intelligence agencies have used the confusion in responsibilities and overlapping jurisdictions to slow down the overall strengthening of the community by highlighting, for bureaucratic reasons, the work of their home agencies. To many, the funding for intelligence, while vast, did not appear to be adequate to make the reforms the community required.

Part of the problem for the intelligence community is its relationship with the Department of Defense. While the intelligence agencies often have somewhat more vague names such as the National Security Agency or CIA, the overwhelming majority of intelligence funding within the U.S. government resides with the Department of Defense. During the Rumsfeld era (2001–2007), that was not sufficient for the secretary to believe he was getting an adequate product even thought the Defense Intelligence Agency and the individual services all produced their own intelligence, at least partially to guarantee a redundancy that would not allow any threats to be missed. Under Rumsfeld, the Office of the Secretary of Defense began its own independent collection and analysis of data for fear that the other intelligence agencies were skewing their intelligence away from threats of major importance (the two most frequently cited examples were Iraq before 2003 and China). This independent source of intelligence has been controversial and raises serious questions about the funding and breadth of reach of the entire intelligence community.

Additionally, questions arose about the intelligence community's activities in the interrogation procedures for national security after scandals at Abu Ghraib prison in Baghdad and at the Guantánamo Bay base in Cuba. Some people, thinking back to the murder of CIA agent Johnny Michael "Mike" Spann at the interrogation facility in Mazar-e-sharif in Afghanistan, wonder if the interrogations have moved too far toward covert activities rather than gaining real-time intelligence.

Department of Homeland Security

In the late 1990s, discussions in the national security community began to include a concern about first homeland defense, then homeland security. This type of mission was being discussed in hypothetical manners should there be attacks on the U.S. mainland as occurred at the World Trade Center in February 1993 and the Federal Building in Oklahoma City two years later. Those discussing the creation of a homeland security agency within the United States pointed to fears about bioterrorism, chemical terrorism, and pandemic illness (naturally occurring or artificially created).

The Bush administration had already started down this path when the 9/11 attacks occurred. One of the most immediate effects of the shock was to galvanize the U.S. government to create the Office of Homeland Security under former Pennsylvania Governor Tom Ridge. Within weeks of the attacks, the administration began discussing elevating homeland security from a White House office to a cabinet department.

In creating the Department of Homeland Security (DHS), the administration sought to shift control into a single, consolidated mega-department. The new DHS absorbed twenty federal agencies into four vast directorates. While the shift has had its advantages, the DHS has proven less successful than anticipated because of remaining overlapping jurisdictions, unclear organizational responsibilities, and associated questions. In 2005, New Orleans and the Gulf of Mexico coastal areas sustained a direct hit from the category-four Hurricane Katrina with disastrous results and inept government aid responses that highlighted problems within the DHS. One of the remaining concerns about DHS is that money has poured into the problem without a clear-cut prioritization of the needs.

Coast Guard

The Coast Guard, long a fixture of the Transportation Department, moved into the Department of Homeland Security where it has assumed a higher-profile position. The Coast Guard has the responsibility of monitoring U.S. ports and coastal areas but now plays a greater role in coordinating with other governments and proposing security initiatives such as monitoring international container traffic to prevent covert attacks. The Coast Guard also increasingly plays a liaison role to protect against drug and human trafficking, weapons of mass destruction proliferation, and other activities requiring coordination between governments around the world.

Department of Justice

The Justice Department has played an important role in the nation's history but never more so than now. The department has been heavily involved in decisions to tighten the nation's borders to prevent entry by terrorists as occurred before 9/11, even though border control is administered by the Immigration and Naturalization Service of the DHS.

The Federal Bureau of Investigation (FBI) is central to the nation's efforts to track threats against national security. One of the concerns voiced by the Kean-Hamilton 9/11 Commission was that the FBI retained too great a concern about financial crime but not enough about international terrorism. There have long been jurisdictional differences between the FBI and the CIA, which also monitors national security concerns. Indeed, the 9/11 Commission pointed out that bureaucratic in-fighting prevented the two agencies from adequately sharing intelligence, along with the third major intelligence agency, the National Security Agency, which monitors signals intelligence. The Bush administration has struggled to correct these deficiencies.

The Justice Department has been crucial in issuing the directives on how to interrogate suspects and what the applications of international law are for the global war on terrorism. Its legal guidance has been controversial at times but remains essential to the national security community today.

The Judicial Role

The courts have arguably the smallest but most enduring part in national security of the three branches of government. The courts only see cases after a controversy has arisen. Because of the doctrine of judicial review, which dates from the early nineteenth century, the courts may weigh in on the constitutional fitness of various legislative and executive positions. In particular, the courts find themselves central to the questions of the detainee interrogation policies as well as the applicability of many executive branch directives on surveillance. The Supreme Court, along with federal appellate courts, has struck down what many see as expansion of presidential authority to grant interrogation rights, as shown in *Hamdan v. Rumsfeld* (June 29, 2006) and several other cases.

Eventually, under the Democratic Congress and the Republican Bush presidency, the 1973 War Powers Act will probably come before the Supreme Court. Many analysts believe that, unlike the first century of the republic, today's political environment domestically draws the judicial branch into all major political debates in the republic.

Summary

This is a thumbnail sketch of the institutions and basics of national security. The remainder of this volume will discuss them from various perspectives such as further resources available, individuals engaged in the decisions, the documents themselves, and the organizations exerting pressures on various concerns.

References

Baker, James A., and Lee Hamilton, *The Iraq Study Group Report*, December 2006, available online at www.usip.org/isg/iraq_study_group_report/report/1206/iraq_study_group_report.html.

Baker, P., and R. Wright, "Pelosi, Reid Urge Bush to Begin Iraq Pullout," *Washington Post*, January 6, 2007, www.washingtonpost.com/wp-dyn/content/article/2007/01/05/AR2007010501080_pf.html (accessed July 31, 2007).

Brown, H. 1983. *Thinking about National Security*. Boulder, CO: Westview.

Bush, G. W. 2002. "President Delivers State of the Union Address." www.whitehouse.gov/news/releases/2002/01/20020129–11.html (accessed July 1, 2007).

Gordon, M., and B. Trainor. 2006. *Cobra II*. New York: Knopf.

National Commission on Terrorist Attacks. 2004. *The 9/11 Commission Report: Final Report on the National Commission on Terrorist Attacks on the United States*. New York: W. W. Norton.

Ricks, T. 2006. *Fiasco: The American Military Adventure in Iraq*. New York: Penguin.

Roemer, T. J. 2007, January 5. Remarks on "All Things Considered," available online at www.npr.org/templates/story/storyphp?storyID= 6730798.

Suskind, R. 2003. *The Price of Loyalty: George W. Bush, the White House and the Education of Paul O'Neill*. New York: Simon and Schuster.

U.S. Government Printing Office (GPO). 2006. *National Security Strategy of the United States*. Washington DC: GPO. http://www.whitehouse .gov/nsc/nss/2006/ (accessed July 9, 2007).

Washington, G. 1796. "Farewell Address." http://www.yale.edu/ lawweb/avalon/washing.htm (accessed July 31, 2007).

Watson, C. A. 2002. *National Security: A Reference Handbook*. Santa Barbara, CA: ABC-CLIO.

2

Problems, Controversies, and Solutions

The United States has had remarkable consensus on national security for much of the nation's history. However, in the forty years since the Vietnam War divided the nation along political lines, few aspects of public policy in the United States generate the heated discussion that national security does because the stakes are so high.

Questions on the Issue of National Security

This chapter examines a number of the controversial issues the nation confronts in the realm of national security. Each of us as citizens might develop a different list, but this is a relatively wide-ranging series of controversies.

Does Terrorism Represent the Same Type of Existential Threat as the Cold War Did?

Once the Soviet Union developed atomic weapons in 1949, the existence of major portions of the United States was threatened on a daily basis as long as the Soviet Union sought to end the United States as a competing ideology. A nuclear exchange, as worried citizens learned in the mid-1980s, could have resulted in the deaths of tens of millions of citizens in less than thirty minutes' time, seriously undercutting the survival prospects of the United States.

Few analysts believe terrorists around the world have the capability to instigate a similar magnitude of threat through terrorism, with the exception of bioterrorism. Terrorists do not appear to have delivery systems to bring nuclear or chemical weapons to these shores; the 2001 attacks were damaging but were relatively isolated. The more likely scenario is that terrorism will be used to sow fears and ongoing anxiety, but it is not, in most people's minds, the same level of threat as the Cold War was.

What Is Included in National Security?

Traditionally, national security has focused on ensuring the physical security of the nation and protecting the population. This was the basic approach up to and through the Cold War, and it remains the basis of how the armed forces defends the nation by protecting its physical security and territorial integrity. One reason this focus has remained is the view that the nation's founding documents guarantee safety.

With the end of the Cold War, however, people began questioning whether national security should include a much broader array of concerns. In particular, many citizens asked what was included in the national interest. Did national interest mean more than physical security? Many citizens cited the Preamble to the Constitution, "to form a more perfect Union, establish Justice, ensure domestic Tranquility, provide for the common Defense, promote the general Welfare, and secure the Blessings of Liberty to ourselves and our Posterity," as an example of why economic issues should be part of national security.

Further, some question why other issues confronting the nation should not be included in national security. For instance, is computer crime, including hacking, identity theft, or placing malicious information on the web, part of national security? Should national security include health issues? The probability of a global pandemic would likely result in significant numbers of fatalities, undercutting the basic sense of security for anyone in the United States. Some advocate using military forces to keep out potential carriers of various epidemics, while others are uncomfortable with asking the armed forces to conduct this mission. Along the same lines, many people view human immunodeficiency virus/acquired immunodeficiency syndrome (HIV/AIDS) as a national security threat because it is spread so easily between humans and has no cure.

In May 2007, a peculiar event attracted attention regarding the dangers of both global travel and diagnosing disease. An Atlanta, Georgia, attorney who travels frequently to the lesser developed world became the subject of medical concern because of a diagnosis of highly drug-resistant tuberculosis, still a deadly disease in much of the world. The attorney had traveled to Greece for his wedding against medical advice that his drug-resistant diagnosis indicated he would be jeopardizing the health of people with whom he came into contact. The Immigration and Naturalization Service alerted its agents to prevent his arrival because of the health dangers he carried, yet the attorney crossed back into the United States with little effort through a Canadian border crossing before medical officials quarantined him in a tuberculosis ward. Within two months' quarantine, the medical community reversed its diagnosis that the tuberculosis strain was highly drug-resistant and the attorney returned to his civilian life after a drug treatment program.

The case raised many national security questions, including, how was he diagnosed as having such a dangerous form of tuberculosis only to have that verdict reversed later? How was he able to travel initially after the first alarming concerns? What dangers did he pose to those he flew with to Greece, then back home through Canada? How did he return to the United States when border agents were watching for him? How easy would it be to carry a highly toxic medical agent that no one was anticipating?

In 2006, former Vice President Al Gore's documentary, *An Inconvenient Truth*, along with numerous reports of climate change, species extermination, and water pollution, raised the specter that environmental threats to national security could rival any other security concerns. When Gore won the Academy Award for his effort in 2007, it reignited the question of whether the environment is a political or national security issue.

Probably the most common controversy over the past decade has related to whether terrorism is a national security threat and how to respond to it. Few people dispute the reality of terrorism after the 9/11 attacks, but whether to confront it here, within U.S. boundaries, or at its source is an open controversy with little likelihood of resolution.

Those who could be described as national security purists insist, however, that by asking the armed forces to defend situations well beyond the physical security of the nation, the military is asked to do too much, which eventually weakens its ability to do anything at all. Curiously, this was the position taken by George W. Bush during the 2000 presidential campaign when he gave a number of speeches claiming that the military had been overstretched into tasks that were bound to denigrate its core capabilities. President Bush, as have a number of his predecessors, has found that conditions confronting the nation made his need to ask more of the armed forces something absolutely unavoidable.

In particular, as a candidate the president seemed uncomfortable asking the military to engage in the types of nation-building activities that are now fundamental to the attempts to reconstruct Iraqi society. Many analysts have asked whether one option for settling this dispute over the definition of national security concerns would be to create special corps of personnel to engage in these specialized activities. An example would be to create a civilian-military specialist category for nation-building activities, as this appears to be a likely national security tool for the twenty-first century. General David Petraeus's March 7, 2007, speech on the evolving security conditions in Baghdad spoke in this vein, as he noted that the armed services cannot engage in these activities alone, but need civilian assistance.

The debate about what is actually national security as the core issue for the nation is unlikely to cease, however, as it arguably should not in a democratic society.

Is the United States More Secure After the Invasion of Iraq?

Support for President George W. Bush's invasion of Iraq was substantial when he first moved U.S. forces against Saddam Hussein over concerns that the dictator had a weapons of mass destruction program. The debate within the United States ultimately led to congressional support for the use of U.S. military forces; the administration believed it had to defend national security, particularly to prevent another 9/11-type attack.

Saddam and his sons are dead. No nuclear weapons or weapons development programs have been discovered. The feared links between Saddam's Iraq and al Qaeda terrorists before 2003 appear to have been exceptionally weak—if they existed at all.

The subsequent four years have seen a tremendous upheaval in Iraq and, more generally, in the world where Islamic adherents believe the United States has undermined their security. Many young Iraqi men have been unemployed for several years. Car bombs, improvised explosive devices, kidnappings, and sectarian violence—Sunni versus Shiite—characterize daily existence in Iraq. The Kurdish population remains somewhat separate from the remainder of the country. Electricity is sporadic, and health care and education are unpredictable. Life in Iraq, in short, is harder than it was before 2003.

Most alarming to many people is the idea that many in the population of Iraq have become radicalized to join terrorist groups around the world. In 2004, most specialists in the world did not believe ties existed between al Qaeda and the Baathist regime in Baghdad, but they now worry that Iraqis are turning to terrorism. Friendly regimes in the region, including Saudi Arabia and Egypt, have warned the United States that it is seeking to address the wrong problems: Instead of answering calls to resolve the Palestinian-Israeli conflict, the United States is pushing a democratic agenda. Similarly, the U.S. Army and Marine Corps are stretched and stressed, and budget expenditures continue to grow.

Regardless of whether Islamists are being bred by this war in Iraq, the sectarian violence of Iraq has made it difficult for many in the United States to believe that promoting democracy, something so core to the national ethos of the United States and a prerequisite for security in the eyes of many, is being advanced in this effort. President Bush and Secretary of State Rice, for example, have pushed as hard as they believe they can to promote the ideals of democracy in Iraq and the Middle East, only to see behavior to the contrary in Egypt, Saudi Arabia, Lebanon, and the Palestinian territories. For some, that lack of consistency endorses the idea that democracy has made the world less safe than before. On balance, many wonder whether the United States is, in the grandest sense, safer than it was before.

Will Russia Become a National Security Threat to the United States?

When the leadership of the Soviet Union did not stop the East German public from beginning to dismantle the Berlin Wall on November 9, 1989, it was immediately obvious that something was changing in the Soviet Union. Just over two years later, the Soviet Union ended its seventy-four years of existence on December 31, 1991, when it dissolved into Russia and a series of independent states from Armenia in the Caucasus region to Tajikistan in central Asia.

The 1990s were a decade of selling off of Soviet assets into private hands and a relatively positive diplomatic relationship between Russian leader Boris Yeltsin and his U.S. counterparts. Issues of difference, such as the Russian discomfort with the North Atlantic Treaty Organization's (NATO) expansion into neighboring states of Eastern Europe, were downplayed by both sides, along with Russia's objections to U.S. actions in Kosovo and other areas of traditional Slavic affiliation with Mother Russia. When Yeltsin stepped down on December 31, 1999, his successor was a former KGB agent, Vladimir Putin, who was considerably younger than the deteriorating president. The overall view in the United States was that Russia was a state in decline, no longer nearly the threat it was during the Cold War between 1947 and 1989 because it no longer had the financial capability or the will to challenge U.S. dominance around the world.

With the September 11 attacks, President Bush welcomed support in antiterrorist efforts from a wide array of leaders around the world, including Putin. In November 2001, Putin visited Bush at the latter's Crawford, Texas, ranch where Bush praised the Russian leader as being so supportive of the pro-Western coalition rather than one of the former Communists that Washington had so long feared.

In the subsequent five years, Putin's Russia has moved steadily and repeatedly away from the U.S. assessment that it was a partner for the future. Russia did not veto the U.S. requests for United Nations support in prosecuting a war with Iraq but neither did it support the action. Russia, virtually bankrupt financially in the 1990s, has enjoyed marked increases in national revenues from spiking energy prices, so it is far less cooperative on attempts to restrain energy prices. At the same time, the energy-producing companies of Russia became increasingly reconsolidated under state control, through imprisoning their civilian owners as corrupt or through simply reinstituting state needs for protecting national assets. This neomercantilist behavior was of great concern but occurred gradually enough that people were too absorbed in the unfolding problems of Iraq to realize what was happening in Moscow.

More worrisome for many is the increased consolidation of power in the hands of Putin loyalists, many former intelligence agents with strong ties to authoritarian governance. Forces within Russia raised alarms about these antidemocratic moves, but many of these voices were silenced through murders or other mysterious circumstances, most notably the poisoning of a former KGB operative in London in November 2006.

The controversy that is growing is whether this emerging authoritarian Russia poses a threat to the international community or whether Russia is merely pursuing its own path of development and governance. Russia has retained a large nuclear arsenal, and there is little prospect for serious arms control debate because of strong nationalist sentiment that the United States does not respect Russia as an important nation. In addition, the Russian military has faced a number of high-profile failures, such as the 2000 sinking of the *Kursk* and loss of the submarine's crew; the botched rescue missions of hostages held by Chechnyan rebels at the Moscow Opera House in 2002 and at a school in Beslan in 2004, both of which resulted in heavy civilian deaths; and the overall military disaster of the campaign to subdue the successionist Chechnyans (1994–2001). Parents and recruits frequently charge Russian military officers with abusing young Army recruits, which has led to a significant number of people ignoring their military service, thus undercutting the military's effectiveness. In short, serious questions about the professionalism of the Russian armed forces lead to concerns that it would not behave predictably should a serious crisis arise between the Russian state and the rest of the world. When this unpredictability couples with a growing sense of Russian nationalist pride asserted with a clear sense that the international community, especially the Bush administration, has ignored Russia's rightful role as a powerful state in the international community leads many to fear that an authoritarian regime in Moscow could take aggressive steps to undermine peace in the world.

The overall picture is one of Russia with power consolidated, directly and indirectly, in the hands of an intelligence agent who prefers operating in a nontransparent, authoritarian political system while also fearing that the nation's position as a major global player has been inappropriately dismissed by the world's superpower. This could be a combustible situation for national security in the future as Russia accumulates wealth from its vast energy assets, thus allowing it to rebuild its military capability to meet its self-image as a respected state.

Additionally, Russia has increasingly made clear its intolerance for U.S. moves to promote pro-Western regimes along the fringes of the traditional Russian empire, such as slicing off Kosovo into its own non-Serbian state; promoting democratic revolutionary governments in Kyrgystan, Ukraine, and other neighboring states; and positioning U.S. missile defense systems in states of the former Soviet sphere, such as the Czech Republic. In each and every one of these instances, Russia has threatened to flex its muscle and, as Washington is increasingly mired in long-term commitments elsewhere, it may become more menacing in getting its way than U.S. national security can allow.

Can "Personalization" of National Security Adversely Affect U.S. National Interests?

The United States has a long tradition of personalizing national security opportunities and threats in the character of an individual. The most positive, recent example of this phenomenon is Colombian President Álvaro Uribe Vélez, who has been, and remains, the embodiment of perceived success in reforming a society. Uribe has instituted a number of major changes to Colombian society. Colombia has struggled with insurgency for more than four decades, and has seen drug trafficking and overall criminality ebb and flow tremendously since the 1980s. Some observers wonder about the likelihood of real institutionalization or permanence of the changes the president has made, but the United States, under the Clinton and George W. Bush adminstrations, has invested dramatically in Colombia's future through foreign and military assistance.

Similarly, Russian President Boris Yeltsin, who abandoned Communism in favor of a free market economy and sold off many state assets into private hands in the 1990s, was considered a pioneering figure in opening Russia to the West and Western values in the years after the Soviet Union and the fear of global Communism. In retrospect, the Yeltsin years appear less upbeat as the president's personal behavior problems, heightened by alcohol abuse, allowed Russian society to deteriorate and contributed to a sense of humiliation that the subsequent Putin regime is trying to erase.

Conversely, U.S. presidents have also personalized national security threats by singling out certain individuals as the root of evil. President Bush's charges against Saddam Hussein before the 2003 invasion are one such example, as are the concerns about Osama bin Laden being the crux of the al Qaeda threat. In both cases, the individuals targeted were important symbols but were not the whole problem. Evidence that Saddam Hussein's death did not alter the fundamental problems in Iraq that have generated a strong insurgency has remained controversial, but the reality is that the insurgency has continued three and a half years past the former dictator's capture and months after his late December 2006 hanging at the hands of the Maliki regime in Baghdad.

With Osama bin Laden, the role of personalizing him as the source of evil around the world is even more apparent. Doubts about whether the Saudi renegade remains alive abound but concerns about al Qaeda have not diminished despite the possibility of bin Laden's diminished role in its operations. New fears about al Qaeda resurgency appear regularly in the U.S. press.

The George W. Bush administration is far from the only one to adopt this focus on an individual as the root of national security concerns. President George H. W. Bush also highlighted Saddam Hussein's evil in the Middle East during the 1990–1991 Gulf War. President Clinton personalized the evil of Serbian President Slobodan Milošević as the root of the problems in the former Yugoslavia in the 1990s. President Ronald Reagan had a strong, vocal antipathy for Libyan strongman Muammar Gadhafi in the mid-1980s as the root of terrorism, evil, and danger to the international system, particularly as Reagan's personal ties with Mikhail Gorbachev and the Soviet leadership improved. For the Carter administration in the late 1970s and early 1980s, the supreme religious leader of Iran, Ayatollah Khomeini, became the target of U.S. angst, despite the fact that the whole of the Iranian society had welcomed back the long-exiled leader after the shah was deposed in 1979. For many in the United States, the aging Iranian cleric became the embodiment of the humiliation resulting from the November 1979–January 1981 hostage crisis where 44 U.S. diplomats and service personnel were held by Iranian radicals.

Currently, the Bush administration is also targeting Venezuelan President Hugo Chávez Frías and North Korean dictator Kim Jong Il, who they fear are challenging the international order the administration seeks to establish. Both leaders are highly critical of U.S. policies and its role around the world and consider President Bush to be the root of evil in the international system. Bin Laden has not disappeared as a symbol of evil, but the apparent difficulty in equatng al Qaeda to Bin Laden is increasingly difficult to rationalize. One of the most frustrating lessons from the past six years since the 9/11 attacks has been the inability to reduce al

Qaeda to a group under a sole individual's control instead of the evolving menace it now appears to be.

The problem with this personalization is that it runs the risk of ignoring the systemic challenges in any society or state. This misunderstanding or simplification of conditions around the world set up the United States and the world public for frustration and disappointment when the individuals are removed from office but the necessary ameliorations of societies do not occur or are less successful than anticipated. The disappointment of the failure to achieve the anticipated transformation of a society once a designated dictator disappears can breed further frustration, impatience, and cynicism that leads to less public participation and understanding in the world. This situation can be exceedingly dangerous for democracy and the political process, and thus is dangerous for national security as a whole.

Is National Security the Concern of Politicians or the Entire Society?

The debate about who conducts national security policy is the most fundamental in the United States. For some, including many of the most intellectual and educated in the country, national security is the prerogative of those in the armed services. For others, national security is the responsibility of each and every single citizen. For still others, national security is handled by the executive branch alone, in the person of the president of the United States. For yet another segment of the nation, Congress, in conjunction with the executive branch and the citizenry as a whole, is the decision maker for national security.

This question has no set, easy answer. As is true with national security threats, the decision maker is in the eye of the beholder. For the executive branch official, Congress is an annoyance to be ignored wherever possible because it slows the process and operates too loosely. For the legislative branch, national security cannot be held exclusively in the hands of the executive branch because this will not adequately represent the views of the 300 million citizens of the nation. And citizens often feel they have inadequate preparation or knowledge to answer these pressing questions. Instead, it takes all of the groups to provide checks and balances, support, and amend the national security process and system.

Is Global Warming Truly the Most Pressing Immediate National Security Issue?

In early April 2007, a commission of the world's most prominent, respected climate scientists released a report arguing that the earth is heating up substantially and that this will result in dramatic effects on the climate within two decades' time (LeTreut and Somerville 2007). This raises the question of whether global warming is the most pressing national security concern facing the nation, because these climate changes appear likely to alter the current lifestyle of many in the United States. Climate changes have been occasionally seen as important as the nation looked at specific, smaller regions such as the Northeast, where acid rain has periodically been a concern or the 1930s dust bowl conditions that drove a significant portion of the poor population of the center of the nation into California and the southwest United States.

Yet the potential global effects of the current climate deterioration appear to be broader and harder to resolve in a manner that will allow the nation to ignore the problem. For some, this global environmental threat is far greater than the threat of terrorism or of any likely war scenarios. For others, such as President Bush, global warming remains only a peripheral issue that the free market will probably address if left to its own devices rather than being forced to react under regulation. The issue is far more broadly discussed outside the United States, especially in Western Europe, than it is here, but its role as a priority national security concern will only generate more debate as climate issues deteriorate in a world where energy and resource consumption continues to increase, especially in China, India, and the United States, to maintain growing economies and higher standards of living.

Does China's Phenomenal Growth Pose a Threat to the Nation's Security?

Thirty years ago, the People's Republic of China (PRC) was still coming to grips with the horrors and excess of the Great Proletariat Cultural Revolution (1966–1976) where Chairman Mao Zedong unleashed radicals within the Communist Party to eradicate opposition and keep society in a perpetual state of upheaval. Mao's death in September 1976 opened the door to gradual stabilization of the Chinese nation under the Second Generation Leadership in the person of Deng Xiaoping. Deng opened the door to reforms in China that redistributed economic power into the hands of the population and sparked the most amazing economic growth in a three-decade period that the world has ever seen, especially when cast against the reality of a population of more than a billion people seeking to improve its standard of living in that short time. While far from all Chinese citizens have fat bank accounts or lush villas outside Shanghai or Beijing, the standard of living for most Chinese has improved greatly in the past three decades.

Along with these changes in economic status are marked steps to modernize the People's Liberation Army (PLA), the collective term for the military in China. The vast force that proved virtually impotent against Vietnam in 1979 has seen its weapons systems improve along with the education levels of its officers and enlisted personnel. Similarly, the PLA has taken steps to enhance its cooperation across its military branches, known as "increased jointness" in Western parlance, and to target its greatest national security goals in its modernization process rather than trying to meet U.S. military capability one-on-one.

Undoubtedly the greatest single security goal for China is to prevent Taiwan, the island of 23 million people located 100 miles off the southeast coast of Fujian province, from declaring independence from the "motherland." Taiwan's split views on whether it wants to declare independence, reunite with the mainland, or continue in the ambiguous status it has held for generations do not comfort Beijing but the urgency and frantic behavior with which Beijing threatened Taiwan between 1996 (when it fired missiles off the northern and southern coasts of the island to affect presidential elections) and 2003 (when it feared the incumbent in Taipei, Chen Shui-bian, would act upon his talk of rewriting the Guomingdong Constitution, which formally linked Taiwan to the Republic of China and, indirectly, the PRC itself) calmed dramatically after 2004. Part of this is due to Beijing's enhanced military capability (Taipei's military has not commensurately improved) and part of this is due to ever-growing economic ties between the PRC and Taiwan businesses.

Many fear that the Communist government in Beijing is not interested simply in playing a peaceful role as a state in the international community, but seeks to oust the United States from its prominent position in east Asia and then dominate, if not subjugate, Asia to traditional Chinese hegemony. One look at a map indicates that most of east Asia *is* China, but many fear that it has nefarious goals and could operate unchallenged, much as the Soviet Union did fifty years ago. People with this view of China's threat point to its unwillingness to defer to the democratic wishes of the Taiwan population along with China's utter intransigence on democratizing itself as major economic reforms occur.

Chinese responses to these sorts of concerns are often dismissive but consistent. The Chinese government refuses to concede that Taiwan is anything other than an internal Chinese matter; under no circumstances will it surrender sovereignty on any and all issues regarding China's development and politics to anyone other than the Communist Party leadership. Additionally, China notes that its military modernization only offers a balance to the dramatic imbalance existing in east Asia under U.S. military presence there. China's leadership proclaims its purely "peaceful" desires to modernize and raise up its population from the dire conditions it faced in the twentieth century.

Some analysts take China at the leadership's word, noting that it is still a rather poor society with half a billion people living on less than two dollars' a day income. These analysts also note that Chinese military modernization appears aimed directly at preventing Taiwan's independence. Others note that China views its role as the center of the world, or the "Middle Kingdom"; thus, it seeks a modern economy and military to achieve the status it envisions for itself and that it held for much of the past five millennia.

In September 2005, a senior U.S. diplomat challenged China to become a "responsible stakeholder" as it assumes an ever greater role in the international system (Zoellick 2005). Others in Washington, particularly in the defense community, fear that the Chinese Communist Party is incapable of modernizing only for a Taiwan scenario, noting that China's goals must extend beyond that island to greater control over Asia. Still other analysts argue that China's modernization has been measured and completely consistent with Deng Xiaoping's placement of military modernization as the fourth of the Four Modernizations announced in the 1970s. The debate about China's goals and aspirations is a fierce and growing one as China plays an increasingly important role in the global financial and diplomatic games.

Less clear but equally controversial is what options are available to address China. Some analysts argue that the United States needs to confront PLA modernization, but this position rarely includes a detailed discussion of how to operationalize that confrontation. Those fearing PLA modernization often discuss enhancing Taiwan's military prowess but the island's political establishment, especially under the pro-independence Democratic Progressive Party, has proven utterly incompetent to increase financial commitment to military modernization, even in the face of obvious PLA enhancements. In the early years of this decade, President George W. Bush strengthened relations with two stalwart allies in east Asia, Australia and Japan, but neither of these states can afford to alienate Beijing for trade and geographic reasons. Japan, in particular, has a long, strained relationship with China, and any sense of military enhancement for the island democracy, such as acquiring nuclear weapons, would send China into a paroxysm of panic because of the World War II experience of a strong military power in Japan. Other friendly states in the region, such as Vietnam and Thailand, are as acutely aware of their geographic proximity as is Australia, not to mention the increasing need these states have to maintain growing access to the Chinese economy for their products.

Other options often mentioned in the United States include decreasing the trade that is making China so much stronger. China is rapidly modernizing its economy by producing a wide array of products with cheap labor abundantly available in the PRC. The United States, with its insatiable desire for consumer goods, buys many of these cheap exports. Additionally, China's growing trade has allowed it to accumulate phenomenal amounts of foreign exchange that it is loaning to the United States to pay its debts. Some wonder why Washington is not trying to stem this behavior if it is seriously worried about Chinese threats to the United States. At present there is no easy solution as the relationship between the two states is increasingly complicated. Thus, the question of how to stop China's modernization may be moot because of the real conditions evolving around the world.

Does U.S. Involvement in the "Long War" Threaten Its Role as the World Leader?

The United States entered Iraq with both mixed feelings and high hopes of a rapid overthrow of Saddam Hussein's government and immediate withdrawal of ground forces in favor of Iraqi efforts to construct a democratic, post-authoritarian state. President Bush had made it clear eighteen months earlier that the war against terrorism would be a long-term commitment that would require prolonged dedication to a difficult cause. The image of U.S. troops helping a crowd of cheering Iraqis overturn a statue of Saddam Hussein seemed to embody the initial view that the war would be over quickly, as did President Bush's proud announcement that "major combat operations in Iraq have ended" when he appeared before a banner proclaiming "Mission Accomplished" on the flight deck of the USS *Abraham Lincoln* on May 1, 2001 (Office of the Press Secretary 2003). Within weeks, the apparent successes seemed to disappear against the specter of a growing insurgency.

The successful termination of war in Iraq has become the primary cause for President Bush. Obviously, the administration does worry about Afghanistan, Iran, Israel, and the global war on terrorism, but the overall issue of Iraq is of utmost importance to the national security leadership. Perhaps the nature of the criticism about the laser-like focus should be labeled the "Islamic world" instead of simply Iraq.

As Washington adjusts to changing conditions in Iraq while seeking to bring about a democratic, stable regime there, many supporters and critics of the administration agree that Washington is so absorbed in this issue that it is missing major changes on the global scene. An obvious concern is about whether the overall Middle East security balance is adversely affected by the growing power of Iran, even without the nuclear program that the international community fears will lead to a weapons program. Iran, as the primary Shiite state in the world, has become a much more powerful player in the region as Iraq has descended into virtual chaos since 2003. The primary U.S. allies in the region are predominantly Sunni states, which do not want to see a stronger Iran in the region yet view much of the U.S. activity within Iraq as helping, rather than hindering, Iran regardless of U.S. intentions.

Similarly, analysts point to increased Chinese prowess around the globe, illustrated by the chairman of the Joint Chiefs of Staff nominee Admiral Michael Mullen in the summer of 2007. In reports on his pending hearings before the Senate, Mullen's concern, symbolic of many in the Navy, is for the U.S. role in the Pacific theater where Chinese power grows steadily as the nation of 1.3 billion strengthens its economy and its People's Liberation Army forces. As China's role in the Pacific grows, its confidence and willingness to act across the world also has expanded. This includes Chinese engagement in Latin America, traditionally an area of virtual exclusivity to the United States, along with utter frustration on the part of Latin Americans with Bush's lack of attention until his March 2007 tour through Brazil, Uruguay,

Colombia, Guatemala, and the Yucatán of Mexico. Similarly, many point to dramatic increases in Chinese involvement on the African continent as it searches for energy and other resources. Chinese-European ties have also solidified but not as significantly as those between India and China since 2007, two states with tremendous populations available for economic exploitation. Finally, Washington seems dramatically slow in turning its attention to the region by trying to create better ties at a time when its role as the major partner for east Asia is being usurped by China's trade relations with virtually all other states in the region, including Taiwan. Despite Taiwan's dependence on its ties with Washington, the state has many businesses that are willing partners for the PRC. Washington's concerns about Iraq seem to have made it less aware of the emergent Chinese involvement, particularly in trade issues, with the rest of the Asian sphere, leaving the United States less interesting as a partner as the states of Asia wonder if the United States would abandon Asia for interests elsewhere. The United States has been the great balancing power in Asia since 1945 but some question whether China's growing role in international politics, trade, diplomacy, energy use, and other fields may weaken Washington's ability to provide that role as a balancing agent.

Fears that Washington is wearing blinders about the world go beyond Chinese involvement. These concerns relate to the increasingly authoritarian nature of Russia and the slowdown of democratic trends in many former Soviet republics. Others cite the aggressive expansion of European ties with Asia.

The question of U.S. strategic blinders relates not only to geographic regions but also to functional concerns. The Bush administration seemed to join the discussions about energy dependence far after most other governments around the world. Washington still argues that global warming is only a theory rather than the widely accepted danger cited by the rest of the world. The administration has proven itself determined to proceed on ballistic missile defense in the face of significant objections by many governments, such as China and Russia.

While the United States is clearly still the predominant military power in the world, changes in world views are important and have consequences for strategic interests. These changing world views have led other states to move forward without the desired Washington endorsement as the role that the United States plays in many areas outside the Middle East is more of an afterthought than the required support it once was.

Is U.S. National Security Threatened by the Nature of Islamic Societies?

When President George W. Bush led the nation in mourning and reprisal against the horror of the September 11 attacks, he explicitly and carefully made clear that the target of retribution was evil individuals and regimes, not Islam itself as a religion. In subsequent steps, he reinforced this distinction by inviting Islamic scholars to the White House and reaching out to the Islamic community.

The wars in Afghanistan and Iraq have been waged in two areas where Islam is the absolutely dominant religion, although with two distinct sects engaging in sectarian warfare in the latter. The distinction between waging war against Islam versus waging war against the bad actions of individuals or groups was played down but still retained.

Over the past five years, however, as terrorist bombings have spread to Indonesia, an overwhelmingly Islamic society, states such as Saudi Arabia, Egypt, Lebanon, and Pakistan have adopted increasingly traditional anti-Western mores. Rare exceptions remain in nations such as the United Arab Emirates but the picture of the Islamic world is one that is moving away from Western, democratic values rather than toward them as the United States has staked its goals over the same time period.

A question arising from these divergent actions is whether Islam is incompatible with the West, and thus a threat to the national security of the United States. In the pluralist society that the United States so richly embodies, this question would almost have been unheard of before this decade. When respected Harvard University political scientist Samuel Huntington asked the question, in the mid-1990s, about a coming "clash of civilizations" between the Christian West and the other cultures of the world, he was accused of massive misunderstanding or simplification of the world, even though the article "Clash of Civilizations" was one of the more cited pieces of the decade (Huntington 1993). Today, a generation later, many in the Christian world are asking precisely these same things.

This point has no absolute, assuring answers as to whether Islam is incompatible with democracy or whether the problem is a series of fanaticals; instead, the response depends on one's views of the world and relative priorities. Many in the Islamic world respond that they have adopted strong beliefs in their faith because they are frightened and discouraged by the unparalleled strength and power of the United States. The United States has millions of Islamic citizens who work hard and have joined the center of national society with entirely peaceful goals, ideals, and hopes as have Methodists, Jews, Bahais, Catholics, Buddhists, Confuscianists, Baptists, Disciples of Christ, and many other religious adherents across the fifty states and around the globe.

The fundamental differences between Islam and the West are great as are those between most religions. Islam has its adherents of absolute doctrinal purity as does any other religion. It does appear to have less compatibility, at this point, with some Western ideals than do other faiths but this is a snapshot in time. At the same time that many fear Islam's threat to the national security, some critics worry about the intransigence of many in the United States and their uncompromising commitment to faith as well. Still others fear the greatest danger to the United States is the increasingly secular nature of the society with no faith at all.

Does Challenging the President's Decision-Making Give Support to al Qaeda or Is It Part of the Democratic Process?

Vice President Dick Cheney has repeated countless times over the past four years that critics of President Bush's policies in Iraq and Afghanistan are validating al Qaeda's strategy of threatening the United States. Critics, particularly after the Democratic takeover of the Congress in 2007, have responded that this criticism of policy is inherent to the checks and balances of the U.S. political system and is the responsibility of those who disagree with the policy. The debate raises questions about how members of the national security community, as well as the decision-making community in the United States, view their influence on opponents (or equally peers) around the world.

The argument that challenging the president supports al Qaeda goals is a variation on a traditional concern in the United States. It essentially notes that "united the nation stands, while divided (on any issue) it falls." This view relegates public debate and democratic practices to a backseat in favor of one branch of elected officials that is ostensibly more knowledgeable than the rest of society.

Countering this position is the view that any adversary of the United States will operate to achieve its goals regardless of national debate or support for the U.S. leadership. On this side of the debate, the challenges to the executive branch will not have any affect on the ruthless behavior of those opposing U.S. national interests.

How Does India, the Largest Democracy in the World, Relate to the United States?

For most of its modern historic experience, India has been influenced by British culture; thus, Washington has often ignored India and its half-century of thriving democracy. During the Cold War, New Delhi's flirtations with the Non-Aligned Movement, illustrated by the 1955 Bandung gathering of "Third World" states in Indonesia, were important to the newly independent India's assertion of its own development as a sovereign state. Viewed by Washington, the Non-Aligned Movement and New Delhi's leadership position were seen as a euphemism for pro-Soviet beliefs, making Washington even less interested in engaging strategically with the burgeoning population, the long-governing Congress Party, the increasing military prowess, and the overall developing state that India represented.

The end of the Cold War coincided with the decline of the Gandhi dynasty and the Congress Party. Prime Minister Indira Gandhi died at the hands of her Sikh bodyguards in October 1984, several months after a government attack on the Golden Temple in Amritsar, the most sacred spot for Sikhs. Her younger son, the heir apparent Sanjay, had died in a plane crash in 1980, but her actual heir Rajiv ruled as prime minister intermittently before he died in a suicide bombing in southern India in May 1991. The successor governments in New Delhi loosened the Congress Party traditions of state-controlled economic policies and gradually began putting out feelers for India to join the broader international community in many ways.

At the same time, India was aware of deteriorating conditions in western neighbor Pakistan, as a result of growing Islamist pressures, as well as military modernization and rapid economic growth in China to the north. India survived the international condemnation of its May 1998 nuclear tests confirming its membership in the nuclear weapons club. The clear evidence that India and Pakistan had nuclear weapons as of 1998 put one more concern into the national security mix for the United States since the two states have such a contentious and war-ravaged history, including skirmishes after the 1947 Partition that created Pakistan and India and a 1971 war that created Bangladesh from the old East Pakistan/West Pakistan formation that had existed for twenty-four years. The extra danger of nuclear weapons heightened concerns after an attack on the Indian Parliament in December 2001, which Indian officials believed had to be condoned by Pakistani leadership. Throughout the first half of 2002, the international community held its breath as Islamabad and New Delhi came perilously close to a war over concerns about the attack on the Parliament. Washington, needing a more peaceful international community where its attentions were not diverted from the pursuit of al Qaeda in the aftermath of the 2001 attacks in the United States, could not ignore the prospect of nuclear war in the subcontinent yet had other priorities it had to consider as well.

In the final year of the Clinton administration, the president made a wildly successful tour of India, where he was able to begin opening doors to better U.S.-Indian relations. When the Bush administration arrived, it chose to push even harder for better ties as a method of balancing Chinese power in Asia. In 2003, however, India—long a major critic of Beijing military modernization and fearful of the evolution underway—tentatively began to open better relations with the PRC, to include more military-to-military exchanges.

Washington has continued to try to capitalize on India's evolving economic and diplomatic policies, which finally appear to be "opening" the country to free market economics and a more pro-Western stance. Unlike China, the Indian regimes have not fully embraced free market economics but are moving far more cautiously toward a free market commitment. The question of whether the United States is better off embracing an India that is fairly unlikely to pursue extremely pro-U.S. policies versus keeping a balanced relationship with Pakistan and India remains a crucial one. Many critics have never forgiven the U.S. administration for turning away from its own nonproliferation goals while advocating for a strict nonproliferation regime. India, never a signatory of the Nuclear Non-Proliferation Treaty (NPT) of 1970, will never sign on to the NPT because of the conviction that the treaty violates Indian sovereignty, yet Washington is abandoning one of its core principles to embrace this relationship. The question of whether this relationship is helpful for U.S. interests in the long run is an important one.

Did Questionable Interrogation Techniques for Prisoners and Saddam Hussein's Execution Undercut the U.S. Global Position?

Many around the world have long identified the United States with pushing a civilized standard of living, ethical behavior, and human values. Although not all agree, the United States has often been seen as protecting rights in a manner important to the world.

Thus, the photographic evidence of questionable and humiliating interrogation techniques at the Abu Ghraib prison in Baghdad and at the Guantánamo Bay detention center undercut this position. Further, the widely held belief that the United States tacitly or more directly supported the taunting and sectarian nature of Saddam Hussein's execution—a charge the Bush administration adamantly rejects—has led many to ask whether the U.S. stature around the world has been seriously undercut. And, if so, does this loss of stature hinder the United States' credibility in condemning human rights abuses in states such as the PRC? The United States has long issued an annual human rights report on issues of concern in other countries around the world, but the Abu Ghraib situation resulted in states such as China issuing their own human rights reports on the United States.

Additionally, the standing of the United States has been in question for many who believe the U.S. behavior in interrogating prisoners has undercut the basic democratic ideal of equal treatment under the law. The Bush administration argues forcefully and repeatedly that the traditional rules of law do not apply in these cases, but this has not silenced all critics, at home or abroad.

Does Funding for National Security Tools Affect Which Tools Become Most Frequently Used?

When people hear the term "national security," some automatically think of the military as the most important implementer in any scenario. Others think of economic power or diplomacy or information. These are known as the "tools of statecraft" and form the basic toolkit available to any leader. National security strategy is the appropriate use of the various tools in a concerted manner to achieve the goals of the nation, allowing for various priorities and understanding that each and every action in the national security realm will generate consequences—some known and others unforeseen until they occur.

In the past thirty years, funding for tools of statecraft to address national security has increasingly been dedicated to the military, to the exclusion of other tools. The need to rebuild the military after the Vietnam conflict (1960–1975), along with the funding required to move from a military draft to an all-volunteer military, meant a significant increase in military expenditure. With President Ronald Reagan's advent to the White House in 1981, defense spending increased dramatically because of fears that the Soviet threat was overwhelming the nation. Additionally, with the revival of the military as a proud arm of the national security, it became known as the most competent aspect of the government, and it probably reached its zenith with the completion of Operation Desert Storm in late February 1991. At that time, it appeared that the military could do anything, do it well, and do it with few casualties, as proven in the 96-hour ground campaign to oust Saddam Hussein's forces from occupied Kuwait.

When defense expenditures rose, similar increases in funding did not occur for the State Department, foreign assistance programs, or other aspects of the government that controlled instruments of statecraft essential for national security. During the 1980s and 1990s, as conservatives won the White House under Ronald Reagan and George H. W. Bush, and then the Congress under Newt Gingrich's leadership in 1994, talk centered on the incompetence and lackluster performance of the nonmilitary instruments. The State Department and the Agency for International Development, in particular, were blamed for mismanaging scarce financial assets, as if altering a situation outside the continental United States were an easy task completely under their control. The idea of the military being the most effective tool of national security found great credibility in the fall of the Berlin Wall in November 1989 and the dissolution of the Soviet Union two years later. Both events were initially often viewed as consequences not of diplomacy but of brute military strength; the reality, however, was that it was the combination of factors known as "national security strategy" that contributed to the inherent weaknesses and contradictions in the Soviet state.

When the Cold War ended in 1989, expectations were high that military spending would decrease dramatically, a concept known as the "peace dividend." Yet the first Gulf War (1990–1991) and subsequent peace operations around the world, in Somalia, the former Yugoslav republics, Haiti, and others, meant expenditures for armed forces did not decrease but continued to increase. The United States was the sole superpower in the early 1990s, so the U.S. military was the shining example of national prowess around the world. It was an outstanding force when there was little to challenge it, prompting Ambassador to the United Nations Madeleine K. Albright to ask the Chairman of the Joint Chiefs of Staff General Colin L. Powell what the point was to having such a magnificent military if it wasn't going to be used, since there were few situations requiring its deployment for traditional reasons (Powell and Persico 1995).

As the 1990s progressed, the military remained an outstanding instrument of statecraft while expenditures for other arms of the government did not receive similar funding. Some elements, such as U.S. Information Agency libraries, closed as a money-saving effort during the severe budget-deficit crisis facing the Clinton administration. Foreign assistance continued to decline in absolute and relative terms as politicians could not justify aid abroad while cuts faced those at home. As a divided government prevented the Clinton administration from getting its diplomatic nominees confirmed by the Congress, military presence by the senior armed forces became the major U.S. presence in many places, Latin America for example, rather than a full complement of all elements of statecraft to show U.S. interests.

In the period after the terrorist attacks of 2001, this situation persisted, and the military continued to be the major and sometimes only tool upon which politicians relied to achieve national security. In the Iraq campaign and the subsequent rebuilding effort, the Pentagon leadership preferred to consolidate all national security functions under its wing, and the White House acquiesced. Once again, the United States appeared to be relying almost entirely on the military tool instead of the range of security instruments.

Many critics charge that the Bush administration would be better off increasing the power and funding of other governmental agencies and decreasing the emphasis on military involvement in achieving national security. This highly charged debate appears unlikely to end in the foreseeable future. In March 2007, the newly installed U.S. commander in Iraq, Army General David Petraeus, made it clear that his forces could not work alone to rebuild the

Middle East but required the concerted efforts of all aspects of the national security team in the U.S. government.

How Has "Globalization" Affected National Security?

In the first decade of the twenty-first century, the immediacy of communication and global activities made globalization an unavoidable fact for many. Some believe the ability of international telecommunication to show events in one area of the world almost instantaneously is a serious threat to global stability and this ability to influence people so rapidly is a dangerous trend that undercuts the rationality of thinking people. Others, however, argue that globalization is nothing more than the logical progression of international change.

The July 1997 Thai baht crisis is an example of how rapidly international capital flows in today's environment. The fickle movement of capital is often viewed by non-U.S. citizens as a means by which the United States manipulates the system, thus undercutting the sovereignty of other states. While U.S. government officials of both political parties view the nation's involvement as a bipartisan activity, other critics argue that the U.S. activities around the world are a manner by which the nation exerts itself in a less obvious manner to influence others. This goal of creating an international environment that would benefit the United States, potentially at the expense of other states, is a controversial position that globalization allows.

Is U.S. Debt a Major Threat to National Security?

In the era after the 2001 terrorist attacks, national security expenses have raised the U.S. budget deficit dramatically. The Republican Congress (1995–2007), long critics of profligate Democratic pork-barrel politics, oversaw a tremendous growth in expenditures for all sorts of pet projects. The budget surplus welcoming the administration of George W. Bush in 2001 rapidly became a deficit as homeland security expenses skyrocketed.

Additionally, the United States has always been somewhat of an anomaly in its inability to encourage national savings. The steady increase in personal consumption by the citizenry, improved access to cheaper goods imported under the World Trade Organization agreements, and the need to increase government borrowing for the expenses have led to a marked increase in foreign borrowing.

The United States saw much of its spending covered by foreigners purchasing U.S. financial instruments. In the 1980s and 1990s, concerns grew about Japanese financing U.S. deficits, which contributed to severe anti-Japanese sentiment in the United States. As Japan's financial conditions declined in the 1990s, concerns about Japan's ability to overwhelm the United States subsided.

The current levels of foreign debt are a greater concern than they were in the 1990s for two reasons. One is that a growing concentration of the foreign funding for U.S. borrowing is in China. Second, China's own economy is growing at a rapid-fire pace that has no clear-cut end in sight. As China's military, economic, and social modernization grows, a significant corps of U.S. analysts worry that the reliance upon China's "help" in paying U.S. bills is a major threat to the nation's long-term security. Other economists and analysts view the relationship as interdependent, meaning China cannot operate without the United States as the market for its goods that are fueling the economic growth upon which the Chinese Communist Party bases its ability and right to continue governing the vast Chinese state.

Where Does National Security End and Homeland Security Begin? [Or are they really the same thing under different terms?]

Since 9/11, the nation has been unclear about precisely how to combat terrorism and enhance national security, partially because of bureaucratic differences between the goals. For many, national security is a broader topic than physical defense, so the need for greater economic opportunities, the need to enhance trade options, and perhaps the controversy of whether to allow more immigrants to do jobs in the United States are also issues playing into national security. Basic goals and premises of homeland security include the need to raise border protection and slow down the flow of people and goods across the boundaries to make certain they are not undercutting our security.

While there is general agreement between these goals for national security and homeland security, there are fundamental conflicts between the two. The redefinition of national security to include broader issues, largely outside of the nation's physical territory, makes this task challenging. Additionally, the difficulty, in a large, modern bureaucracy stressed by budget constraints and human limitations (for example, the armed forces that are engaged outside the nation in huge numbers), of determining which agency conducts which operations can be significant.

While the 2002 realignment of two dozen federal agencies into the Department of Homeland Security was intended to clarify responsibilities, in 2005 the Hurricane Katrina debacle along the Gulf Coast unveiled the depths of the existing problems in this area. Calls to realign the agencies, particularly the Federal Emergency Management Agency, may result in change, but the massive size and exceptional competence of the National Guard and regular, active-duty forces make it likely that they will still be called on to engage in homeland operations at times.

For a vibrant democracy such as the United States, the homeland security versus national security issue also raises questions about how traditional values bump against the new conditions. Many fear the United States is losing its core values by allowing the requirements to track terrorists to override such core values as privacy and executive-legislative branch relations. Time will tell how this balance comes out over the long run, but these calls of concern illustrate that not everyone believes homeland security is the same as national security, and those people prefer not to lose ideals that have been cherished in the four centuries of the national experience.

How Can the Nation Retain Its National Character in the Face of the Terrorism Threat?

One of the most fundamental arguments since 2001 has centered on whether the changes wrought by the terrorist attacks are fundamentally altering the nature of the United States. The decisions by President Bush and attorneys general John Ashcroft and Alberto Gonzalez to engage in domestic surveillance have led many on both sides of the aisle to question whether protecting national security requires the nation to ignore its basic tenets such "innocent until proven guilty" and freedoms under the First Amendment. The Bush administration, in response, has argued that the need to preempt the new type of terrorism outweighs any fears of infringement on individual rights and liberties.

Many citizens also question the new approach of waging preventative wars as opposed to waiting until the United States has been attacked to launch massive military operations. President Bush, former Secretary of Defense Donald Rumsfeld, and Secretary of State Condoleezza Rice rebut this concern, noting that the Constitution requires the government to protect the population and that this policy of prevention merely tweaks long-existent U.S. doctrine. Critics charge that the change undercuts our traditional view that the United States is a peaceful nation that only takes military action to defend itself. As the Iraq campaign drags on, the debate is likely to persist. Once congressional control moved from the Republicans to the Democrats in the 2006 elections, the debate on this point became more vocal and more heated but it remains far from ended some six years into the war against terror.

What Is the Proper Balance between Defending National Security and Protecting Civil Rights and Liberties?

Fears that Bush-administration covert policies aimed at rooting out foreign threats to the United States are undercutting civil rights and liberties are immense. In late 2005, revelations that the government had been monitoring domestic phone calls, in direct contradiction of Watergate-era reforms to the intelligence community, led many people to question whether the loss of civil liberties in the United States was a victory by terrorists. The administration, trying to keep these actions out of the press, argued that the United States could only protect itself by not telling potential adversaries they were being monitored. Even telling the courts and Congress might expose these programs, thereby compromising both the programs and, by extension, national security. The United States, in short, could not operate as openly as it had in the past, and that openness was probably a reason for being attacked.

Civil libertarians, in contrast, rebut the administration's actions and assert that they are the actions of a nondemocratic government that is not accountable to the public. Civil libertarians argue that the accountability of the three branches of government far outweighs anything the government seeks to do. As the Bush administration finishes its term with a Democratic Congress, civil liberty issues will continue to be debated.

Should the Nation Return to a National Draft or Retain a Voluntary Force?

President Richard Nixon ended mandatory military service in 1973. Later that decade, President Jimmy Carter reinstituted registration for military obligation, but the United States has had an all-volunteer force for three and a half decades. Until the Iraq conflict, this national choice has worked fairly well, depending on the particular context of any moment. However, the mounting conflict in Iraq has affected military recruiting, raising concerns over the length of the conflict and the number of casualties. At several times in the past several years, Representative Charles Rangel (D-NY) has suggested that the nation return to a mandatory draft to make the national service commitment uniform. Rangel and others have long believed military service has become too often a function of those not linked to government decision making. He also fears that military service increasingly falls to those at the lower socio-economic ranges of society, disproportionately involving the Hispanic and African American populations. Rangel is concerned that the nation's leadership is asking other young men and women to go to war when their own children are not among those who are potentially giving their lives for the nation; thus, a return to a draft would make everyone more cognizant of the sacrifice the young are making. Few people seriously support Rangel's suggestion, but his concerns illustrate a sense of frustration on the part of many about how the United States engages in national security decision making.

The constant strain on ground forces—primarily the Marine Corps and Army—in Iraq and Afghanistan, along with small deployments across the globe, still raises the question about the sustainability of the current force. Reenlistments have been less predictable than in nonconflict periods, and the National Guard and the Reserves, in particular, show major stress. The likely response will be a major increase in the congressionally established levels for the armed forces, but that will be neither cheap nor all that easy to fill in an era of relatively strong economic expansion and continuing long tours away from loved ones in places far away.

Should Those Seized During Conflict Be Treated as Prisoners of War or as Nontraditional Combatants?

One of the issues that has generated the most international and domestic controversy about the post-9/11 world is how the United States treats the nontraditional military combatants it captures. In the aftermath of the Afghan campaign in late 2001, the Bush administration decided to consider the Taliban supporters that it captured as nontraditional combatants on the grounds that the war on terrorism is a new form of warfare, thus not subject to the Geneva Conventions, a series of agreements forming the basis to the global norms for humanitarian treatment of captured individuals. The normal rules of the Geneva Conventions (1949), for example, were not invoked when men were incarcerated in Guantánamo Bay or other facilities around the world. Men were not publicly charged nor were they given representation in court, on the grounds that this endangered national security. The men were often held indefinitely and based on suspicion rather than the habeas corpus rules of law enshrined in the Constitution. These actions have been highly controversial.

The 2004 revelation, through numerous photographs, that the incarceration procedures being used in Iraq were in direct opposition to many tenets of Islam, the faith of the overwhelming majority of the prisoners, inflamed the already heightened anti-U.S. sentiments around the world, but especially in the Islamic world from Indonesia to Morocco and to Great Britain as well. Many critics at home and abroad charged that the procedures violated the 1949 Geneva Conventions. The photographs illustrated men being humiliated by women, by animals, and by being forced into degrading activities. Apologies and comments by administration officials only reinforced the sense that the United States not only did not understand Islamic populations but also sought to engage in a crusade against Islam rather than terrorism.

Administration officials argued strongly that these interrogation and incarceration techniques were essential to getting the intelligence needed to fight the global war on terrorism. Critics asked whether the war on terrorism outweighed basic U.S. values and whether the actions were not creating more terrorists than curbing them. The July 2005 underground and bus bombings in

London were cited as evidence of the failure of the policies. It is not clear whether all or any of the individuals who have been in custody for questioning held for several years offer any valuable intelligence at this point, but holding these people clearly sends a signal around the world that the United States is serious about stalking and capturing terrorists. Six years into the war in Afghanistan and four years into Iraq, the United States retains its interrogation and incarceration facilities in Guantánamo Bay, Cuba, and various other locations.

How Much Is National Security Worth if Faced with a Massive Budget Deficit?

The massive costs of enhancing national security over the past several years have created a burgeoning budget deficit. This situation has not been exclusively caused by national security, as Congress has spent much on pork-barrel projects, and President Bush has rarely vetoed any bills coming across his desk, but the escalation of security expenditures and the rapidly growing and apparently unanticipated economic toll for Iraq have led to budget-breaking expenditures. Critics of the administration ask whether the enhancements are worth the costs. As the goal of creating a larger permanent armed force for the nation becomes clearer after late 2006, the expense involved is also clearer. The larger military will require a much higher expenditure as well as more women, men, and weapons. Getting and retaining a quality military requires education and training, materiel, family benefits, post-conflict health care and assistance, and various other costs that are often hidden. As the Bush administration closes out its second term, the debate appears likely to grow as Congress and potential presidential candidates question these decisions.

How Does the Nation Balance National Security in the Private and Public Sectors?

One of the more interesting aspects of warfare in the new millennium is the use of private-sector employees to accomplish much of what used to be military activities. The outsourcing ranges from privatizing janitorial services in the Pentagon, to providing food to troops in northern Afghanistan, and to providing security for the leadership of Iraq in the Green Zone. This has reduced staffing levels for the Department of Defense and other federal agencies but has created a host of unintended consequences.

Contractors are not governed by the same Uniform Code of Military Justice that establishes rules for their behavior in the field. In the Abu Ghraib scandal, one of the more sensitive issues was the accounts of interrogations by civilian contractors, who went much further in their sordid techniques than did the young soldiers who were ultimately court-martialed and jailed. For some, this contradiction of civilians seemingly ungoverned in their actions, potentially unpunished, was profoundly unhelpful to the U.S. national security goals of forwarding the rule of law, not rule of an individual, in the Middle East. In other cases, private contractors appear to get in the way of the traditional forces in the field and these contractors have no willingness to get out of the military's way. Accounts of this challenge have been rife from Iraq.

Still others raise the question of whether a nation wants to hire out its most fundamental obligation to a segment of the population over which it has virtually no control. Private contractors may be more concerned about costs than safety, which can affect the level of security, or they may not feel obligated to meet all of the stringent requirements to protect civil rights or civil liberties that government strictures require. Alternatively, private contractors might be more expensive in the long term than the costs of continued government staffing for all obligations, as contractors probably pay a premium for their workers that the traditional national security paid by the government would not require.

Finally, for many in the United States, the idea of bearing arms is purely a governmental activity rather than one of private citizens, even when they are working for a contractor. People who hold this view are uncomfortable with the idea of leaving the business of warfare in the hands of any single private group within society.

Should the Nation Be Preparing for Traditional Warfare or for Counterinsurgency and Other Types of Nontraditional Conflict?

One of the most challenging issues for the nation is what preparation is best for the men and women of the U.S. armed forces. The traditional U.S. view of warfare is that it is abnormal and once it is ended, the international system and nation return to the status quo ante. This leads to a large buildup of forces for a traditional conflict, often described as "force on force conflict," as occurred in World War I or II.

Back to at least the Korean War of the early 1950s, however, a different type of warfare has arisen. In this latter form, large battles are less relevant as the nation confronts more irregular conflict. This irregular conflict is often known as "asymmetrical" warfare, as the weaker adversary seeks to find a technological niche by which it can defeat the stronger force. In this latter case, conflict is less military but more psychological and political. Counterinsurgency, as practiced in Vietnam and increasingly in Iraq, addresses less predictable attacks against larger, slower massive forces of a military superpower like the United States.

Secretary of Defense Donald Rumsfeld assumed his office with a promise to wean U.S. forces from their dependence on units that were too big and too slow to move with the agility required of the twenty-first-century battlefield. Not only would this enhance war-fighting skills by making the armed services better able to confront problems more quickly, but this would create cost savings that could be used for other military responses, particularly national missile defense.

Before the March 2003 Iraq invasion, Army Chief of Staff General Eric Shinseki predicted it would take "several hundred thousand men" to invade and stabilize Iraq. Deputy Secretary of Defense Paul Wolfowitz and others roundly dismissed Shinseki's professional assessment, resulting in the deployment of fewer than 150,000 troops, a relatively small number by many military estimates, to Iraq. These forces were led to believe their tours of duty would be relatively short—some estimated as low as a few months' duration, by which time Iraqi forces were anticipated to take control of the security situation.

Instead, over the five years since the invasion, the need for much more heavy military protection and a significantly higher number of troops to accomplish the stabilization mission became apparent. Along with this troop strength argument was the question of what these forces should be prepared to do once in country. Nation building is generally seen as a radically different mission from traditional war fighting, but U.S. forces have typically not seen the two as compatible, and presidential candidate George W. Bush, in his 2000 campaign remarks (Bush 2000), cited the need to decrease nontraditional military tasks in favor of highlighting those activities the U.S. armed services did best: traditional war fighting.

Some five years into the conflict, fundamental debate about the types of forces needed remains one of the cornerstones of U.S. debate about national security. Military men and women often cite the need for what is referred to as the Powell/Weinberger Doctrine, which advocated massive force before going to war, as occurred in the first Gulf War (1990–1991). Others besides Secretary Rumsfeld have argued that technology and absolute U.S. military dominance make overwhelming force less important than responding swiftly and decisively to problems around the world.

With the shift from a Republican to a Democratic Congress in 2007, the overall discussion of whether the conflicts on the horizon will be traditional or new types became a much more heated one. The military released a new *Counter-Insurgency Manual*, FM3–24, in December 2006, which recognized the need for a new study and focus on the particular form of conflict represented by Afghanistan, Iraq, Somalia in the 1990s, and several other more recent conflicts. Lieutenant General David Petraeus, the man President Bush appointed as head of forces in Iraq in early 2006, had primary responsibility for redrafting this manual. His emphasis on gaining a more personal, close knowledge of the small areas of cities and villages in hopes of winning the "hearts and minds" of local populations has been a resounding cry for many who look at the conditions faced in these new theaters.

At the same time, many senior officials in all services continue to fear a more traditional conflict as they assess the growing military modernization program of the PRC. Believing a conflict with the PRC might erupt over the island of Taiwan, the need to make certain of the U.S. capabilities in case of a major military exchange with a powerful, large Chinese PLA is paramount. Trying to balance these concerns with adequate preparation for the future is one of the greatest challenges facing the nation in national security.

Is the United States Safer by Creating Governance in States around the World or by Allowing Others to Determine Their Governments and Fates?

One of the self-assessments characterizing citizens of the United States is a sense of exceptionalism in the world. The United States has always believed it held the strongest, if not a unique, commitment to democracy as a form of the government along with attendant values and ethics. This sense of a national ethos, which differs from other states and cultures, is seen as providing the nation with a greater responsibility and right to help the rest of the world find this obvious option as a "better" way in the world.

In today's post-9/11 world, the United States has taken an aggressive stance to advocate democratic governments over any other. As a democratic republic, the United States has always had an affinity for democracy but it has also, albeit uncomfortably at times, always recognized that citizens in a sovereign state have the option of choosing their forms of government

The attitude and strategy after 9/11 altered that traditional view. President Bush adopted an approach to mold the world aggressively into one of democratic states in a global arena. This was a shift from the historic experience and one that made many of our allies uncomfortable. The move to impose democracies seemed in stark contrast to the U.S. unwillingness to entertain calls from citizens at home and abroad to give Iraq more time to answer adequately the world's doubts regarding weapons of mass destruction before launching an invasion.

Many ask whether any outside state can impose a form of government on a people. This debate goes to the heart of how any population governs itself or what sovereignty means. In this instance, the questions are all the more important because the U.S goal of imposing democratic governance has been vital to the administration's attempts to maintain an international political consensus. Whether the assumption behind the goal is correct remains unclear because the goal implies that democratically governed states cannot threaten the United States. This assumption is not obviously true but nor is it demonstrably false.

Is the United States More Susceptible to Threat by Engaging in Conflicts in Iraq and Afghanistan?

In the early days of 2007, President Bush fine-tuned his new military strategy for Iraq and, by extension, possibly for Afghanistan. In neither conflict is the U.S. victory—which once seemed so obviously likely if determined exclusively by size and military prowess of its force in invading these relatively weakened states— completely ensured. Thus, President Bush decided to "surge" U.S. forces into Iraq to increase the troop strength for a relatively fixed period of time, to stabilize conditions on the ground in the hopes that Iraqi forces can then take over to create a stable, democratic government and a peaceful environment.

Embedded in the debate about surging troops is the condemnation that the Iraq and Afghan conflicts, which have both turned out to be considerably more military force–intensive than envisioned earlier, are breaking the resilience and strength of the U.S. military. Concerns revolve around the frequency of troop deployments in the theater (many Army and Marine units are in Iraq for their third deployment in four years); the inability to recruit highly skilled and better educated forces; the severe financial strains on the armed services, which will not only require significant recapitalization but will require that the country forgo further defense research and development at the levels desired; and the real probability that enlistments for the Reserves and National Guard, neither of which has ever faced during the all-volunteer-force era the frequency of deployments that each confronts today, will tumble. In short, many fear, as former Chairman of the Joint Chiefs of Staff General Colin Powell said in mid-December 2006, that the Army (and Marines) are nearly broken.

For President Bush, this is an irrelevant argument because he believes that the threats posed by the Taliban in Afghanistan and the Saddam Hussein regime in Baghdad were utterly and completely consuming to the nation's security. For those who viewed this war as not a war of necessity but one of choice, the long-term threat to reduce the quality of the armed forces at a time of other possible concerns around the world (North Korea and Iran with nuclear weapons, an increasingly dictatorial Russia, and a growing might in China) is a bigger concern to be remembered.

Is the United States Better Off Waging a "War of Choice" than a "War of Necessity"?

Many critics of the Bush administration charge that it waged a "war of choice" in Iraq instead of following the traditional U.S. view that war is conducted only when it cannot be avoided. World wars I and II were considered wars of necessity, particularly after Pearl Harbor. Indeed, most analysts view the war in Afghanistan, which began in October 2001, as a war of necessity after the 9/11 attacks.

The situation in Iraq, however, was less clear cut. President Bush opposed Saddam Hussein but the threat to the United States was not as clearly true, the timing was not as compelling, the goal was somewhat undefined, and the overall goals beyond "major combat operations" ousting Saddam were unsettling.

As the United States looks at other possible conflicts around the world, such as a nuclear-armed Iran, the debate about war of necessity versus war of choice will continue. Each president, as commander-in-chief, has to make decisions based on his best understanding and analysis, as did President Bush. The president rarely has unanimous support in a democracy; it is the nature of the system. But this absolutely fundamental concern frames the heart of the national security issues that confront a superpower in its sole position as able to fight any war it so chooses.

Does the United States Still Recoil from Service Personnel's Deaths or Has the Nation Overcome the "Vietnam Syndrome"?

The Bush administration has been cautious about reporting body counts, releasing information about deaths, showing pictures of caskets arriving at Dover Air Force Base in Delaware, and many of the public images that had undercut public support in Vietnam. At the same time, the globalized world provides images and reports of events going on regardless how hard the administration may try to spare the nation the angst of addressing its dead and, particularly in this war, severely wounded. As the United States has come to grips with more deaths in Iraq than were accumulated on September 11, public support has sagged dramatically. What is not clear is whether this is a new version of the Vietnam syndrome, where people do not support a war that sacrifices U.S. human or financial resources, or whether U.S. citizens simply do not see Iraq as central to the war on terrorism as President Bush does. Has the administration not adequately spelled out its goals and elucidated support for those goals? Is the nation tired of fighting a war that appears to have no relevance to the Iraqi people's desires? Is the United States losing its sons and daughters as Iraqis engage in civil war? These are unanswered but growing questions about the current involvement in Iraq, reminding many of the debates about body counts in Vietnam.

Is Traditional National Security No Longer Relevant?

For many in the national security field, this is the broadest, most overarching question. Each analyst's perspective on the international community will determine the likely outcome of the question. As the nation debates what it wants to spend, what type of military it wants to field, which path is the correct one for cooperating or confronting the international community, and various other associated concerns, the issue of whether traditional views of national security are relevant remains central to the debate. National security, if defined as purely defensive actions for protecting the homeland and the physical safety of citizens, is relatively straightforward. Once more complex definitions are applied, however, the debate becomes much more complicated, more enduring, and harder to afford.

Clearly, the events of 2001 indicated that the United States is not immune from terrorism. But that was true as early as April 19, 1995, when a U.S. citizen, Timothy McVeigh, blew up the Alfred P. Murrah Federal Building in Oklahoma City. Terrorism has never been exclusively a foreign-born phenomenon.

The question of whether conventional national security is out of date, however, depends on the analyst's orientation and definition. To many, national security will always mean protecting the physical attributes of the country and its citizens, nothing more, nothing less. For others, terrorism and that arbitrary, unexpecting sense of national danger far outweigh the old view, thus requiring the vigilance be transformed into an aggressive preemptive defense. This question has no absolute answer, nor is one ever likely to emerge through national consensus.

Have Discoveries of Poor-Quality Veterans' Care Standards Altered the Debate about National Security?

Early in 2007, the *Washington Post* published a series of highly critical stories on conditions for veterans at the Walter Reed Army Medical Center, and by extension the entire army medical structure nationally ("Walter Reed and Beyond" 2007). The stories of mold-plagued rooms, the need for massive rehabilitation, and unreliable predictions of how long veterans can anticipate care ignited a firestorm within the armed forces as well as on Capitol Hill. Eventually, the secretary of the army and the surgeon general of the army both retired under pressure from the new secretary of defense, Robert Gates.

The questions of commitments to those who have been injured while serving the nation have become more public and less comfortable for society as a whole. With the tremendous advances in medical care in the field, soldiers are surviving many wounds that would have been fatal a generation ago, but many are left with injuries and disabilities that will plague them for the rest of their lives. How the country treats these people's sacrifice will resonate with the veterans for the rest of their lives.

Is the Whole Nation Sacrificing for This War or Are Only Those in the Armed Forces Affected?

Historically, one result of universal military service was that all citizens were involved in wars the nation was fighting overseas. During World War II, for example, the sacrifices of the public at home were embodied in the campaigns to create Victory Gardens and buy war bonds. U.S. personnel returning from war went to school on the G.I. bill almost as an entire generation. Veterans' benefits were an important part of the nation's debate, and everyone was part of the war effort.

With changes in national commitment after the war in Southeast Asia, the United States ultimately chose to abandon the idea of universal military service in the early 1970s. One reason for that change was that, increasingly, those who were wealthier appeared to have the options to withdraw from this universal national commitment by staying in school through education deferments. The overwhelming majority of political figures in the United States in their fifties and sixties today did not serve in uniform in Vietnam, for instance. Senators John Kerry and John McCain, both Navy veterans, are exceptions.

When the Nixon administration chose to take the path of an all-volunteer force, people were able to choose their commitment to the military. The idea, still well-supported, was that those who were more highly committed to service would provide a much more effective, less controversial force. Military incomes rose, benefits increased, and the idea of a career in the armed services took on wide appeal for some in society.

With the war on terrorism, however, a confluence of issues has led those sending their young to war to question this national commitment. The war in Iraq has proven that signing up for a tour in the National Guard or the Reserves is not just a "weekend warrior" job as many had thought in the 1970s and 1980s. Multiple tours in the military theater are taking people away from their regular civilian jobs and separating them from their families for far longer than anticipated. Even those who are regular-duty forces are facing multiple and extended deployments in a military environment that is stagnant, rather than improving dramatically as anticipated in the early days of the conflict when many believed the U.S. deployment of troops to Iraq would be brief.

More irritating and of concern to many in uniform and their families is a sense that they alone are fighting this war, not the nation. The nation appears able to carry on its traditional lifestyle without the sacrifice that is being asked of those who are sending their daughters and sons to war. This raises questions about the nobility of the patriotic mission as well as the nation's ability to assume these soldiers are merely "hired guns."

As the wars in Afghanistan and Iraq continue, reenlistment and retention concerns continue within the active-duty and reserve components and the National Guard. It begs the question whether these young men and women will be willing to continue this personal commitment unless they have no options, which is not the basis upon which the all-volunteer force began. The creators of the all-volunteer force never intended it to be a place of "last resort" but a military force where people joined because they believed in its missions, ethics, and goals. Those in uniform want to believe their fight is noble and sanctioned by their friends and neighbors as a whole, and not that they are merely part of a hired force operating while the remainder of the country looks the other way.

Are the Disagreements on National Security Priorities between the President and Congress Threatening Troops in the Field and the Nation's Security?

Upon taking control of Congress in early 2007, House and Senate Democrats made clear their absolute determination to force the return of U.S. service personnel from a highly unpopular conflict in Iraq. The first three months of their control over the Congress largely focused on crafting a military budget that would give a specific date for the initial withdrawal of combat forces.

President Bush and several senior figures in his administration made clear their belief not only that this was not the best strategy for the nation but that this was inappropriate behavior on the part of one branch of government. This argument centered on the premise that the commander-in-chief has the constitutional responsibility to make decisions about the use of force while the role of Congress is to fund these decisions.

The debate underlying this constitutional point is an important one for national security. When the president believes it his sole responsibility and right to make decisions relating to use of force, force deployments, and overall orientation of national security strategy, it puts the power in a single hand, albeit one elected by the nation. Under the premise that Congress is an equal player to the president, the decision making becomes the purview of as many as 535 individuals representing smaller district concerns around the nation. This creates factions and coalitions, and it is virtually impossible to orchestrate through any single voice.

Some see this issue as merely a political, partisan debate between the Democratic Congress and the Republican White House. President Bush and Vice President Cheney have made this point repeatedly as they argue that the "surge" policy should have an adequate time to work in Iraq. Alternatively, the question of constitutional responsibility as the basis to the debate raises broader issues of popular participation, links to other constitutional responsibilities, and various other aspects of the fundamental struggle characterizing the U.S. political system. It also raises issues about the need to maintain the checks and balances so fundamental to the U.S. political ethos.

Should the United States Be the Global Police, Keeping the World in Line with U.S. Goals?

U.S. exceptionalism has always made citizens believe it has had and always will have a special role in the world, especially in national security. Historically, the United States has approached many of its relationships with the goal of projecting its goals and values in what many find an almost naive eagerness. The arrival of U.S. Protestant missionaries in China or various Middle East countries exemplified this strain of beliefs.

In the fifteen years since the breakup of the Soviet Union, the United States has had a unique opportunity to carry out the mission it has long seen for itself and its citizens. This has been an era of great involvement in countries around the world through all aspects of national security strategy: Somalia, Haiti, Bosnia and Herzegovina, Kosovo, Colombia, Afghanistan, Iraq, Taiwan, Yemen, Liberia, and more. Some of these involvements have been military interventions (Iraq and Afghanistan) while others have provided humanitarian aide (Somalia, Haiti, Liberia) or military assistance (Colombia and Taiwan). The United States has been attacked on the homeland in 2001 and its citizens have been the victims of terrorism in Indonesia as have been the citizens of its allies from Australia, Spain, and Britain. In short, violence has certainly continued and increased around the world, indicating that the international scene is not purely a benign place where a series of individual threats may affect citizens, but is a complex place where the goals of individuals, groups, or states may lead them to violent action to achieve their goals. Whether a single nation can control that environment as a policing agent is open to debate.

An issue that underlies much of the debate about interventions in Iraq and Afghanistan is the gradual recognition that, under the current global configuration, the United States is likely to be the major state called upon to solve problems no matter where or what they are or what they cost into the foreseeable future. If this is true, have citizens or only the government signed up for this awesome responsibility? Is the United States willing to carry this financial responsibility? Does the nation want to send its daughters and sons to fight all of the world's battles? Is the world willing to take on permanent responsibilities for national security problems such as Taiwan, Colombia, or Israel? Each of these countries has a commitment to protect itself but requires a major, sustained responsibility on the part of the United States to make financial and other assistance virtually permanent. It is unclear whether the nation as a whole has made the commitment to engage in this sustained support.

Should the United States Carry Burdens of National Security Alone or Work with Greater Numbers of Allies and Partners?

The United States has long been skeptical of the institutions that have populated the international system during the twentieth and twenty-first centuries. As a society the United States has largely adopted a "realist" view of the international system. This view emphasizes the role of both states and power, the desire for states to achieve their national interests regardless of the needs or interests of others, and the desire to prevent any state from achieving a dominance of the international system that would allow those states to overwhelm the international system. And as a result of this realist view, the United States did not trust international organizations to protect our nation's interests in the face of other states' concerns.

In particular, the United States has had little true use for the United Nations (UN) over its sixty years' existence. Washington wanted the organization to be headquartered in the United States to ensure that Washington could weigh in on its activities, but over time, the United States proved less willing to pay its fair share of operational and maintenance costs. In the 1990s, at precisely the time the UN appeared to overcome the many enduring criticisms of its lack of accomplishments, the United States withdrew even further from the organization by arguing it would only pay its fair share (seen by most in the United States as too high) when the UN underwent serious management reform. This was ironic as many of the international civil servants operating the organization were from the United States but did not operate under Washington's direct control.

In the lead-up to the Iraq war in 2003, the United States turned its back on the UN on the grounds that it was not adequately protecting the international system against Saddam Hussein's weapons of mass destruction because Washington felt the UN-sponsored inspectors were being duped (or allowing themselves to be duped) by Saddam. The UN clearly did not support the action in Iraq but was unable to dissuade Washington and London from involvement.

After it became clear that Iraq would be a more enduring reconstruction effort than originally envisioned, many in the United States expected the UN to assist with the reconstruction tasks. The UN had much experience with these activities around the world, but the body had withdrawn from Baghdad after the August 2003 suicide bombing that killed the secretary general's personal envoy.

As the Iraq and Afghan efforts continued, Washington began looking for assistance. The North Atlantic Treaty Organization became involved with small troop deployments to Afghanistan but fewer troops from allies went to Iraq. With the withdrawal of British forces later in 2007, Washington will be even more isolated in its role in Iraq.

The question at hand is what other options are available in an intervention that is highly unpopular outside the United States. It remains unclear who will assist Washington for the long haul.

References

Bush, George W., 2000. "The Second Gore-Bush Presidential Debate," Winston-Salem, North Carolina, October 11, 2000, www.debates.org/pages/trans2000b/html (accessed August 4, 2007).

Geneva Conventions. 1949. www.unhchr.ch/html/menu3/b/92.htm (accessed April 30, 2007).

"Hearing Set for Choice to Head Joint Chiefs," *Morning Edition*, interview by Steve Inskeep of Tom Bowman, *National Public Radio*, aired July 31, 2007.

Huntington, Samuel. "The Clash of Civilizations?" *Foreign Affairs*, summer 1993.

LeTreut, Hervé, and Richard Somerville, "Historic Overview of Climate Change Science." In *Intergovernmental Panel on Climate Change: The Physical Basis of Climate Change.* United Nations Environmental Panel, April 27, 2007, at http://ipcc-wg1.ucar.edu/wg1/Reports/AR$WG1_Print_Ch1.pdf (accessed October 1, 2007).

Office of the Press Secretary. 2003. "Commander in Chief Lands on USS *Lincoln*." www.cnn.com/2003/ALLPOLITICS/05/01/bush.carrier.landing (accessed August 13, 2007).

Petraeus D. H. 2007. March 8. Remarks to the press.

Powell, C. L., and J. Persico. 1995. *My American Journey: An Autobiography.* New York: Random House.

"Walter Reed and Beyond: The Wounded Warrior at Home." 2007. *Washington Post.* www.washingtonpost.com/wp-srv/nation/walter-reed/index.html (accessed April 30, 2007).

Zoellick, R. 2005. September 21. "Whither China? From Membership to Responsibility" (speech before National Committee on U.S.-China Relations). www.ncuscr.org/articlesandspeeches/Zoellick.htm (accessed April 30, 2007).

3

Worldwide Perspective

The U.S. perspective on national security is unique in the global environment for several reasons. The discussion in this chapter will focus on these unique characteristics and how they affect security and U.S. options around the world. It is drawn from observations and reactions gathered over a long period of time rather than specific articles or statements. While virtually any of these individual points could tolerate much expanded discussion, the focus of this volume is on U.S. national security, so the chapter is relatively brief in its discussion of the differences.

Geographic Imperative

The United States has a radically different view of national security than the rest of the world because of certain advantages the nation has. The major and enduring advantage the United States has over virtually any other country in the world is its geographic location. The People's Republic of China (PRC), for example, has borders with more than a dozen states, one of those borders being thousands of miles long with few natural inhibitions to the easy movement back and forth of anyone who seeks access to Chinese territory. People frequently forget that the Great Wall, which spans much of northern China, was not built as a tourist curiosity, but to prevent the incursions of outsiders threatening the Chinese state at various points in history. Russia, with whom the Chinese share such a long border, has had a historic animosity over much of the last millennium that has forced many Chinese dynasties to worry about their ability to maintain national control or keep out marauding invaders.

Similarly, one of the reasons for the fragile and seemingly dysfunctional state of affairs in much of Africa is the lack of respected or even clearly defined borders. Constant and ongoing fears that these borders must be protected redirect national energies in a substantive manner that can be highly disruptive to other national priorities. Even in Europe the need to protect the nation against others who sought to redress an existing "wrong" in borders has led to many wars, such as the long-running dispute between France and Germany over the area of Alsace-Lorraine.

The United States has had a geographic advantage shared by few other areas of the world. With two vast oceans on the east and west, the nation developed a strong sea service to facilitate shipping and defense, but the centrality of the oceans to protecting the nation against outside intervention has been obvious. Similarly, having two neighbors with relatively weak and benevolent intentions has given the United States a cushion that people appreciate in today's world where geography is infrequently studied or appreciated. The United States could hardly have created two more favorable neighbors than Mexico and Canada, even though many critics of the Mexican immigrant phenomenon would argue that this cross-border trafficking is a major threat.

Canada, with its wide territorial expanses and relatively calm, measured political tradition, shares the longest unarmed border in the world with the United States. While some Canadians would argue that they have been threatened by the United States and its goals over the years, the relationship between the two states is a relatively strong one and has led to Canada being one of the three closest allies with the United States (along with Great Britain and Australia). Tensions exist between the states over trade and other issues at times, but the overall shared beliefs are high and sustained.

Although Mexico's history, culture, religious experiences, and world view have been somewhat different from that of the United States, Mexico is still a relatively benign neighbor, despite the fact that a substantial portion of the Mexican territory was ceded to the United States after the War of 1848. Mexico's Catholic culture stood in stark contrast to the U.S. Protestant experience, which was heavily weighted toward accepting new immigrants who would become ingrained in the new culture instead of retaining their home views of the world.

The United States has periodically worried about the border with Mexico, fearing that individuals could bring "trouble"—often meaning different views or a different standard of living—over the boundary or that the general instability that so often characterized the Mexican political system in the decades after independence in the 1820s would bring chaos to the orderly expansion occurring in the vast region west of the Mississippi River. For instance, during World War I (1914–1918), which overlapped with the Mexican Revolution (1910–1927), the greatest social upheaval in Latin America in the twentieth century, the United States sent troops to buttress the U.S. defenses, but that was the rare instance when the nation needed to use force to ensure its physical border security. Other tensions developed as a result of the statist activities of the Mexican regimes under the *Partido Revolucionario Institucional* (Institutional Party of the Revolution), such as nationalizing foreign petroleum firms in 1938 or perpetuating the single-party rule between 1927 and 2000, but Mexico's stability was a relatively sure condition upon which U.S. security analysts could rely. While immigration and illicit drug trafficking have been periodic concerns for the United States over the years, the depth of worries about Mexico has never been anywhere as deep as they were about the Soviet Union and the threat posed by nuclear weapons in the Cold War, even though the relationship between Mexico and the United States is arguably the most important for either state on a daily basis.

With this imperative, or state of affairs, the United States occupies a position unparalleled in the international system. This creates a different view of what is required to achieve national security. For the United States, the seemingly easy relationship between it and its neighbors allows for the U.S. view that peace is the norm but war is an aberration to be addressed and quelled, and then the norm of peace renewed.

Other states are always aware that conflict is a continuation of politics by other means, to paraphrase the great Prussian strategist Karl von Clausewitz from his perennial wisdom in *Von Kriege* or *On War*, reflections from the Napoleonic wars of the early nineteenth century (Klinger 2006).

Economic Imperative

The United States also views national security differently from other states because it has the economic wherewithal to do so. No state in the world spends nearly as much on defense as does the

United States. The United States has the vast resources available through its multi-trillion dollar economy, unparalleled by any other state in history.

Secretary of Defense Robert Gates oversaw the submission of a budget request for an aggregate $716.5 billion for fiscal year 2008, including anticipated spending of $141.7 billion for Afghanistan and Iraq as well as more than $90 billion to finish off 2007 spending for these theaters. The regular defense budget for fiscal 2008 amounted to $481.4, an increase of more than 11 percent over the 2007 allocation (Matthews 2007).

In fiscal year 2007, the U.S. defense budget allocation was $471.5 billion, exclusive of the supplemental submissions for Iraq and Afghanistan (Department of Defense 2006, 5). By comparison, China, thought to be the second-highest spending nation in defense terms, announced a defense budget increase of 17.8 percent for 2007 over its acknowledged outlays equivalent to $36.6 billion in 2006 ("China's Defense Budget" 2007).

A frequently cited statistic is that the United States spends more on its defense than do the next fourteen states combined, including the PRC, Russia, the United Kingdom, Japan, France, Germany, India, the Kingdom of Saudi Arabia, South Korea, Italy, Australia, Brazil, Canada, and Turkey (Shah 2007). While many in the United States and abroad question whether the Chinese numbers are accurate for the People's Liberation Army (PLA) expenditures, few question that it still represents only a small portion of the U.S. outlays. The Chinese admit PLA expenditures are rapidly growing but note that early expenditures for the PLA were a pittance compared with what the United States spent on the military at the end of the Cold War, roughly the period that coincided with PLA modernization.

The reason the United States can spend as much as it does on defense is its economic strength; the U.S. economy has long been the dominant economy in the world. The U.S. economy has proven resilient in instances of exogenous crisis, such as the September 11 terrorist attacks, and in instances of economic downturn, such as the October 1929 or 1987 massive stock market sell-offs. The United States has been able to spend a significant amount of money on defense because it is still a relatively small portion of the federal budget and of the gross domestic product.

Historically, U.S. defense expenditures have been high when the threat was accepted as worth that level of national commitment, such as the 1945 defense budget of 34.5 percent of the gross national product. During the Cold War, which many national security specialists viewed as the single most threatening period in the nation's history, the U.S. defense budget amounted to 11.7 percent in 1953 and 8.9 percent in 1968, both "war years," while in the Reagan administration the budget decreased to 6.0 percent in 1986. In 2005, defense accounted for 3.9 percent of gross domestic product (Baker 2006). By contrast, the European Union's (EU) military arm, the European Defense Agency, spent 1.8 percent of the states' gross domestic product on defense in 2005, amounting to less than 4 percent of *governmental expenditures* by EU states that year (Bitzinger 2007). In short, the United States outspends Europe on defense by three to one.

Spending on Defense versus Nonmilitary Tools of Statecraft

The United States has the single largest budget and economy in the world; thus, it is not surprising that it spends the most on national security. The spending is far from balanced, however, because the overwhelming majority goes to a single tool of statecraft, the military. At the same time, the United States has a decidedly lower view of the value of the nonmilitary tools, such as foreign assistance for development purposes. While the United States certainly contributes a substantial amount to foreign assistance in gross terms, as a percentage of the gross domestic product or of its budget expenditures the United States spends far less than, say, Japan or Norway, for comparison.

Part of this comparative approach indicates the U.S. propensity to engage in an odd view of the world: a view that conflict is not the norm yet armed solutions are frequently the desirable approach. Part of this is because the military, particularly in the two generations since the conflict in Vietnam, has the reputation of being more efficient than other tools of statecraft. This probably relates to the fact that the U.S. armed services retain an autonomy, strictly adhering to U.S. direction rather than being put under the control of foreign commanders, much to the irritation of U.S. allies.

Foreign aid has long been controversial in the United States because it does not go to U.S. hands but into the control of others. Long-standing critics of U.S. foreign assistance in national security, such as former Senator Jesse Helms, the North Carolina Republican who ran the Senate Foreign Relations Committee in the 1990s, argued that assistance often went to corrupt foreign bureaucrats who were more interested in enriching their own pockets than helping their people. The United States, especially in the past quarter of a century, has decreased its foreign assistance dramatically as skepticism about the utility of such aid has increased.

Similarly, all spending on tools other than the military has remained low. The military, in the era of the all-volunteer force after 1973, has been viewed as an efficient, competent, and professional force that has utility in virtually all instances where applied. Instances where the military has been used for purposes beyond traditional military operations include domestic disaster relief (e.g., southern Florida after Hurricane Andrew in 1992 and the Gulf Coast after Hurricane Katrina in 2005) and international relief efforts (e.g., Operation Provide Comfort for the Kurdish areas of northern Iraq in 1991 and in the Indian Ocean basin after the December 26, 2004, tsunami). Beyond disaster relief activities, the military has become the major instrument of stability, security, reconstruction, and transition operations, as noted by the Pentagon in a Department of Defense order of 2005 (Department of Defense 2005). The lack of resource allocation to these efforts made any other instrument of power exceptionally challenged to accomplish what repeated U.S. administrations believe the armed forces are best able to do.

The PLA has a similar role in *domestic* national security efforts in China because of its historic links to the people of China. The PLA, as a politicized arm of the Chinese Communist Party, views itself as a tool of the people, an instrument of achieving and responding to the goals and needs of the people. The view, however, is somewhat different from that of the U.S. professional military. The U.S. military is an instrument of achieving national security, while the PLA is a mechanism by which the Communist Party stays in power, theoretically for the benefit of the people.

In many states of the former third world, the role for the military revolves heavily around border enforcement, a role that is not a normal obligation for the U.S. national security community. National security for these other states often relates to protecting the security and integrity of the physical area of the country, largely because the neighbors and the borders of these states come under frequent assault, which does not happen in the United States.

Latin America has historically had a peculiar variation on national security with its self-arrogated role in defending the *patria. Patria*, historically, has meant more than the territory; it encompasses the soul, history, culture, values, soil, blood, and absolute essence of these societies, as defined by the military, which did not believe civilians could be trusted to defend the society. Some believed the militaries were thus engaging in a form of nation building that could be done by no one else but was required to keep these states safe from Communism and associated stains. The "national security states" of the 1960s through 1989—Brazil, Uruguay, Chile, and Argentina, which had brutal dictatorships that seized power with the full intention of remolding their societies to achieve a sound, uncorrupted nation—were quite different from the national security understandings of the rest of the world. The post-1989 world, devoid of any monolithic Communist entity, appears to have erased this view of the military tool in these countries, but the possibility of national security defined by the bearers of arms in those countries will always remain a background issue.

Unilateralism versus Multilateralism

An area that strongly differentiates the U.S. view of national security from that of the rest of the world is the role of unilateralism versus international organizations and multilateral activity. Ironically, one of the greatest proponents of multilateralism in the world, Scottish-born Andrew Carnegie, made his wealth in the United States and tried to use that wealth to enhance multilateral activities around the world to prevent war. But in the United States itself, the citizenry has tremendous suspicions of *spending on* multilateral institutions on the grounds that these might lead to the creation of a world government imposing its views on top of the individual rights guaranteed by the Bill of Rights or because people fear the institutions have highly bloated, inefficient bureaucracies. National security in the United States is the responsibility and the right of the nation on its own, not outsiders who might compromise the nation's values for the ideas and goals of others. Yet, people in the United States often say, when asked, that multilateral approaches in the abstract are good for our national security.

As a result, the United States has a love-hate relationship with the multilateral organizations while much of the rest of the world, especially Western Europe, prefers multilateralism to balance the overwhelming power of a single large state. The United States has long paid to have a significant role in international organizations; for example, it funded the creation of the Pan-American Union and the subsequent Organization of American States and funded their headquarters in the United States. While many critics of international organizations accuse non-U.S. members of being less willing to carry their financial weight than the United States, evidence suggests that Washington prefers these groups to have their headquarters in locations where the United States can exercise considerable influence.

In the 1990s, The U.S. refusal to pay its full United Nations (UN) dues was a perfect example of a lackadaisical, if not hostile, view toward the organization while the other member states were somewhat baffled by U.S. foot-dragging. With such a large budget and ability to contribute to this international effort, many around the world dismiss U.S. assertions of its willingness to pay for an efficient organization. Too often other states of the UN note that the United States bullies the organization and ignores it at will. Arguing that the UN was full of extreme mismanagement and gross waste, the United States, particularly Congress, would not pay its full dues assessment until Secretary General Kofi Annan implemented major management reform. Without a doubt, the UN had a tremendous mismanagement problem as is true of many governments and organizations around the world. However, the irony of the situation was that much of the upper management of the UN throughout this period was led by U.S. citizens who were on loan to or direct employees of the organization. Rather than seeing the UN as a tool of statecraft, the United States preferred to ignore it in many instances when it could have been used more readily.

As a subset of multilateralism, the United States has a particularly strong view regarding the national willingness to have U.S. military forces serve under a foreign commander. The United States, in the current era of alliances and multilateral operations, requires U.S. forces to be in a chain of command exclusively headed by a U.S. officer. Even as the United States has sought to broaden and strengthen those alliances and operations, it has maintained the need for U.S. armed forces to be under a U.S. chain of command. In practice, however, U.S. forces have not exclusively been in a chain of command under U.S. officers. After NATO assumed responsibility for stabilization efforts in Afghanistan under the International Security Assistance Force mission in October 2006, the commanding officer was a European. Since the United States has forces in NATO, he commanded U.S. troops on the ground in Afghanistan (ISAF 2007).

The rest of the world often shares that goal of wanting to maintain control over its national troops but typically cannot keep control as easily as the United States can because of the latter's size and military prowess. The United States is the senior partner in all alliances, providing the greatest portion of the financing, materiel, and often both troop strength and transportation requirements. Other states frequently receive benefits from the national security relationships with the United States, but trade-offs are involved.

Sovereignty: The United States versus the World

One of the most important differences between the views of national security in the United States and the rest of the world is the respect and centrality of sovereignty to their assessments of national security. The United States has rarely seen its sovereignty clearly violated, a notable exception being the September 11 attacks. For the geographic and economic reasons discussed earlier in this chapter, the United States has been relatively isolated and thus sovereign, able to control its own destiny as an independent nation for nearly all of its history..

For the overwhelming majority of states around the world, sovereignty has not been as attainable. Instead, many states—including Mexico, Canada, China, Iraq, Afghanistan, Egypt, and South Africa—and peoples—such as the Palestinians, the Jews, and the Kurds—believe they have not been able to control their destinies.

To the Chinese, the most fundamental need of national security is retaining the ability to control its future without the influence of others who seek to keep China in a subservient role. Rarely does one ever hold a conversation, even in today's emergent, excited, increasingly confident, and aggressively involved China, where the term "century of humiliation" does not appear. This period was characterized by China's inability to determine its own future through policies and self-governance. It extends from the signing of the Treaty of Nanking in 1842, which gave Hong Kong to the British, through the creation of the People's Republic on October 1, 1949, when China believed its future was invariably determined by outsiders who were bent on depriving the Middle Kingdom of its rightful role as a central state in world affairs. This period of humiliation actually ended in 1997 when Hong Kong formally reverted from a British Crown colony to a Special Administrative Region within China. The reversion agreement specifies that the special status will continue until 2047.

Today, rare is the instance in which China does not adhere firmly to a principle of not intervening in the affairs of another state (with the notable exception of Taiwan, which it does not deem a sovereign state but an internal Chinese issue). This policy equally precludes outside involvement in the case of humanitarian crisis (such as the Darfur region of Sudan) or absolutely appalling government (such as Saddam Hussein's pre-2003 government in Iraq).

Similarly, the former states of the third world have seen their borders and rights to self-determination violated for centuries; thus they are hypersensitive to sovereignty questions. These states frequently resent, if not outright reject, the idea that the United States can bring some sort of outside "wisdom" to their particular and peculiar problems and concerns. Many states in Africa, Asia, and Latin America are distinctly uncomfortable with the paternalism and outside involvement Washington brings to the table, yet are also too weak, in most occasions, to prevent these ideas from being imposed on their development agenda. This means that these states, fearing the power of a single state in Washington that does not seem willing or able to listen to their views, are more open to the alternative leadership that Beijing or New Delhi or Pretoria offers in contrast to Washington's lecturing tone, as the other capitals at least imply that they will listen to the needs of others.

Unipolarity versus Multipolarity after Bipolarity

The world view that the United States and Soviet Union had between 1947 and 1989 was known as bipolarity, the concept that the nations of the world fell into one of two camps, supporting either the United States or the Soviet Union. After 1955's Bandung Conference of nonaligned states, many of the states in Latin America, Africa, and Asia sought to take a "third" position that was neither Eastern (Soviet) nor Western (U.S.) in orientation, but the two superpowers still viewed these other states as supporting one camp or the other. Thus, scholars began to describe the political configuration of the world as bipolar.

The demolition of the Berlin Wall on November 9, 1989, ended this bipolarity. No longer were East Germans segregated behind the Iron Curtain under pro-Soviet governments aligned with Moscow's view. This monumental shift in the world's structure continued until the dissolution of the Soviet Union on December 31, 1991. This series of events marked a remarkable, once-in-a-generation opportunity to rebuild the international system.

China, the largest state still retaining a somewhat Communist view of the world, believed the end of the Soviet Union and demise of the Cold War could only result in forcing the world— including the United States—into a much more multipolar environment. This would allow multiple centers of power to develop, one of which might be China, thus dispersing power across the international community. India and the European community, to a lesser extent, had similar hopes for greater power dispersion.

The United States itself had various assessments of what would result in the post–Cold War environment. Some analysts believed multiple power centers would result while others believed peace, instead of conflict, would be the norm in the international system, and power would essentially melt away all together. One prominent view that attracted much attention was the one that said the United States would become the dominant state, based on its vast economic power and overwhelming military prowess, and it must not allow the development of alternative power centers to challenge the U.S. dominance. Known to some as the Wolfowitz doctrine, this idea allowed that a single state, with its superior moral, economic, military, and political stances, could be the dominant state of the world so that no one could threaten the nation (Gellman 1992).

The Balance-of-Power World

The Wolfowitz doctrine differed dramatically from the view of most of the world for several fundamental reasons. While political scientists around the world discuss alternative approaches to explaining the global political system, probably the most common one was what is referred to as "balance of power" or realpolitik thinking. Balance of power is a view that says the international system operates to preclude the creation of a single overwhelming state that can exercise virtually unrestrained power or hegemony over the remaining states. The measure of power that matters most to those espousing this world view is military power, although economic power is nearly as important. The reason the world view is also called realpolitik is that states will pursue their national interests with whatever power is available to them, often military but occasionally other types of power. For this reason, measuring power in terms of bullets, ships, and missiles became a crucial measure of a state's role in the international system.

Under the balance-of-power view of the world, the creation of a single superpower is not desirable; thus, states will come together in alliances to prevent that single superpower from occurring. These balancing actions, based on military and other forms of power, are only temporary but are used to prevent any single state from doing precisely what some in the United States sought to do in the immediate post–Cold War world.

The need to prevent such a single dominant state became apparent to many in the international community after the Gulf War of 1991 when the United States, although nominally leading a coalition to reverse Saddam Hussein's August 1990 seizure of Kuwait, clearly had an overwhelming military superiority over any other state in the world. The emergence of a single state with such economic, military, and political power relative to any other state on the planet made many around the world highly uncomfortable. This state of affairs made many states adopt pro-U.S. democratic regimes and free market economic models but for others these moves went against fundamental cultural and historic norms, such as in Latin America where the role of the government in society and economics had been a historical reality even before the Spanish colonial experience.

For other states with large populations or significant economies, such as India, China, and the European Union, the overwhelming U.S. superiority was uncomfortable and undesirable. These states began expanding their relations with each other without shutting the door on U.S. connections. A common misunderstanding about balance of power is that it must be swift and initially successful to achieve its goals. However, balance-of-power responses to the international system may be slow, systematic, and gradual to achieve the overarching goal of preventing a single supreme state.

In the two decades since the end of the Cold War, more states have come to fear that a single superpower would try to eliminate regimes with which it differed. President George W. Bush's 2002 State of the Union speech, with its reference to the "axis of evil," bred unease abroad (Bush 2002). The subsequent invasion of Iraq in March 2003 proved further to these observers that the United States did not respect sovereignty in principle but would overthrow regimes that Washington did not want to continue. Cuba's long-running Castro government had to be expecting to be in the queue for U.S. actions.

Under the balance-of-power perspective of the world, the natural state of affairs is one of conflict and violence, a view that is frequently associated with the early seventeenth-century English political theorist Thomas Hobbes. Hobbes's experience during the English Civil War led him to argue that man lived in a natural state that was violent, harsh, and aggressive. This natural state of affairs was, thus, a pessimistic one in which man needed to have the strength to defend himself, as outlined in *Leviathan* (Hobbes 1651).

Most of the measures of power discussed in the balance-of-power view of the international community include military, economic, and other tangible or measurable indicators. The tremendous shock for the global population resulted from those who argued that the real danger posed by the United States was to cultural or religious systems across the world. The war that al Qaeda wages is specifically against the cultural norms that the United States holds most dear and is attempting to export around the world: democracy, tolerance, and religious diversity. The al Qaeda view of the world is a shift from Western tolerance for diversity, where ecumenicalism and discussion are more expected than the orthodoxy al Qaeda seeks to impose on adherents to Islam as well as apparently for the entire world that does not currently embrace Islam. This lack of common language or genuine exchange of ideas that the al Qaeda view requires is fundamentally at odds with the basic U.S. perspective of the world, even though the United States has its own advocates for orthodoxy and reversing the diversity so characteristic of U.S. society.

The United States is far from a monolithic entity, in any sense of the word. The national unity resulting from the September 11 attacks may have been the closest the nation has ever come to unanimity. The political measurements of the nation's unity, national elections for Congress or the presidency, have shown remarkable results since the end of the Cold War. As a society, the United States clearly does not like the overwhelming single-party supremacy in its domestic political system that makes the rest of the world uncomfortable at the nation-state level in the world system. A minority Democratic president had only two years of a friendly (that is, Democrat governed) Congress before his adversaries took over in 1994, even though Clinton won reelection to the White House two years after the massive defeat of his party in congressional elections. The 2000 presidential election had the narrowest margin in U.S. history with the Republican victor, George W. Bush, losing the Senate to the Democrats when a fellow Republican sought refuge as an independent. President Bush won a similarly razor-thin victory in his reelection effort in 2004, only to see his party lose Congress two years later, at least to a great extent because of the public's doubts about the efficacy of war in Iraq. In short, the United States is a country where its public is not comfortable giving power to a single party or branch of government, much like the rest of the world is not comfortable with a hegemony by any nation at the global level.

A Concrete Example of Differences: The United States and Asia

Asia, during the first decade of the twenty-first century, offers three distinct areas of possible concern that illustrate why Washington's views are so different from the international perspective: the China-Taiwan dispute, the India-Pakistan question, and nuclear developments in North Korea and Iran. The three issues are quite different from one another but have a common thread: a major threat to the peace of the international system, with Washington believing it can manage a situation that could easily spin out of control. In some ways, Washington appears condemned if it does and condemned if it doesn't, to paraphrase a popular phrase, on these highly sensitive questions.

China-Taiwan: Three Different Interpretations of the Status Quo Ante

Many international security specialists believe the only situation on earth where two highly armed nuclear states could get into conflict is over the question of Taiwan and its status with regard to the PRC. Taiwan offers a conundrum for U.S. strategists, one where the position Washington takes is almost alone in the global community. Taiwan has an elected, democratic government that has maintained the position for more than fifty years that Taiwan is not a part of the PRC, although its status is not entirely clear or agreed upon by its citizens.

Originally inhabited by aborigines, then traders from the mainland, but only loosely under Beijing's control until the Qing Dynasty's arrival in the seventeenth century, Taiwan fell under Japanese political control between 1895 and 1945. At that point China was in the terminal stages of a long civil war, and Taiwan became the refuge for the remnants of the Guomingtang (GMD), the Chinese Nationalist Party that ruled between 1927 and 1949, albeit with fits and starts. The GMD waged a campaign to retain power against the Chinese Communist Party under Mao Zedong but the vast corruption and poor governance record of the GMD made the Communist victory possible. In 1949, GMD President Chiang Kai-shek declared the Republic of China relocated from its headquarters on the mainland to the island, beginning a myth that the Republic of China would eventually reclaim the mainland as an anti-Communist regime.

The United States chose to back the GMD in the civil war, thus recognizing the Taiwan government as the only one for China until President Richard Nixon's historic February 1972 visit to Beijing, which opened the door to U.S. relations with long-standing Communist adversaries. The 1972 visit, followed by President Jimmy Carter's decision to "normalize" (meaning "recognize," in diplomatic parlance) China on January 1, 1979, complicated the situation for the United States in east Asia because Beijing would only accept formal U.S. diplomatic relations with "one China," a position to which Washington acceded. But Washington was exceptionally uncomfortable completely abandoning an anti-Communist ally of more than thirty years' standing, so Washington set up a parallel, nonformal diplomatic system to maintain a fiction that Washington respected Taiwan as an entity and it was not succumbing to Beijing's position that it was a part of China only awaiting further reintegration into the motherland. Neither Beijing nor Taipei was happy, nor were countless U.S. supporters of Taiwan. As long as Taiwan had virtual military superiority over the mainland's PLA, however, the fiction was an uncomfortable but acceptable one.

With the end of the "century of humiliation," marked by significant PLA modernization and vast Chinese economic advancement, the context had shifted in important ways. The PLA began modernizing in the 1980s but accelerated that process after the Chinese economy began growing substantially in the 1990s and even faster the following decade. More money in the system allowed the PLA to receive a bigger budget slice consistently over the past two decades. At the same time, the Taiwan defense community saw its expenditures decrease significantly, partially because the Taiwan economy went into recession in the late 1990s when its economic expansion of the post–World War II period slowed dramatically. Thus, the PLA was increasing its capabilities for China at the same time Taiwan's defensive military edge was stagnating and eventually declining from the status it had maintained since the 1950s when the United States had begun taking a major role in helping Taiwan with its defense needs.

Additionally, a major shift in the Taiwan political scene produced unintended consequences. From Chiang Kai-shek's arrival on the island in 1949 until his son was about to leave power in the mid-1980s, Taiwan was far from a democracy—it was a hard authoritarian regime that brooked little political opposition or debate. The United States conveniently looked away from the repressive system on the grounds that it was anti-Communist and had to be tolerated. Chiang Ching-kuo (1910–1988) began removing many of the antidemocratic conditions in Taiwan, resulting in a truly open, democratic presidential election in 1996 and a non-GMD president four years later. This change in political landscape meant a much freer, open debate that did not guarantee that national priorities for spending would result in the defense community receiving all of the funding it believed necessary. Instead, the political debate during the two-term presidency of Chen Shui-bian became a much more fragmented one that resulted in stalemate instead of overall agreement on national priorities. As a result, Taiwan, with a supportive U.S. Congress and White House, did not purchase the long list of military modernization programs that both Washington and Taiwan military officials had argued were necessary.

Finally, Chen's government, based on the Democratic Progressive Party's strong independence stance, seriously unnerved Beijing for much of the first decade of the century. The Communists had hoped he would not win in 2000, and certainly not in 2004, fearing that his actions would force armed action against what the mainland refers to as their "Taiwan brothers," thus threatening Beijing's growing modernization and economic progress. The Communist government in Beijing values its survival as the ruling party above any other goal but has long believed that the Taiwan reunification problem remains the last unsolved issue from the Chinese civil war, thus an item about which the Chinese people might blame the Communists and threaten their control over the society. So for Beijing, the minimum tolerable condition through Chen's tenure is that Taiwan not try to alter the status quo ante that Beijing defines as a Taiwan that has not formally declared independence, is not recognized by most other states around the world, and is ultimately—at some unspecified but expected date—going to return to the historic Chinese Middle Kingdom.

The difficulty is that both Washington and Taipei define status quo differently. For Taipei, the Chen government defines status quo as meaning it is a de facto sovereign state merely awaiting the recognition by the rest of the world, one not to be threatened or manipulated by their Chinese "cousins" across the strait. Thus, Taiwan's desire is a codification of a radically different view of the world than that of Beijing.

Yet a third definition is that held by Washington: a "single China" policy but with an understanding that the views of the Taiwan people will be taken into consideration in what the United States hopes will be a peaceful resolution to the disagreement. In fact, the United States is obligated to help provide Taiwan with defensive articles, under the Taiwan Relations Act of 1979, but it is not required to intervene in any potential conflict between the two. But many analysts wonder whether the president of the United States, particularly after George W. Bush, will be able to deny military assistance to a Taiwan subjected to direct Chinese aggression as Taiwan is a democratic government. Precedent was set when President Bill Clinton decided to send two carrier battle groups to the Taiwan Strait area in 1996 when Beijing shot missiles across the north and south shores of the island.

In sum, Taiwan is a complicating factor in a growing Sino-U.S. relationship in east Asia. Many argue that Taiwan represents the only likely flashpoint over which the United States and another nuclear-armed state could enter military conflict. Others believe cool, rational thinking would preclude warfare. In any case, the Taiwan question remains one where views are quite split and seemingly irreconcilable at present.

The India-Pakistan Nuclear Standoff

India and Pakistan are the two highly populous but polar opposite states that resulted from the partition of the British Raj in 1947. India tends to have highly educated Hindu and other populations, whereas neighboring West and East Pakistan (the latter of which evolved into Bangladesh in 1971) have a mostly Muslim population facing staggering poverty and hopelessness. Many conflicts remain between the religious groups in both states, and the territorial dispute over Kashmir, a largely Muslim population governed by India, remains highly tense. For most of the sixty years of these states' existence, the United States was satisfied to see tensions and conflict between the two remain relatively contained on the subcontinent.

The Indian detonation of a "peaceful nuclear device" on May 18, 1974, loosened that comfortable situation a bit, but the May 1998 nuclear weapons tests by each state changed that relative complacency. The reality that New Delhi was building nuclear weapons was disquieting, particularly as the United States began pushing states to focus on governance and raising the status of the populations rather than allowing the fomentation of radicalized groups in society.

U.S. concerns about a Pakistani nuclear bomb were more profound. Pakistan has a markedly smaller population but since the 1970s has felt the need to produce an "Islamic bomb" to counter India and, by extension, protect Islamic interests (Weissman and Krosney 1981).

Even more important for a longer period of time, U.S. leadership began to realize that Pakistan had become a fundamental battleground in the war of ideas between Islam and the non-Islamic west. President Pervez Musharraf, formerly a general, offered a serious test to the U.S. goal of promoting good governance and democracy since he had seized power but he was seen as a desirable option to the Islamic hardliners, often referred to as Islamists or Islamic fundamentalists, who had growing ties to the Taliban in Afghanistan and al Qaeda and clearly sought to erase the secular trends at work in Pakistan's governance. India, in turn, perceived itself to be the target of such Muslim extremism. In one such conflict, Indians charged that Kashmiri militants masterminded the December 2001 terrorist attack inside India's parliament that killed a dozen people. In short, both India and Pakistan seemed more important to U.S. national interests in 2001 than they had almost thirty years earlier.

The December 2001 attack on the Indian Parliament was arguably an even more flagrant reason for an Indian national response than the 9/11 attacks in the United States as it was an attack on a seat of national power. Everyone around the globe recognized that the passions involved in the India-Pakistan tensions, along with the accusations involved, could have generated a nuclear response between the two states. For the first half of 2002, the international community held its collective breath for fear that India would attack Pakistan and a catastrophic war would result. By the second half of the year, the two sides began tentative talks but the reality that two highly volatile national entities had the military capability to inflict significant damages on each other was not lost on anyone.

Washington has close ties to the Musharraf government but also notes that the two governments have differences over several major issues, such as arms proliferation and especially how closely the Pakistanis are pursuing the Taliban across the border in Afghanistan. Washington fears pushing too hard on Musharraf, however, for fear his government will fall and an anti-U.S./pro-Taliban government will result. Similarly, Washington would like to see India play a bigger role in balancing Chinese growth in Asia as well as opening the economy to U.S. products. But at the core of the south Asian concern is the reality that these two states—both allies and both possible adversaries, depending upon the context—offer an exceedingly dangerous border tension with other states because they have proven nuclear weapons stockpiles, albeit small by U.S. and European standards. How the tensions will be resolved in the long term is not clear, but in 2002 the two states appeared intent on going to war, with or without nuclear weapons. Only the power of time softened the tensions. Washington recognizes only too well that the nationalism of 2002 could easily rise again and that cooler heads might not prevail, yet in the increasingly interdependent world, the United States cannot simply return to a position that this part of the world is no longer of interest.

New Nuclear Players: Iran and North Korea

The United States has shown serious concern about the proliferation of nuclear materials to potential new nuclear states as far back as the Indian blast of 1974. In particular, the United States has worried about nuclear weapons falling into the hands of those states whose objective is to hurt U.S. national interests in a meaningful way. The September 11 attacks brought this possibility to the forefront of national concerns, as it became clear that threats to the United States are proliferating and that weapons of mass destruction may be as small as airplanes.

President George W. Bush highlighted his concerns about North Korea and Iran threatening the United States in his second State of the Union address in 2002. In those remarks, the president talked of an "axis of evil" that included Saddam Hussein's Iraq, the Islamic Republic of Iran, and the Democratic People's Republic of Korea. The president noted his fear that the axis states sought to threaten the United States in many ways, but his greatest concerns were over states with weapons of mass destruction such as biological, chemical, or nuclear weapons.

In the autumn of 2002, some analysts were surprised when the United States acknowledged that it feared the advancement of North Korea's nuclear program. The United States had worked to thwart a nuclear program in the remote North Korean system in 1993 when the Clinton administration pushed for the "agreed framework" in exchange for a "cease and desist" in North Korea's goal of achieving a thriving nuclear system. Clinton's Republican opponents and others criticized the agreement on the grounds that the North Koreans had no intention (or track record) of adhering to their promises. While the efficacy of the agreed framework was controversial, U.S. government officials did not accuse the North Korean government of pursuing nuclear weapons until the autumn of 2002.

The North Koreans, extraordinarily closed and withdrawn as a society, have had a range of responses on the nuclear concerns, according to press accounts. At times their negotiators have agreed with the U.S. diagnosis of their behavior, while at other times they have fiercely denied the accusations. In the years since 2002, the United States, in conjunction with the PRC, Japan, the Republic of China, and Russia, have negotiated in the Six-Party Talks, hosted by the Beijing government. The process has been tedious, plagued by fits and starts, and often discussions were not convened for months at a time. In early 2007, however, the Bush administration announced a breakthrough thought to signal North Korea's intention to scale back its program after receiving financial, technical, and food assistance from the Six-Party partners. Critics in the United States, frequently former Bush administration officials such as former Ambassador to the United Nations John Bolton and Ambassador Bob Joseph, have argued that this agreement is no better than the one made more than ten years ago. Many critics believe North Korea will continue its nuclear program and that the United States can only guarantee security in the region through regime change in North Korea, a move that Washington is clearly unable and uninterested in orchestrating at present.

The concerns among Asian participants raised about North Korea during the Six-Party Talks are quite different from those raised by Washington. While the nonproliferation agenda is an important one in Washington, partners in Asia are far more concerned with the possibility of a forced collapse of the Pyongyang government than they are of nuclear weapons. The nearby states, particularly the PRC and South Korea, worry a great deal about the potential crush of refugees from a starving North Korea should the Communist government fall. Northeast China, where the refugees would flood into the PRC, already faces unemployment problems, so this possibility would be quite unwelcome. And although the South Koreans would like to see the reunification of the many families separated since the 1950s, they have evidence of the vast expenses that the two Germanies incurred in their reunification process more than a decade ago. The economic levels of North and South Korea are far more varied than were the two Germanies, meaning even greater costs for any potential reunification. And in the case of a Pyongyang collapse, those costs might be even higher. Furthermore, the capital of South Korea, Seoul, is within artillery range of North Korea, meaning South Koreans do not want to see the North Koreans pushed into a position of acting desperately.

The endgame for North Korea's nuclear program remains unclear. For the United States, the goal remains keeping that government from ever getting nuclear weapons, but Washington's single-minded approach to the problem is at odds with the views of other states in the region, which may push those states to differ from the United States on policy options in the future.

Iran also represents a significant challenge for the United States because the Iranian Republic is the largest population in the region and a major petroleum repository. Its possession of nuclear technology would threaten many allies in the region yet many in the Gulf region believe that U.S. actions in Iraq have made Tehran stronger, not weaker, to the disappointment of Sunni-led neighbors. Washington's wearing involvement in Iraq has tied its hands, lessening its options to address Iran's threat. Additionally, some abroad were slow to abandon hopes for greater economic relations with Iran, thus impeding attempts to pressure the Iranians to abandon their nuclear efforts. Beijing, in particular, needs to continue importing petroleum to fuel its economic growth yet pressuring Teheran might threaten one of the Chinese sources. China is reluctant to threaten its primary goal of economic growth by pushing Teheran on nuclear activities; Beijing believes its interests at home outweigh the international threat at present. The United States broke diplomatic relations with the Iranian government in the late 1970s when the U.S. ally, Shah Reza Pahlavi, fell from power at the hands of the Ayatollah Khomeini and his Iranian Revolutionary Guard. The November 1979 seizure of hostages at the U.S. embassy in Iran, a crisis that lasted for 444 days, reduced the possibility of some sort of improvement of ties between the states.

Iran has long desired nuclear weapons, beginning in the 1970s when the Shah took preliminary steps to develop a nuclear weapons program before his ouster. It remains unclear when the Revolutionary government resurrected the idea, but it had become evident by 2002, which earned Iran and its radical government a place in President Bush's axis of evil. The Bush administration also had to deal with Iranian President Ahmadinejad's volatile government. President Ahmadinejad has questioned whether the Holocaust actually happened, and has proclaimed that the state of Israel should be wiped out. These statements have upset non-Iranian governments around the world and made many people question his basic sanity.

The United States is not alone in its concern about Iran's behavior but few states feel the urgency Washington feels. Many states are uncomfortable with U.S. intelligence claims about nuclear weapons in Iran because of botched intelligence claims in Iraq. Critics wonder if Washington is more interested in regime change than stopping nuclear weapons. Additionally, many states around the world need the vital petroleum that Iran has in vast quantities. These states, especially China, appear less willing to lean on the Iranian regime about its nuclear program than the United States would like to see. These states fear that pressuring Teheran would further constrain their access to petroleum, which is crucial to economic growth. Finally, some states are simply not comfortable with Washington's willingness to violate sovereignty to satisfy its concerns.

What Do These Cases Mean?

These three Asian cases represent concrete examples of differences in perspective between Washington and much of the rest of the world. They are neither clear-cut nor easy to resolve; each of them presents a series of complex effects on other U.S. and foreign national interests. These cases also show that each state has its national security interests, which it will protect, often contrasting and conflicting with the interests, of others around the world. National security strategy attempts to resolve these differences without conflict but this is not always possible. But the cases exemplify how Washington prioritizes national security concerns differently from many of its allies and major interlocutors.

Conclusion

The United States is different from the rest of the world because of its power, values, and approach to the international system. Yet it values national security in a manner similar to other states because protecting a nation's citizens is arguably the highest requirement for any government to meet, and failing to do so can hardly characterize a successful regime or state. The United States has an unparalleled set of conditions, physical and economic, to produce the national security spending vital to the post-9/11 world. At the same time, the United States is operating in a world without radically different views of national security, views being acted upon by adversaries who seek to thwart the United States along with allies who simply evidence discomfort with U.S. actions.

The nature of national security for the United States in today's world, however, is learning to react to those different approaches to the world that may threaten the nation or slow down its achievement of national interests. The bigger question is how long the United States can afford to answer each and every one of these challenges. At no point in world history has any state had unending patience and political will or inexhaustible resources. The United States appears likely to see those issues arise.

References

Baker, S. 2006. "Defense Spending." *Issues 2006*. The Heritage Foundation. Washington DC: Heritage. www.heritage.org/Research/features/issues/issuearea/Defense.cfm (accessed May 4, 2007).

Bitzinger, R. 2007. May 4. "European Defense's Never-Ending Death Spiral." *ISN Security Watch*. www.isn.ethz.ch/news/sw/details .cfm?id=17457 (accessed May 4, 2007).

Bush, George W., "State of the Union Address," January 29, 2002. www .whitehouse.gov/news/releases/2001/01/20020129–11.html (accessed August 5, 2007).

"China's Defense Budget to Rise 17.8 Percent in 2007." 2007. March 4. *People's Daily Online*. http://english.people.com.cn/200703/04/ eng20070304_354130.html (accessed August 13, 2007).

Department of Defense. 2005. "Military Support for Stability, Security, Transition, and Reconstruction Operations," Directive 3000.5, issued November 28, 2005. www.dtic.mil/whs/directives/corres/pdf/300005 .pdf (accessed August 13, 2007).

Department of Defense. 2006. *National Defense Budget Estimates for FY2007*. www.defenselink.mil/comptroller/defbudget/fy2007/ fy2007_greenbook.pdf (accessed May 4, 2007).

Gellman, B. 1992. "Keeping the U.S. First; Pentagon Would Preclude a Rival Superpower." *Washington Post*, March 11.

Hobbes, T. 1651. *Leviathan*. http://oregonstate.edu/instruct/phl302/ texts/hobbes/leviathan-contents.html (accessed May 4, 2007).

International Security Assistance Force (ISAF), "NATO in Afghanistan," www.nato.int/issues/afghanistan/index.html (accessed 13 August 2007).

Klinger, J. "The Social Science of Carl von Clausewitz," *Parameters* Spring 2006: 78–89.

Matthews, W. 2007. April 29. "The GDP Argument." *Armed Forces Journal*. www.armedforcesjournal.com/2007/03/2545232 (accessed May 4, 2007).

Shah, A. 2007. February 25. "World Military Spending." www .globalissues.org/geopolitics/armstrade/spending.asp (accessed May 4, 2007).

Weissman, S., and H. Krosney. 1981. *The Islamic Bomb*. New York: Times Books.

4

Chronology

Although it is artificial simply to choose a date for this chronology's starting point, space does not allow any other course of action. Therefore, 1978 has been chosen because at that point, a new generation of leaders around the world brought fundamental changes to the international system and the threat to U.S. national security, such as Ayatollah Khomeini preparing to return to Iran from a prolonged exile and Deng Xiaoping returning from the internal exile of the Great Proletariat Cultural Revolution. Both proved crucial to today's national security concerns for the United States. This is not an ideal arrangement, but it is unavoidable. Starting earlier would put too much focus on the Cold War, which is but a distant, if not entirely unknown, memory for many alive today.

1978   In consolidating power at the Eleventh Communist Party Congress, Chinese Communist Party Chairman Deng Xiaoping reiterates Zhou Enlai's 1973 theme of "Four Modernizations" to reverse Mao Zedong central control over many aspects of Chinese society, especially the economy by introducing economic reforms to achieve "Strong Country, Strong Army." The Four Modernizations are intended to bring China out of the Cultural Revolution and improve its shaky position in the world. These modernizations, in order of priority, are agriculture, industry, science and technology, and the military.

A non-European cardinal, Karol Wojtyla, becomes Pope John Paul II, and he has a virulently anti-Communist context for viewing the world.

1978   Massive protests begin in Tehran, Iran, in the fall,
(*cont.*) leading to calls for the shah, Mohammad Reza Pahlavi,
          to give up the Peacock Throne.
1979   On the first day of the year, the United States reverses
          its thirty-year recognition of Taipei as the govern-
          ment of China in favor of Beijing. The status of Taiwan
          becomes a complicated issue in U.S. national security
          because Congress passes the Taiwan Relations Act
          later in the year. Washington appears to promise its
          support to both sides.

          Iran's long-standing strongman, the shah, flees
          the Iranian Revolution orchestrated by Shiite Ayatol-
          lah Khomeni. Upon his return later in the year from
          many years in exile, Khomeni declares Iran an Islamic
          republic with what the West labels "fundamentalist"
          Islamic governance, based on the sharia.

          In July, the *Frente Sandinista de Liberación Nacional*
          (FSLN) removes long-term U.S. supporter Anastasio
          Samoza Debayle from power in Nicaragua. Many in
          the United States see this as a threat to national secu-
          rity because of FSLN ties with Cuba.

          In November, Iranian students seize the U.S.
          Embassy in Tehran, taking the employees and Marine
          guards hostage. While a number escape with the help
          of the Canadian Embassy, most are held for 444 days—
          they are released on the day Ronald Reagan succeeds
          Jimmy Carter as U.S. president in 2001.

          In November, Islamic radicals take hundreds of
          hostages at the Grand Mosque in Mecca during the
          Hajj, threatening the global pilgrimage to the holiest
          spot in Islam. The rescue efforts by Saudi and French
          commandos are bloody—250 are believed killed and
          600 injured.

          In December, the Soviet Union invades Afghani-
          stan, beginning a disastrous eight-year involvement
          there. Almost immediately, Islamic men flock to Paki-
          stan to arm in an attempt to oust the infidel Commu-
          nist force. To U.S. strategists, the involvement of the
          Islamic fighters means the United States can avoid
          direct confrontation with Soviet troops while still mak-
          ing progress toward the crucial goal of stopping Soviet
          expansionism. The long-term effects prove somewhat

different, however, because the Islamic fighters become the basis to the Islamic radical Taliban movement in the 1990s.

1980 An obscure but motivated Polish worker in the Gdansk shipyards, Lech Walesa, becomes one of the founders of the first independent labor union, known as Solidarity, in Communist-controlled Poland.

A young Seattle entrepreneur, Bill Gates, negotiates with IBM to provide the code or software for its anticipated new product. His company, Microsoft, becomes a global behemoth through the creation of the MS-DOS operating system. Microsoft's product makes the newly created personal computers accessible to many by allowing nontechnical people to use a relatively sophisticated instrument with virtually no training. This in turn moves many companies to think about computerizing activities—particularly with the parallel development of the "World Wide Web"—that had traditionally been done manually, allowing for the ultimate advent of globalization and instant communications that affects national security today.

In September, Iraqi dictator Saddam Hussein attacks Iran, leading to an eight-year war that will kill at least 600,000 in the two states.

In December, four Roman Catholic laywomen are murdered in El Salvador. Suspicions center on El Salvadoran soldiers as the culprits.

1981 In January, Ronald Reagan assumes the presidency, promising to return pride to the nation while addressing what he believes to be a growing threat to U.S. security from the Soviet Union.

An inexplicable new disease, appearing overwhelmingly in gay men, earns the title "human immunodeficiency virus/acquired immunodeficiency syndrome," or HIV/AIDS. A quarter of a century later, it remains a potent, unsolved medical problem confronting some of the poorest nations of the world and representing a significant health security challenge to all societies, including the United States. Since then, millions have died around the globe and tens of millions remain carriers, often undiagnosed.

1981
(*cont.*)

Israel attacks the Osiraq nuclear power plant in Iraq to stop a feared nuclear weapons program.

IBM introduces the personal computer, or PC. The following year, rival Compaq begins to provide competition in this commodity. Smaller, less expensive computers open the door to greater use by average citizens, increasing the communications and virtually all other forms of interaction around the world. This has positive effects on speeding up many processes but also adversely affects national security by allowing illegal activities and dangerous linkages, such as drug trafficking or terrorism planning, to flourish in a more stealthy manner that is harder for security specialists to control.

In October, Egyptian President Anwar Sadat, presiding over a military parade, is the target of an Islamist assassination. Experts would later recognize that this was a key event in the rise of Islamic militancy.

The Soviet-inspired government of Poland, under Wojciech Jaruzelski, declares martial law by sending tanks into the streets to prevent the Solidarity movement from spreading. Pope John Paul II endorses the movement's actions.

1982

Argentina launches an invasion of the Islas Malvinas, better known as the Falkland Islands by their British administrators, in the south Atlantic. Over a two-month period, Britain launches a tremendous armada to prove its commitment to the islanders, getting much covert U.S. assistance in the effort. Argentine military rulers are stunned that the Reagan administration chooses to support Britain, even though at the time the Argentines are engaged in secretly training *contrarevolucionarios*, or "contras" as they are popularly known, to oust the U.S.-opposed Nicaraguan Sandinista regime. The virulently anti-Communist government in Buenos Aires was training the contras because Washington faced opposition at home in supporting forces trying to overthrow the leftist Nicaraguan government that had itself ousted a decades-long U.S. ally, Anastasio Somoza Debayle. The Sandinistas were viewed by some in the United States as far less threatening than the Reagan administration feared, creating a highly charged atmosphere in the United States. Additionally, many in the United States feared that the contras were learning from a military in Argentina that had engaged in massive human rights violations against its own population, where thousands of Argentine citizens were being made to "disappear" by their government for their ideological beliefs. U.S. critics feared the contras would import the same sort of ideological purity to Central America.

The Israelis, led militarily by Ariel Sharon, move north of their traditional operating space within southern Lebanon into the capital, Beirut, to oust the Palestine Liberation Organization (PLO) and prevent further attacks on Israel. This becomes a much more difficult operation than advertised, causing serious political debate within Israel and considerable international disapproval. The newly elected Lebanese president and head of the Christian forces, Bashir Gemayel, dies from a bomb blast in the captial. Israel allows its Christian Lebanese allies, the Phalangists, to root out any remaining Palestinian "terrorists" at the Shatilla and Sabra Palestinian refugee camps. A massacre ensures in retaliation for Gemayel's assassination, and an estimated 700 to 3,500 people die in the two refugee camps.

The Reagan administration decides to deploy Marine Corps forces to Lebanon to stem the civil war by helping international peacekeepers evacuate PLO forces from Beirut.

Leonid Brezhnev, long-serving chairman of the Communist Party in the Soviet Union, dies. Yuri Andropov, head of the KGB, the State Security Committee, succeeds him.

1983 In a single remarkable speech, President Reagan notes the concerns his administration has with Cuban involvement in the Caribbean island of Grenada and advocates the Strategic Defense Initiative to alter the nuclear condition known as "mutually assured destruction." The Initiative immediately becomes known as the "Star Wars" plan after the George Lucas–produced movie.

In August, the unarmed civilian flight, Korean Air Lines 007, en route from the United States to South

1983 (*cont.*)	Korea, is the target of a Soviet missile because the flight crossed into Soviet airspace. The international community expresses outrage at the unprovoked action.

Two crucial events occur within a few days of each other in October. First, the U.S. Marine barracks in Beirut, Lebanon, is the target of a massive truck bomb, which many analysts call the first suicide bombing. Then, President Reagan sends U.S. troops into Grenada to rescue medical students believed threatened in a chaotic political situation that the administration thought was orchestrated by Soviet and Cuban forces.

1984	Apple Computer introduces the Macintosh computer, working off a non-Microsoft operating system. This icon-based operating system made computers more accessible to use for virtually anyone who could get onto one since the technological impediments were gone. This greatly increased the proliferation of computers around the world, including putting them into the hands of disreputable figures and outright terrorists.

Andropov's short-lived regime ends with his death in February; Konstantin Chernenko succeeds him as chairman of the Communist Party in the Soviet Union.

A massive poison gas leak at a Union Carbide plant in Bhopal, India leads to tens of thousands of deaths and perhaps 120,000 injuries.

1985	Konstantin Chernenko dies after a short period in office. Mikhail Gorbachev succeeds him as chairman of the Communist Party in the Soviet Union. Gorbachev begins introducing small steps that he notes will modernize the Soviet system. In the autumn, Gorbachev holds a summit in Geneva, Switzerland, with U.S. President Ronald Reagan.

The cruise liner *Achille Lauro* becomes victim of a Palestinian hijacking, culminating in murder of a wheelchair-bound American Jewish passenger. The introduction of terrorism to the high seas of the Mediterranean is further evidence of the growing anti-U.S. sentiments as well as actions against U.S. citizens at seemingly innocent locations abroad.

1986   As Gorbachev consolidates power in the Soviet Union, he advocates a *glasnost,* or opening, of the society, especially in politics. In conjunction with the restructuring known as *perestroika,* he begins economic and political changes that ultimately lead to the end of the Soviet Union three years later.

     An accident at the Chernobyl nuclear power plant in the Ukraine causes widespread radioactive fallout, resulting in global concerns about nuclear radiation and questions about how well the Soviet bureaucracy is functioning since it proved poor at coping with this problem.

     The Goldwater-Nichols Department of Defense Reorganization Act fundamentally alters the relationships of the armed services as they provide national security to the nation. Goldwater-Nichols, as it was called, gives considerable power to the chairman of the Joint Chiefs of Staff as the primary advisor to the president of the United States but also affected professional military education, the role of "jointness" in the U.S. armed forces, and various other wide-ranging issues.

     Gorbachev and Reagan again meet, in Reykjavik, Iceland, for a summit, where Reagan's spokesman says the presidents seriously discuss changing the nuclear balance to reduce risks.

     Congress passes sanctions against the apartheid regime in the Republic of South Africa, trying to end the legal segregation in that nation.

     Reports begin seeping out that the United States has been negotiating with Iran to release the hostages in Lebanon by selling arms to fund covert training and support to the contras in Nicaragua. This complicated relationship becomes known as the Iran-Contra scandal as its details surface through congressional investigation.

1987   President Reagan appeals to President Gorbachev to "tear down this wall" in Berlin, Germany.

1988   In March, Saddam Hussein uses chemical weapons against the Kurds, who he sees as undermining his rule in the north of Iraq. The attacks kill at least 5,000.

     Panamanian strongman and former U.S. ally Manuel Noriega comes under indictment on drug charges

1988
(*cont.*)

in the United States. After eighteen months of attempting to convince him to leave power, the United States invades Panama in Operation Just Cause after a U.S. military person and his wife are harassed by Panamanian forces. Noriega evades capture only briefly and served a sentence in a U.S. federal prison.

The USS *Vincennes* mistakenly shoots down an Iranian airliner departing Bandar Abbas, identifying it as a warplane instead of a passenger flight with 290 aboard.

In August, the secretary general of the United Nations, Javier Pérez de Cuéllar, convinces both Iraq and Iran to accept a cease-fire. The international organization's role in ending the conflict heralds a renaissance for the concept of peacekeepers.

The Armenian Socialist Republic suffers a massive earthquake to which the Soviet government has extreme difficulty in responding with aid. Humanitarian help pours in from outside, but few seem to recognize that this inability to provide aid is an indication of a failing Soviet empire.

1989

On June 4, the People's Liberation Army moves into Tiananmen Square under orders from the Chinese Communist Party to quell student protestors. The final death toll remains controversial, but the government sentences many student leaders to serve time in jail for their actions, while others go into exile.

Eastern European states Hungary and Czechoslovakia begin facing a growing number of East German citizens trying to cross the border into Austria rather than stay under a Communist regime.

After weeks of decaying conditions, the Soviet-allied government in East Germany does not stop protestors from bringing down the Berlin Wall, the symbol of division between East and West since its construction in 1961.

In the closing weeks of the year, Romanian strongman Nicolae Ceaucescu and his wife, Elena, become the target of protests, and they are ultimately ousted and put to death.

Presidents George H. W. Bush and Mikhail Gorbachev hold a summit in Malta, against the inclination of many in the new U.S. administration. They declare the Cold War to be "over."

1990 After more than twenty-five years in prison, African National Congress leader Nelson Mandela is released and becomes the most respected political figure on the African continent. He negotiates with F. W. de Klerk, the Afrikaner president, to end the legal separation of races in South Africa and open the state to genuine democracy. Mandela serves as president of South Africa for much of the 1990s.

The occupying powers of World War II—Britain, France, the Soviet Union, and the United States—agree to the reunification of East Germany and West Germany, ending the most obvious sign of the Cold War.

In August, Iraqi President Saddam Hussein sends troops into Kuwait, ostensibly to regain a lost province. President George H. W. Bush starts the campaign to create an international coalition to support action to oust Iraq from Kuwait.

1991 The international coalition against the Iraqi invasion of Kuwait launches air strikes on Iraq in January, following up in February with a ninety-six-hour ground invasion that forces Iraq from Kuwait but does not remove Saddam from power. An uprising in the Shiite section of southern Iraq does not receive U.S. military support, but humanitarian operations help the Kurdish population of northern Iraq, who need massive assistance.

In June, Croatia and Slovenia declare their independence from Yugoslavia under a Serbian strongman, Slobodan Milošević. Independence movements gradually surface in the remaining non-Serbian portions of the former Yugoslavia. The breakup of the former Yugoslavia takes the better part of a decade and results in over a hundred thousand deaths and thousands displaced from their homes.

On December 26, the Soviet Union ceases to exist; it is replaced by sovereign entities allied as the Commonwealth of Independent States, led by the most powerful state, Russia.

1992 The United States sends humanitarian forces to Mogadishu, Somalia, to alleviate death and starvation resulting from tribal violence orchestrated by warlords.

1992 (*cont.*)	Repeated allegations of Serbian attacks on Bosnia and Herzegovina's Muslim population reintroduce the concept of genocide into European debate.
1993	Shootings outside the gates of the Central Intelligence Agency (CIA) in January, followed five weeks later by a partially failed bombing at the World Trade Center in New York City, indicate that Islamic extremism has arrived in the United States. Although six people die in the February incident, the possibility of tens of thousands dying in the massive two-building structure is shocking to many in the national security community. Perpetrators of each incident have links with Pakistan. Mir Aimal Kasi attacks people outside the CIA to protest bombing of Iraq by U.S. forces as well as interference in Islamic states by outsiders bent on humiliating adherents to the faith. An al Qaeda operative, Ramzi Yousef, ultimately goes to jail for his terrorism after another spectacular attack on U.S. citizens fails in the Philippines.

The Clinton administration cancels the Strategic Defense Initiative, but the concept of ballistic missile defense continues to receive funding.

Israeli prime minister Yitzhak Rabin meets PLO head Yasir Arafat in the Rose Garden of the White House to sign the Oslo Accords, an initial step toward resolving the Israeli-Palestinian morass. Through the Palestinian Authority, the Palestinians ultimately get the ability to self-govern in portions of the West Bank and Gaza, and a Jewish student assassinates Rabin in 1995 for giving away too much to the enemy.

The U.S. forces in Somalia take fire from warlords, bringing down two Blackhawk helicopters and allowing marauding crowds to desecrate the bodies of dead soldiers in the streets of Mogadishu. The U.S. forces withdraw the following year.

1994	The president of Rwanda, Juvenal Habyarimana, and his senior aides die in a suspicious helicopter crash in early April. Resulting ethnic violence leads to genocide and the death of more than a million Rwandans within weeks while the international community stands by.

The U.S. Congress ratifies the 1992 North American Free Trade Agreement with Mexico and Canada, even though President Bill Clinton loses his party's majority in the Congress in the November midterm elections.

1995   In April, a former U.S. serviceman, Timothy McVeigh, detonates a massive bomb outside the Alfred P. Murrah Federal Building in Oklahoma City, Oklahoma, killing 168. The worst domestic-engineered act of terrorism in U.S. history results in McVeigh's execution under the death penalty in 2002.

Led by neoconservatives such as former U.S. Representative to the United Nations Jeane Kirkpatrick, the cries for U.S. intervention to stop "ethnic cleansing" in Bosnia push the Clinton administration to send air strikes against the Serbian regime in Belgrade. In November, the Clinton administration hosts negotiations that result in the Dayton Accords, which form the basis of the Bosnia and Herzegovina peace.

1996   The People's Republic of China sends short-range missiles over the northern and southern ports of Taiwan, Chi-lung, and Kao-hsiung in an attempt to intimidate the Taiwan presidential elections. President Clinton responds by sending two aircraft carrier battle groups to the region to indicate the level of U.S. concern over China's actions.

In June, a U.S. housing facility for Air Force personnel deployed in the eastern portion of Saudi Arabia becomes the target of a massive suicide truck bomb, killing nineteen servicemen.

1997   The international community signs the Kyoto Protocol to begin restricting greenhouse gases, thus beginning to control global warming. The George W. Bush administration's subsequent decision to withdraw from this accord becomes a measure of much world distrust of U.S. intentions in the following decade.

1998   India and Pakistan both test multiple nuclear devices, to the disappointment of the international community.

Massive car bomb attacks on U.S. embassies in Nairobi, Kenya, and Dar es Salaam, Tanzania, begin awareness in the United States of an entity known as al Qaeda, along with its mysterious Saudi-born leader, Osama bin Laden.

Former Army officer and coup instigator Hugo Chávez is the unlikely victor of the Venezuelan

1998 (*cont.*)	presidential election, winning on a platform of wiping out the corruption plaguing the nation.
1999	As part of its campaign against Serbian repression in Kosovo, the U.S. Air Force mistakenly bombs the Chinese embassy in central Belgrade, provoking strong protests by Chinese citizens, including attacks on U.S. diplomatic representatives in the People's Republic of China.

In July, Taiwan President Lee Deng-hui declares to a German media outlet that Taiwan and the People's Republic of China need to operate on a state-to-state basis. Beijing is unhappy because this alters the status quo across the Taiwan Strait.

Destructive riots by antiglobalization mobs transform Seattle into an armed camp during the International Monetary Fund meeting there.

The United States signs up to help Colombian president Andrés Pastrana Arango wipe out the insurgency and violence plaguing his nation, offering funding for "Plan Colombia," a multiyear program designed to attack the difficulties from multiple approaches. Critics charge that the U.S. funding priorities are militarizing the solutions.

The Senate defeats the Comprehensive Nuclear Test Ban Treaty ratification, undercutting U.S. efforts to encourage nuclear nonproliferation.

2000	In March, the Democratic Progressive Party candidate and former jailed lawyer Chen Shui-bian wins the close Taiwanese presidential election, even after Beijing's Premier Zhu Rongji verbally intimidates Taiwanese citizens

In October, the USS *Cole*, a warship refueling in the Yemeni port of Aden, is the target of Islamists seeking to sink it with a bomb brought alongside the ship on a small dinghy. Seventeen sailors die; more than three dozen are injured.

2001	A Chinese fighter collides with an EP-3 (a U.S. observation plane). The fighter crashes into the South China Sea while the U.S. EP-3 crew is taken hostage for several days after its pilot, Lieutenant Shane Osborn, heroically lands the wounded craft.

On September 11, suicidal hijackers dedicated to martyrdom as Islamists with links to Osama bin

Laden's al Qaeda pilot four planes into infamy. Two fuel-laden commercial planes attack the World Trade Center in New York City; the resulting fire collapses both towers. Simultaneously, a plane attacks the Pentagon. A fourth plane crashes into a south-central Pennsylvania field after the hijackers are thwarted from hitting a national landmark by passengers' efforts to stop the attack. The incidents kill 2,700 people on the ground and in the planes. Immediate results include grounding of all air traffic in the United States, including all flights to and from abroad, for several days. Airport security reaches a heightened level never before seen. Homeland security becomes synonymous with national security in the United States.

On October 7, President George W. Bush orders U.S. forces, in concert with British forces, to invade Afghanistan to pursue Osama bin Laden and penalize the Taliban government for sheltering him.

Later in October, five citizens in Florida, suburban Washington, D.C., Connecticut, and New York City die of anthrax contracted when they open letters laced with the bacterium. This act of domestic terrorism remains unsolved despite years of investigation. Because the Senate Democratic leadership received some of the letters, one of the Senate office buildings remains closed for months as investigation and cleanup continues.

Planning for an invasion of Iraq begins, and major U.S. administration officials are determined to link Saddam Hussein with al Qaeda terrorism.

In December, U.S. forces believe they have found Osama bin Laden in the heavily mountainous Tora Bora region of Afghanistan near the Pakistan border. Despite the major goal of capturing him, bin Laden remains at large.

2002   In August, President Bush hears from his secretary of state and former chairman of the Joint Chiefs of Staff, Colin Powell, that invading Iraq will be problematic and that the president must remember the concept of "if you break it, you buy it" in this context.

In Nashville, Tennessee, at the Veterans of Foreign Wars convention, Vice President Dick Cheney asserts

2002
(*cont.*)

that little doubt exists that Saddam Hussein has weapons of mass destruction.

In October, Islamists attack popular foreign nightspots on the Hindu island of Bali, Indonesia, killing more than 200 tourists, mainly Australians.

The United States accuses North Korea of trying to build a nuclear weapon in violation of the 1993 agreement to end such activities. This initiates a process of attempting to bring the Pyongyang regime to a position of terminating the program, but discussions over more than five years result in little progress.

International pressure against invading Iraq grows, but none of the other five permanent Security Council members (China, France, and Russia) dissuades the United States and its partner, Great Britain, from pursuing an increasingly determined position to go after Saddam Hussein.

2003

On February 5, at an appearance before the United Nations, Secretary of State Colin Powell argues that the regime of Saddam Hussein is a clear and present danger to the world because of its desire to achieve a successful weapons of mass destruction program.

Bush administration officials scoff at concerns that any invasion of Iraq will unleash destabilizing forces within that state and the Middle East, arguing that Iraqis will welcome the invaders as "liberators." The chief of staff of the Army, General Eric Shinseki, receives administration condemnation for his observations that a force of "hundreds of thousands" would be necessary to secure Iraq. Deputy Secretary of Defense Paul Wolfowitz directly challenges this assertion in public a few days later.

A strange flu-like virus appears in Hong Kong, killing many who come into contact with it. Stories begin spreading of its appearance throughout eastern China, Taiwan, and Southeast Asia. It also strongly affects health care workers in Toronto, Canada. The virus is named severe acquired respiratory syndrome, or SARS. After the spread of the syndrome slows, the international health community realizes that the virus began in China but was covered up by the Beijing government for several months rather than addressing it as a medical problem of the first degree.

On March 19, a coalition of forces, predominantly American in strength, launches an invasion of Iraq to oust Saddam Hussein. By April 9, Hussein's government is deemed destroyed. The image of U.S. soldiers helping Iraqis topple a massive statue of the former dictator in front of the international media comes to symbolize the end of that dictatorship but makes the U.S. nature of the new occupiers absolutely clear. At the same time, vast amounts of looting of antiquities and common thievery occurs in Iraq, while U.S. leadership appears completely unprepared for this turn of events.

On April 15, the head of the Office of Reconstruction and Humanitarian Assistance, retired Army Lieutenant General Jay Garner, arrives in Baghdad, but finds conditions worse and significantly more demanding than planning had anticipated. Garner serves less than four weeks in his position.

In May, Lieutenant General Garner departs as a successor, Ambassador L. Paul "Jerry" Bremer, arrives as the de facto governor of occupied Iraq. Bremer's governance is under the Coalition Provisional Authority through June 2004. Almost immediately upon arriving as "pro-consul," Bremer issues two decrees that create massive unemployment and sow bitterness in post–Saddam Hussein Iraq. One decree encourages "de-Baathification" by disallowing former Baath Party members to serve in the new government, while the other virtually shuts down the Iraqi armed forces.

Deterioration of a long-simmering civil war in Liberia leads President Bush to send in a U.S. task force to help evacuate people from the country, while offering suggestions for a long-term peacekeeping force to help tame the situation

In August, a car bomb attack targets a popular Western hotel in Jakarta, Indonesia, highlighting the Islamic tension within that society and the animosity directed against the West.

2004   A series of digital photographs begin circulating on the Internet showing interrogations of Iraqis incarcerated

2004
(*cont.*)

at Abu Ghraib prison in Baghdad. These photographs indicate ritualistic humiliation of Iraqi prisoners by U.S. military personnel, including women degrading men with obscene gestures and laughter, actions especially humiliating to Muslim men.

Two and a half years to the day after the September 11 terrorist attacks in the United States, massive bombs detonate on commuter trains going into Madrid, Spain, killing just under 200 and casting doubt on Spain's support for the U.S. invasion of Iraq. Less than a week later, the conservative government in power loses the general election; the new prime minister is determined to withdraw Spanish forces in Iraq.

In a bizarre ending to the campaign, an assassination attempt is made on Taiwanese president Chen Shui-bian and his vice president, Annette Lu; each receives a grazing injury. The incident appears to tip the election the following day in their favor, and they win a 30,000-vote victory. The opposition does not accept the outcome for months. Beijing remains unhappy that Chen might, in his second term, revise the Constitution to declare independence.

The Abu Ghraib prison scandal escalates to congressional hearings about the nature of U.S. interrogation processes. Secretary of Defense Donald Rumsfeld takes responsibility but does not resign. An internal Army report names lower-level soldiers, but a single Army reservist brigadier general is the only senior leader cited for responsibility in this disgrace. Several junior Army personnel face court-martial and imprisonment. The Islamic world erupts in fury as the feeling that the United States dishonors Islam begins to grow in Middle Eastern states and important allies such as Pakistan and Indonesia.

In November, PLO founder Yasir Arafat succumbs to an undisclosed illness, leaving the Palestinian Authority struggling to address the needs of its people in the West Bank, Gaza Strip, and scattered around the world

President George W. Bush wins reelection in another extraordinarily thin margin over Massachusetts Democratic Senator John F. Kerry. The focus of the election was whether the Bush or Kerry administrations would create a safer nation in the next four years.

On December 26, a massive earthquake off the coast of Aceh, Indonesia, sets off a tsunami of devastating proportion, killing unknown numbers along the Indian Ocean coastlines in its path. Nearly a quarter of a million die in Indonesia, Thailand, India, Sri Lanka, and other countries. President Bush orders U.S. armed forces to respond swiftly to provide humanitarian assistance, proving again that national security for the United States now encompasses activities that were not traditionally deemed security.

2005   A virulent strain of avian influenza begins spreading from Southeast Asia and China through the rest of the world. Deaths initially remain closely correlated to those who have touched birds, but many fear a repeat of the 1918 Spanish flu, which took more lives than World War I.

In July, attacks on the London Underground and surface buses result in the deaths of 52 and injury of 770. Two weeks later, additional attacks on a bus and a two Underground trains result in minor blasts. In all instances, the perpetrators are Islamic adherents, many of whom are British born (a major difference from the September 11 terrorist attacks).

2006   In June, the U.S. Supreme Court rules that the Bush administration's approach to incarcerating and interrogating terrorist suspects is unconstitutional. The administration asks Congress to endorse its policies to satisfy the Court, but Republican senators John Warner, Lindsey Graham, and John McCain block the administration's moves three months later.

In August, British officials stop trans-Atlantic air traffic upon suspicion of a pending attack on British-originating airliners going to the United States, using fluids as weapons. British officials substantially curtail in-cabin luggage while U.S. officials cite this as an example of the continuing threats and limit the types of materials that may be carried in the passenger cabins.

Iran announces that it will not bow to international pressure to open its nuclear facilities to international scrutiny. The United States, European allies, and

<table>
<tr><td>

2006
(*cont.*)

</td><td>

Chinese governments each have a different approach and level of concern about the depth of the threat. In his appearance at the United Nations General Assembly in September, Iranian leader Mahmoud Ahmadinejad mocks President Bush as a leader of the international system.

Less than a week before the fifth anniversary of the September 11 terrorist attacks, the Senate Select Committee on Intelligence releases a report indicating that there were no ties between Iraqi dictator Saddam Hussein and the al Qaeda terrorist network in the years before the attacks. President Bush acknowledges the existence of long-reported CIA secret interrogation camps abroad. Although he argues that his administration must continue protecting the nation's security through these interrogations and through greater use of domestic wiretapping, both practices are quite controversial among civil rights advocates within the United States.

On September 11, the nation commemorates the fifth anniversary of the terrorist attacks, but there is significant political divisions about the path ahead.

The midterm election campaigns discuss the Iraq war as the central campaign theme in many parts of the country. Upon the Republicans' inability to maintain control over either the House of Representatives or the Senate, President Bush substitutes former CIA Director Robert Gates for embattled Secretary of Defense Donald Rumsfeld.

President Bush, anticipating the congressionally mandated bipartisan Iraqi Study Group recommendations four weeks later, announces he will engage in considerable consultation across the nation about Iraqi policy but simultaneously announces he will not accept a military strategy for defeat in the Middle East.

The final quarter of 2006 is a period of dramatic increases in combat deaths in Iraq as well as civilian casualties. December sees the highest level of casualties since early 2005.

The United States ends 2006 with a stalemate with Iranian and North Korean diplomats over budding nuclear programs in their respective countries.

</td></tr>
</table>

North Korea remains the center of ongoing Six-Party Talks facilitated by the Chinese government in Beijing, but no movement is on the horizon. Various states try pressuring Tehran to allow inspections and abandon its positions, but the pressure is insufficient to achieve anything.

2007   During the initial week of 2007, President Bush elevates his Iraq ground commander, General George Casey, to the position of chief of staff of the Army. He replaces Casey with a commander, Lieutenant General David Petraeus, who advocates a more clear-cut counterinsurgency doctrine for the war-wracked country, based on his doctoral studies at Princeton University as well as prior tours in Iraq. Bush also surprises many by nominating a Naval aviator, Admiral William Fallon, for the position of head of Central Command, a position long held by a "ground pounder" because of the nature of the theater of operations—ground troops instead of predominantly naval or air assets. The change to a naval officer indicates the decision to shift emphasis dramatically in the Central Command. Similarly, the president moves career ambassador Ryan C. Crocker, a senior diplomat with extensive Iraq experience, from his post as ambassador in Pakistan to Baghdad to replace Zalmay Khalilzad, who assumes the United Nations representation replacing the controversial appointee John Bolton.

The People's Republic of China accomplishes the goal of destroying an earth-orbiting satellite that leaves many defense analysts around the world worried about the militarization of space. Beijing denies such an intent, but proves uncoordinated in its response to these concerns, leading some to worry about the rising power of the People's Liberation Army within the Chinese decision-making system.

After fits and starts, the Democratic People's Republic of Korea agrees to the Six-Party Talk negotiations to shut down its nuclear program in exchange for desired assistance from the international community. Critics such as John Bolton argue that the North Koreans will not adhere to their side of the agreement, but the leadership of the nations engaging with North

2007
(*cont.*)

Korea show obvious relief that the North Koreans appear to have backed down from creating a massive weapons program.

Prime Minister Tony Blair announces that Britain will withdraw a significant portion of its 7,500 troops from their multinational coalition role in southern Iraq at Basra. A day later, the prime minister notes that British troops are likely to augment the North Atlantic Treaty Organization forces deployed in Afghanistan in light of fears of a Taliban resurgence there.

Eight helicopters crash in Iraq in the first eight weeks of 2007, leading to questions whether the insurgents have found an ability to bring down U.S. forces or whether the law of averages is affecting U.S. military efforts.

The Palestinian chaos long characterizing the Gaza area continues as Palestinian organizations Hamas and the Palestinian Authority differ on two counts: whether to recognize the legitimacy of Israel to exist and whether to decry the use of violence to achieve Palestinian goals. Cracks appear in the coalition between the United States and Europe on pressuring the Palestinians.

Secretary of State Condoleezza Rice announces a renewed commitment for U.S. engagement in the Israeli-Palestinian conflict, some six years after President Bush made clear his reluctance to have the United States place its credibility on the line as his predecessor President Clinton did during negotiations between the two parties at Camp David in the summer of 2000.

The Bush administration charges that many of the attacks on U.S. forces in Iraq result from massive Iranian intervention in the neighboring state. Critics voice concern about the accuracy of the charges because of intelligence failures preceding the 2003 intervention in Iraq, but the administration maintains its position that Iran is behind much of the unrest.

A series of investigative stories in the *Washington Post* highlights the failure of the military services to offer what most deem necessary post-conflict health care to returning veterans. In particular, the Walter Reed Army

Medical Center becomes the target of critics who cite its deteriorated physical conditions and unsatisfactory care. The secretary of the Army as well as the Army's top physician are both forced from office.

At the end of February, the United States decides to begin including Iran and Syria in regional discussions about the future of Iraq. The Iraqi Study Group in Washington had advocated this move in its December 2006 recommendations, but the Bush administration had been reluctant to deal with a regime unwilling to adhere to international nonproliferation regime monitoring.

Zimbabwean president Robert Mugabe throws himself a terrific birthday party and tells his critics around the world to stay out of Zimbabwe's affairs. Political opponents of the long-ruling president confront physical intimidation by his government's internal police, resulting in condemnation from Western governments such as the United States and Great Britain. A March meeting of the heads of state in southern Africa does nothing to condemn Mugabe for increasing repression at home and does little to encourage Mugabe to alter his behavior even though the U.S. ambassador and Europeans argue that conditions are bound to deteriorate even further in Zimbabwe. Common people in Zimbabwe live in substandard conditions with no prospect for improvement.

Weeks after the Six-Party Agreement with North Korea, U.S. intelligence officials soften their charges about the level of success in Pyongyang's uranium enrichment program. North Korea claims it might still renege on the agreement if its financial accounts are not freed. The financial transaction problems between the states continue into April.

President Bush visits Latin America for a week, promising that the United States is indeed committed to the region. His nemesis, Hugo Chávez of Venezuela, taunts him and says the United States only exploits the region.

In March, Congress passes a funding bill for Iraq and Afghanistan that cites a specific date for the

2007
(*cont.*)

withdrawal of U.S. combat forces from the theater. President Bush vetoes the bill but the polarization of the nation on this topic is apparent.

In early April, an international commission of scientists argues that definitive data support the damning conclusion that global warming will create major national security concerns around the world within twenty to thirty years. Some members charge that the United States and China sought to water down the report, but the overall conclusion about the strongly adverse effects of humans on global climate is no longer in dispute.

New House Speaker Nancy Pelosi, a San Francisco Democrat, makes a foreign policy tour of the Middle East, including a stop in Syria. The Bush administration strongly criticizes her for undermining the president's strong stance on the authoritarian government of Bashir Assad in Damascus. Pelosi retorts that the Constitution calls for the legislature to work with the executive branch in foreign affairs, noting that her positions in the region did not undermine the president but supported his positions.

The U.S. intelligence community acknowledges that the evidence of links between Saddam Hussein's Iraq and al Qaeda before the 2003 invasion were tentative at best and probably insignificant in the overall equation of international affairs. Vice President Dick Cheney continues to assert the strength of al Qaeda ties with Iraq under the Saddam Hussein government.

On Easter Sunday, Pope Benedict XVI calls for the end of "slaughter" in Iraq, but truck bombs targeting Iraqis and targeted attacks on U.S. service personnel continue. The evidence for success of President Bush's "surge" strategy, announced in January, remains open to interpretation.

Nicholas Sarkozy, son of a Hungarian immigrant, wins the French presidential election, meaning that one of President George W. Bush's most vocal critics in the international scene, Jacques Chirac, will no longer be an obstacle to U.S.-European relations.

A rash of public stories on pet food impurities, toys with lead paint, and other Chinese products raise

questions about quality control in China. Officials pro-
claim that they will redouble efforts to ensure quality
of their exports but U.S. consumers begin asking questions about what they are buying.

The number of deaths in Iraq increases over the
spring and early summer months as a result of bombings. U.S. leaders note the successes of the "surge"
probably increased local resistance, but suggest waiting until General Petraeus reports back to Congress on
the surge's success in September. In early August, U.S.
forces in country reach 162,000. Officials speak carefully of tactical successes resulting from the surge.

Prime Minister Tony Blair steps down in late June
as planned. His successor, Gordon Brown, moves up
from the Chancellorship of the Exchequer. In less than
a week after taking the job, he confronts an attack on
the Glasgow airport by Islamic terrorists and police
find cars laden with explosives in central London.

Russian President Vladimir Putin visits President
Bush at the family retreat in Maine but the meeting
produces few solid results and illustrates the growing
tension between the two leaders. Within weeks, Russia
proclaims its navy has sailed below the Arctic icecap
to claim natural resources on the seabed for Russia's
exclusive use.

Domestic protests that began with General Pervez Musharraf trying to oust the head of the Pakistani
Supreme Court in March culminate in a bloody siege at
the Red Mosque in Islamabad. Islamists seek to impose
a greater Islamic lifestyle on Pakistan while General
Musharraf and the Pakistani military want to maintain
a secular state. Pakistani commandos ousted the 100
militants holding the mosque but at a high cost in lives,
further polarizing the already tenuous society.

As General Petraeus hopes for success from the
surge, Sunni members of the Al-Maliki government
resign, focusing attention on an increasingly dysfunctional Iraqi state.

5

Biographical Sketches

S ome theorists of international affairs believe states alone
affect relations, while others believe systems do. Still others
believe individuals are the fundamental building blocks in
international affairs. In any case, people are a crucial component
to understanding national security. This chapter discusses some
of the most prominent persons in the field. As is true with other
materials in this volume, the choices here are based on the person's prominence and key decision-making roles, but the list is,
regrettably, not exhaustive.

John Abizaid (1951–)

John Philip Abizaid, the Lebanese-American Army general head-
ing U.S. Central Command from 2003 to 2007, was crucial in
waging the wars in Iraq and Afghanistan. Abizaid was born in
California but attended the U.S. Military Academy at West Point.
He studied at Princeton University and served as director of the
Joint Staff, a powerful position in formulating the overall national
military strategy for the nation. Abizaid replaced Army General
Tommy Franks at U.S. Central Command. Abizaid voiced caution
about increasing the troop strength in the Iraq enterprise at December 2006 congressional hearings and subsequently announced his
intention to retire in March 2007. His replacement was a Naval
aviator, Admiral William Fallon, a radically different leader for
this traditional ground-oriented theater.

Mahmoud Ahmadinejad (1956–)

The president of Iran, Mahmoud Ahmadinejad has proven a highly controversial figure. Many believe he was one of the masterminds of the November 4, 1979, takeover of the U.S. Embassy in Tehran, which ignited a 444-day hostage crisis for forty-four U.S. citizens. Ahmadinejad, a committed member of the revolutionary generation, is not a cleric but a highly devout Shiite. Much to the surprise of many, he became president through national elections in 2005. A strident nationalist, he earned a reputation as an anti-Semite almost immediately upon assuming office when he gave several speeches that discussed his desire for a Middle East without Israel, either through moving or destroying the Jewish state, as well as publicly questioning the idea that the Holocaust occurred.

Although Ahmadinejad served as the mayor of Tehran and in the Revolutionary Guards before he assumed the presidency, he has proven a poor governor of the Iranian economy, which is in a virtual standstill as the young population of the Islamic Republic grows and makes more demands. Ahmadinejad has proven able, however, to alarm the West as he has spoken repeatedly of Iran's rights to enrich uranium, leading to fears of an Iranian nuclear weapon. The United States, under President George W. Bush and Secretary of State Condoleezza Rice, has warned the Iranian president to stop the nuclear enrichment program while trying to rally European, Russian, and Chinese support to thwart him, but the rest of the world has been lukewarm to another potential conflict. Additionally, many of the nations that are potential U.S. partners in this effort have lucrative energy ties with Tehran. As the war in Iraq has deepened, U.S. officials in early 2007 argued that the deteriorating conditions were instigated by Iran. Washington also worries that Ahmadinejad is meddling in events in neighboring Iraq to create a pro-Iranian Shiite government in Baghdad.

Madeleine Korbel Albright (1937–)

Madeline Albright was the first female secretary of state, serving in the second Clinton administration between 1997 and 2001. The daughter of Czech diplomats who first fled the Nazis, then the Communists, Madeleine Jana Korbelovà was raised a Roman Catholic but learned later in life that her family hid her Jewish heritage to survive during World War II. Albright became a U.S. citizen in 1957 and did her undergraduate work at Wellesley College before marrying newspaper heir Joseph Albright in 1961 and raising three daughters. She later studied with Zbigniew Brzezinski at Columbia University, where she earned a doctorate in government.

Albright taught at the Georgetown University School of Foreign Service before moving to the National Security Council staff in the Carter administration and the staff of Maine Senator Edmund Muskie before he became secretary of state in 1980. Albright took on a foreign policy advisory role in the Democratic Party after she cofounded the Center for National Policy, a foreign affairs think tank. Albright was a primary foreign affairs adviser to the failed 1988 presidential campaign of Massachusetts governor Michael Dukakis. In 1993, President Bill Clinton named Albright his first ambassador to the United Nations, where she earned the scorn of conservatives in the Clinton administration (who felt that military forces ought to fight wars and exclusively defend the homeland) by asking then-chairman of the Joint Chiefs of Staff, General Colin L. Powell, why the United States had such a superb military if it was not going to use it, implying that she would greatly enhance the use of military for foreign policy activities beyond traditional defense. Albright's tenure at the United Nations coincided with U.S. frustration over involvement in Somalia and failure to act to thwart the Rwandan genocide of 1994.

As secretary of state, Albright, so profoundly affected by the global unwillingness to stop Nazi atrocities in the 1930s, argued for greater U.S. actions to stop Serbian strongman Slobodan Milošević's "ethnic cleansing" in Bosnia and Herzegovina, then Kosovo, in the 1990s. She also sought to moderate U.S. policy toward the reclusive, unpredictable regime of North Korea, traveling there in the later months of the administration.

Grand Ayatollah Ali Husaini Sistani (1930–)

The spiritual leader of many Shiites in Iraq, Grand Ayatollah Ali Husaini Sistani has been a pivotal figure in the years after Saddam Hussein's ouster in 2003. Respected by the Shia community for his religious wisdom, Sistani has been pivotal in lowering sectarian tensions. The Shiite community of Iraq suffered tremendous persecution under Saddam Hussein and his Baathist regime from roughly 1968 through 2003, but Sistani remained a figure of immense calm and perseverance. In 2003, after the invasion of Iraq by U.S.-led forces, Sistani signaled his tolerance for the activity by not directly criticizing U.S. actions. A major figure in the religious realm, he has proven a cagey politician, avoiding the turmoil created by many younger clerics, such as Moqtada al-Sadr, who would prefer to oust the United States and reach to the Shiite community abroad as Iraq rebuilds itself after the dictatorship.

Kofi Annan (1938–)

A long-term United Nations (UN) employee who rose through the ranks, Kofi Annan was the secretary general of the United Nations between 1996 and 2006, during some of the most challenging years for the international organization. A Ghanaian married to a Swede, Annan studied abroad, where he became a model for the type of international civil servant that he became within the UN bureaucracy. Heavily involved in refugee issues, Annan assumed the position of secretary general of the United Nations from the Egyptian Boutros Boutros-Ghali in 1996. During his decade as secretary general, Annan faced major pressure from the U.S. Congress—which preferred not to pay its UN dues until its demands for reform of the organization were met—along with growing tensions on use of force in places like Kosovo and Afghanistan. Before the 2003 Iraq War, Annan thinly veiled his skepticism about the need to oust Saddam Hussein over the issue of weapons of mass destruction. In August 2003, after Annan sent a UN delegation to Baghdad under his friend and personal envoy Sergio Vieira de Mello of Brazil, a truck bomb destroyed the UN complex and cost Vieira de Mello his life. The UN gradually pulled back from its work in Iraq. Annan fulfilled his tenure as secretary general but left behind a wounded organization with many challenges facing it.

Osama bin Laden (1957–)

A tall, willowy character who roams the international Islamic world seeking to stay out of U.S. hands, Osama bin Laden is credited with being the architect of the attacks on Washington and New York on September 11, 2001. Son of a Yemeni construction engineer with patrons in the Saudi royal family, bin Laden grew up a serious, religious child in the Saudi Kingdom. Drawn to Afghanistan in the late 1970s to fight against Soviet imperialism, he was seen by some as a major supporter of the mujahideen, Islamic Afghan fighters who drove the Soviets out of the mountainous state in the late 1980s. Others believed bin Laden was a dilettante who provided funding from his vast personal wealth but was not seriously engaged in the fight against the Soviets. Regardless, by 1990 bin Laden was personally appalled by the al-Saud family welcoming Western soldiers into the Kingdom to ward off an Iraqi invasion as had occurred in Kuwait. At this time, bin Laden began moving from one Islamic state to another, wherever he could find protection, as he advocated increasingly strong action against the West, specifically the United States as purveyors of a system to destroy Islam.

In the 1990s bin Laden turned up in Pakistan and Sudan but he lost his citizenship in his native country when he vocally attacked the Saudi royal family. The United States first began discussing bin Laden after the August 1998 attacks on the U.S. embassies in Dar es Salaam, Tanzania, and Nairobi, Kenya, but he was not captured in follow-on raids. In the 2000s, bin Laden has been thought to operate in Afghanistan or the Waziristan section of Pakistan in the northwest frontier. He continues issuing statements on his intentions to bring destruction to the West, but some wonder whether he has died in the attempts to capture him and most observers believe his personal role in al Qaeda has probably lessened as the organization has evolved to try to outlast the international pursuit brought about by the September 11, 2001, terrorist attacks and subsequent ouster of the Taliban government in Afghanistan.

Anthony "Tony" Charles Lynton Blair (1953–)

A charismatic leader who brought the Labour Party of Great Britain back to power after almost two decades of Tory power, Prime Minister Tony Blair served until 2007. Born to a middle-class family, Blair attended Oxford University in the 1970s where he was known for his rock-and-roll band. Blair married a fellow barrister, Cherie, before becoming heavily active in politics. Blair won his initial seat in the House of Commons in the June 1983 election, which was largely disastrous for the Labour Party. Margaret Thatcher's successful leadership in the South Atlantic War (1982), as well as public perception that Labour was too far to the left, helped the Tories resoundingly defeat Labour. Blair remolded Labour's image by his personal commitment to social responsibility. In addition, he used the slogan "New Labour" to craft a party that looked more like Bill Clinton's centrist Democratic Party than the traditional leftist party of the United Kingdom. Blair's 1997 and 2001 victories for Labour were historic in their scope. The BBC noted that Blair's 2001 win was the first time a Labour government in Britain had ever governed for two full terms.

Blair was a key ally for President Bill Clinton as the latter tried to achieve some unity with Europeans on how to address Slobodan Milošević's brutality in the former Yugoslavia in the1990s. In addition, Blair and Clinton had both brought their respective parties to power after "years in the wilderness," and their personalities were somewhat similar. Surprisingly, Blair became an arguably closer ally to President George W. Bush, especially after the September 11, 2001, terrorist attacks.

Blair ultimately alienated many at home as he increasingly supported the U.S.-proposed moves against Saddam Hussein. Blair and Bush argued that the weapons of mass destruction that they believed Saddam had were justification for ousting the dictator. The majority of the British population opposed Blair on this policy, but he remained firm in supporting Bush and providing British forces for the coalition to defeat Saddam. As events subsequent to the March 2003 invasion began to sour the British public on British involvement, Blair's popularity plummeted. He stood for a final term in 2004, but the Labour majority declined substantially. Blair remained Bush's steadfast ally but shifted his priorities from those of his Washington ally, strongly criticizing the U.S. decision to withdraw from the Kyoto environmental treaty, for instance. Blair himself pushed the international leadership to emphasize the needs of the poor, especially in Africa. Before the 2004 election, Blair declared that he would not run for a subsequent term. Much of his final term centered around trying to get the international community to pay more attention to African issues, a pet interest on his part. In 2006 his government became the center of a scandal about political contributions for "honors" by Queen Elizabeth II but the main reason that Blair left office in late June 2007 was his low standing resulting from the Iraq War. Within days of surrendering 10 Downing Street and the prime ministership to Gordon Brown, Blair became a special envoy to the Middle East.

L. Paul "Jerry" Bremer III (1941–)

A career diplomat, Paul "Jerry" Bremer served as the head of the Coalition Provisional Authority in Baghdad, Iraq, from May 2003 through June 2004. Before that, Bremer had served in the State Department in many positions, including deputy chief of mission in Oslo, Norway, and ambassador to the Netherlands. During the final years of his State Department tenure, however, Bremer began to concentrate on terrorism, which led Speaker of the House Dennis Hastert to name him to the National Commission on Terrorism in 1999. After retiring to the private sector, Bremer worked for Kissinger and Associates, a private consulting firm founded by former Secretary of State Henry Kissinger, and a crisis consulting company in the nation's capital. A month after Saddam Hussein was forced from power as a result of the U.S.-led invasion of Iraq, Bremer succeeded former Lieutenant General Jay Garner as head of reconstruction. None of Bremer's prior government jobs had been in reconstruction and nation-building areas, but he became the administration's key figure in reconstruction and humanitarian activities. In his thirteen months of de facto governing of Iraq, Bremer introduced a number of controversial directives that some argue have fed the insurgency plaguing the country two years after Bremer's departure. Bremer's most controversial decision was to "de-Baathesize" the Iraqi Army: Any former members of the Baath movement were consciously excluded from the post-Saddam army. This created significant unemployment, which many critics argue generated a larger pool of insurgent recruits. Other criticisms against Bremer's governance included his concentration on the petroleum industry to the advantage of the United States; too little attention to the power grid, which is not producing nearly what it did in the pre-conflict environment; not asking for sufficient troops to accomplish the U.S. mission; and the overall view that he created a weak regime to get the United States out of Iraq instead of engaging in the nation building that the invasion had in fact required. Bremer left Iraq in the summer of 2004, after an agreement had been reached on how and when to conduct democratic elections in

Iraq. Bremer wrote a memoir, *My Year in Iraq: The Struggle to Build a Future of Hope* (Simon and Schuster 2006).

George W. Bush (1946–)

The former governor of Texas won the presidency in two controversial elections in 2000 and 2004 and has governed with an aggressive and controversial style. Born in Connecticut but raised in Midland, Texas, Bush received a bachelor's degree in history from Yale and a master's degree in business from Harvard University. He then returned to Texas to try his hand in a number of businesses. During the Vietnam War, Bush served in the Texas Air National Guard, but this service generated controversy during the 2004 election when his participation was questioned. Bush became a co-owner of the Texas Rangers baseball team (baseball being one of his passions) before defeating incumbent Ann Richards in the 1994 gubernatorial election. Bush was reelected in 1998 and then began his presidential campaign in earnest in the lead-up to 2000. Bush won the 2000 election with the thinnest margin in history as the decision hinged on controversial ballots in Florida, where fewer than 600 votes separated Bush from his main challenger, Vice President Albert Gore, Jr.

Eight months into his first term, Bush faced the most dramatic attack on the territory of the United States, the September 11 terrorist attacks. He immediately declared a "war on terrorism," and a month later the United States invaded Afghanistan to oust the Taliban government, which was thought to be protecting the masterminds of the terrorist plot. Simultaneously, the administration began quietly preparing for war to oust Saddam Hussein from Iraq, even though many specialists and the 9/11 investigation commission noted there was no evidence of a connection between Saddam Hussein and the terrorists. Bush gave two of the most famous speeches of the past fifty years on terrorism and U.S. strategy as he marshaled forces in these causes. In the first of these, his 2002 State of the Union address, he described Iraq, Iran, and North Korea as an "axis of evil." In the second speech, at the commencement ceremony for the U.S. Military Academy at West Point, the president moved from advocating defensive responses to terrorism to advocating prevention of these terrorist activities; some foreign policy analysts were stunned by the perceived expansion in scope of actions and strategy.

In the summer of 2002, the president's administration began pushing forcefully for an invasion of Iraq, ostensibly because of Saddam's weapons of mass destruction. As 2002 progressed, Bush retained the support of British Prime Minister Tony Blair, but few other world leaders, and he faced a divided population at home. Arguing that this was a war of necessity, not a war of choice, the administration's pressure for the war grew through Secretary of State Colin Powell's February 5, 2003, appearance before the UN Security Council to present evidence of the weapons.

On March 19, 2003, with much of the world protesting, U.S. forces moved into Iraq. Bush's administration appeared to have only thought through the war stage, however, relying on an absolutely best-case scenario for post-conflict planning purposes. As Bush declared on May 1, 2003, that "major combat operations" were over in Iraq, in front of a banner saying "Mission Accomplished" on the aircraft carrier USS *Abraham Lincoln*, the administration fundamentally underestimated the difficulties of post-conflict rebuilding while overestimating Iraqi desire for a non-Saddam regime. Bush's national security governance has aroused considerable debate as he chose to ignore a number of laws to guarantee civil liberties on the grounds that he was chasing terrorists and that as commander-in-chief, the Constitution authorized him whatever steps he deemed necessary to protect the nation against security threats. Critics, including some in his own party, strongly disagreed.

In his national security approach, Bush has continued to push states toward democratic governance but this has not assuaged many concerns around the world that the United States is not protecting itself against terrorists, but is exploiting its military weight to remake the world to its benefit. Bush has paid scant attention to Latin America for most of his presidency except for his concern about the Venezuelan President Hugo Chávez, but has increased visibility to the plight of Africa. He has pushed for democracy in the Middle East while alienating many around the world with his absolutely unwavering support for the government of Ariel Sharon in Israel, which many critics fear has cost the United States dearly in terms of popular support internationally. The wounds the European allies sustained as a result of the debates in the run-up to the Iraq War have not healed, and Bush remains extremely unpopular in Western Europe, although less so in the states of the former Warsaw Pact.

Bush's views on Asia are somewhat unclear. He has pushed for closer ties with Japan, yet there appears to be a serious split within his administration about the future of Sino-U.S. relations. For instance, many believe China will threaten the United States, yet others see it as an unavoidable economic partner. As Bush reaches the middle of his second term, the futures of Iraq and Afghanistan are murky, even though he repeatedly vows that the United States will "stay the course" for "victory." His other major intractable national security concerns are stopping nuclear programs in Iran and North Korea, although neither of these nations seem the least bit interested in seeing the position that the president advocates.

George William Casey, Jr. (1948–)

A graduate of Georgetown University, General George Casey became Chief of Staff of the Army in 2007. Casey grew up in a military family, although his father, Major General George Casey, died in a helicopter accident in 1970. Casey earned a master's degree in international relations from the University of Denver and he held a fellowship at the Atlantic Council of the United States. Casey is an Army Infantry officer who has served in assignments around the world but has not spent not much time in the Middle East. His prior jobs included working with stabilization forces in Bosnia, director of the Joint Staff, and director of plans for the Joint Staff. Beginning in 2004, Casey replaced Lieutenant General Rick Sanchez as the head of multinational forces in Iraq. Sanchez and Ambassador L. Paul "Jerry" Bremer had not gotten along, and Casey was supposed to mend relations between civilians and uniformed officers in rebuilding efforts for Iraq. In that position, Casey tried to lead the United States out of the Abu Ghraib prison scandal, which had damaged U.S. prestige and respect around the world. He has also had to address the persistent, violent insurgency that has led a number of coalition partners, such as Japan, to withdraw their forces. In June 2006, Casey announced a program for possible troop reductions in Iraq by late 2007, as long as the insurgency conditions have improved, but he will be overseeing the conditions from Washington, where President Bush named him Army chief of staff in early January 2007. His final months in Baghdad were marked with a serious increase in sectarian violence. Casey's successor, General David Petraeus, has seen some improvement in limiting violence as a result of the "surge" in troop strength up to 162,000 but the initial months after Casey's departure have been marked by a dramatic upturn in violence, resulting in increasingly vocal calls on the part of many in both houses of Congress for a withdrawal of U.S. forces.

Fidel Castro (1926–)

Fidel Castro has been arguably the greatest thorn in the side of the United States for the nearly half-century he has governed his nearby island nation. Castro was born to an upper-class farmer in the 1920s. He studied law in Havana and witnessed the periodic political upheavals that characterized post-1898 Cuba as it struggled with its economic and political dependence on U.S. sugar companies. As a young activist student, Castro attended the April 1948 founding meeting for the Organization of American States in Bogotá, Colombia, where the assassination of a domestic politician, Jorge Eliécer Gaitán, led to the outbreak of a tremendous violent period that lasted for fifteen years, *La Violencia*.

In the 1950s, Castro gathered a band of armed activists to fight for political change on the island. The group unsuccessfully attacked the Moncada Barracks in July 1953. Castro fled to nearby Mexico to regroup. He brought his guerrillas back to the island three years later, challenging the rule of U.S. supporter Fulgencio Batista y Zaldívar. The increasingly unpopular Batista was heavily corrupt and had direct ties to the interests of U.S. sugar companies, which controlled virtually all aspects of industry on the island. Living in the hills, from which they raided government forces and tried to undermine the Havana regime, Castro and his group spent the years between 1956 and 1959 trying to bring down the Batista government. Castro's younger brother Raúl and the Argentine doctor-turned-revolutionary Ernesto "Che" Guevara were part of the movement. A U.S. journalist with the *New York Times*, Herbert Matthews, traveled to the hills where he profiled Castro, thus giving him credibility in the minds of some critics. In 1958, the Eisenhower administration indicated that it would not protect Batista, who fell from power on January 1, 1959, when Castro and his guerrillas marched into Havana, declaring themselves in charge.

Whether Castro was originally a Communist, a manipulator, or an ardent nationalist has long been in dispute. The Eisenhower administration was not favorably inclined toward his actions, and the bilateral Cuban-U.S. relations were strained but not broken between 1959 and 1961. Castro, seeking to leverage Cuba's position against U.S. dominance, increasingly turned to the distant Soviet Union for assistance. This coincided with the Soviet doctrine of supporting wars of national liberation, and Castro's moves to prevent the United States from dominating Cuba again fit the bill. Castro took steps to nationalize the massive landholdings of foreign sugar companies, which made most Cubans landless workers. His seizures were aimed largely at those who had fled Castro's government to the United States and abroad.

Moscow was also interested in cultivating a relationship with a state so close (100 miles) to the U.S. coast, because a Soviet military presence on the island would mirror the U.S. forces based close to the Soviet Union in Turkey. The Kennedy administration destroyed any hopes for improved relations with Cuba by supporting the Eisenhower-inspired Bay of Pigs invasion in April 1961. The United States encouraged Cuban exiles who claimed that their arrival on the beaches of Cuba would inspire a massive uprising that would overthrow Castro and welcome the exiles with open arms. The operation almost immediately went wrong: it was revealed in newspapers, and the United States did not support the exiles. After their capture, Castro paraded the raiders in the international media to show how the United States sought to overthrow his increasingly Communist regime. The failed uprising was a major embarrassment for the Kennedy administration and caused it to restructure its domestic national security apparatus.

Eighteen months later, the tension over Cuba grew once again as the Kennedy administration detected Soviet medium-range ballistic missiles on the island. After a two-week give-and-take, the Soviets removed the missiles, but not without creating more suspicion in Washington that Castro's Cuba was a danger to reckon with, if not destroy. Over the following forty years, Washington has made clear it would like to see Castro ousted, but he has survived assassination attempts, domestic political intrigue, and the cutoff of Soviet aid under Mikhail Gorbachev in the late 1980s. The opposition to Castro, largely concentrated in southern Florida, where exiles fled after he assumed power in 1959, is a powerful political force in the United States, making Cuba virtually a hands-off topic. While the United States retains an economic embargo that went into effect in the early 1960s, the overwhelming majority of the world has normal relations with Havana.

The basis to the U.S.-Cuban disagreements is Castro himself, who is rapidly approaching his ninth decade of life, but there are legal disputes between the U.S.-based companies whose lands were expropriated by Castro ("nationalized" in his parlance) in the early 1960s. As Castro ages, he is more marginalized in the changing global community but still a tremendous irritant to Washington, which fears he will offer Chinese or Venezuelan interests, among others, access to his island to harm the United States and/or its interests. In August 2006, when he developed a serious medical problem, Fidel transferred power to his brother, Defense Minister Raúl Castro. A year later, the elder Castro brother remained in convalescence, but the stories of impending death appear to have been overstated as were expectations that without him the Cuban Communist regime would easily collapse.

Ahmed Chalabi (1945–)

Ahmed Chalabi was a major conduit to U.S. Defense Department officials before the 2003 invasion of Iraq. A nonobservant Shiite from a long-standing, politically active family, Chalabi left Iraq in the 1950s, landing at times in Great Britain with other periods in the United States. He helped organize antigovernment activities in the Kurdish section of the country in the north, then from outside. Chalabi studied mathematics at the Massachusetts Institute of Technology and University of Chicago, ultimately earning a doctorate. Chalabi then moved to Beirut, Lebanon, where he taught mathematics until 1977 and was increasingly involved in banking operations. Questions have arisen about his role in the collapse of a Jordanian bank in the 1980s.

Chalabi is now a British citizen, based in London, where he has had an important role in the Iraqi National Congress, one of a number of exile groups raising money and working to overthrow Saddam Hussein before 2003. Chalabi was not trusted by a significant portion of the U.S. government, however, especially the State Department, because they believed he had virtually no political support within Iraq, but was widely trusted in other elements including the Defense Department. Chalabi argued that there was wide support for an overthrow of Saddam Hussein, which would occur once U.S. forces supported an invasion, and he claimed his supporters would be the core of a new, pro-Western, anti-Baathist society. Despite concerns about his credibility, Chalabi's views were widely circulated in the U.S. government and led to optimism that U.S. forces would be welcomed with open arms. From this set of assumptions about Iraq spread the view that the reconstruction of a democratic, pro-Western government in Baghdad would be a relatively simple process.

Chalabi has operated in the post-Saddam Iraq but has not attracted much support. With his credibility under attack, Chalabi broke with Washington and is now aligned with one of the many factions trying to establish itself as legitimate within the chaotic Iraqi political landscape. He does not appear to have popular support, however, because many Iraqis fear he is a proxy for the United States and because he was gone from the country for so many years.

Hugo Rafael Chávez Frías (1954–)

The son of two teachers, Hugo Chávez has been the president of Venezuela since December 1998. Chávez graduated from the Venezuelan Military Academy in 1975, trained as an engineer. Chávez had a relatively conventional military career until February 1992, when he was an organizer of the coup attempt against the democratically elected government of Venezuela. The coup was the first in Venezuela since it had embraced democracy in 1958, yet the problems within the government were obvious. The regime in Caracas had been pressed to respond to international demands that the government raise subsidized prices to undercut burgeoning budget deficits. In addition, the democratic governments of post-1958 Venezuela had suffered from tremendous corruption and political manipulation at the highest levels of society.

Chávez and the other coup plotters argued that they would ensure that Venezuela would respond to the needs of its citizens. The plotters argued, as did those attempting a later coup in 1992, that Venezuelan politicians were giving the resources of the nation, including its vast petroleum reserves and revenues, to imperialist outsiders who were seeking to exploit the *patria*, that exquisitely Latin American sense of nationhood built upon the soil, blood, culture, history, and unique aggregate experience that the military pledged to protect.

Chávez served jail time from 1992 to 1994 for his antigovernment activities, but he returned to society as a civilian with a cause and a following. Chávez declared himself a candidate for the 1998 presidential election, running on a platform of strident nationalism and anti-U.S. sentiment. Upon his election, Chávez almost immediately suggested a national referendum on rewriting the national constitution with an eye toward protecting the Bolivarian character of the nation (named after *El Gran Libertador* of northern South America, Simón Bolívar). In December 1999, the referendum passed, and it included provisions allowing Chávez a second term as president.

In subsequent years, Chávez has taken more stridently anti-U.S. positions, such as advocating cutting off petroleum to the United States, visiting ostracized Iraqi president Saddam Hussein in Baghdad before his overthrow, publicly supporting the anti-U.S. sentiment of Cuban president Fidel Castro, and advocating for the leftist guerrillas in neighboring Colombia. In 2006, U.S. Ambassador William Brownfield and Chávez became more publicly estranged as Washington believed the Venezuelan's actions were destabilizing not only his nation but also nations in the northern tier of Latin America. While Chávez has acquired a number of neighbors with relatively similar political outlooks, such as President Evo Morales in Bolivia, he is noticeably ignored by many in South America. Chávez won reelection in December 2006, but with a token amount of opposition. During President George W. Bush's March 2007 swing through six Latin American states, Chávez dogged him with taunts about the lack of serious U.S. commitment to the region. Bush, uncharacteristically, ignored his Venezuelan counterpart.

Chen Shui-bian (1950–)

A minority president in two elections, Taiwan President Chen Shui-bian is the first Taiwanese-born president of the island nation. Born in southern Taiwan after the Guomingdang (Nationalist) Party arrived to rule Taiwan in the aftermath of losing the civil war on mainland China, Chen grew up relatively poor in a society where native-born Taiwanese were significantly disadvantaged. He studied law and became a prominent civil rights lawyer. He eventually became more involved in a political party and had aspirations to govern Taiwan as well as to achieve Taiwan's independence from mainland China.

In 1980, Chen defended a number of Taiwan nationalists who fought against the dictatorial political system under Guomingdang rule in Taiwan. He joined the process through his election to the Taipei City Council. Through the remainder of the 1980s, he became more involved in politics while seeing his personal freedom curtailed: he was imprisoned on libel charges and his wife was permanently handicapped when his political adversaries attacked her. Chen went on to serve in the Legislative Yuan as a member of the Democratic Progressive Party (DPP) and then as the mayor of Taipei.

In 2000, Chen ran for president as the DPP candidate. Because the DPP has an independence perspective, the mainland government, which has claimed it will not tolerate any sort of movement toward independence in Taiwan, was severely critical of Chen running for the office and threatened to take military action if he was elected. Nevertheless, in March 2000, in Taiwan's first truly open political election, Chen won the presidency as a minority candidate because the Guomingdang was split between two rival factions. No military actions occurred, but Beijing has remained unhappy with the Chen regime, because Chen has flirted with openly declaring independence.

Chen's party was not successful in 2000 or subsequent elections at gathering enough support to take control over the Legislative Yuan, so he has governed as both a minority president (having won less than 40 percent of the popular vote for president) and without the support of the legislative branch. Chen's party was ill-prepared for governing, having been an opposition party throughout its history, and his government has been relatively gridlocked. While Chen has raised the issue of Taiwanese independence several times—in August 2002 when he discussed the concept at a party conference, in October 2003 when he advocated rewriting the Taiwan constitution, and in the spring of 2006 when he abolished the National Unification Guidelines—he has not actually taken the step that China has deemed unacceptable. Further, Chen's DPP has moved away from some of its more stridently environmental positions, such as opposing importation of petroleum to establish a strategic reserve, that have left Taiwan more vulnerable to international pressure, as it relies on the international system for its energy and many other needs. The DPP has not lessened its opposition to nuclear power for the resource-poor island, however.

Chen won reelection in 2004 by fewer than 30,000 votes after a controversial incident where he and his vocally pro-independence vice president, Annette Lu, were shot a day before the balloting, while on the campaign trail in the south. Chen and Lu survived, but many in the Guomingdang believe this incident threw the election to Chen. Chen's unpredictable actions have presented problems to the Bush administration. In April 2004, Bush stated that the United States would support Taiwan, as legally required by the Taiwan Relations Act of 1979. What President Bush did not say, however, was that the United States would give any government in Taiwan carte blanche to announce steps that would aggravate China to the point where it had to respond to Taiwan independence moves.

Chen has flirted with declaring independence and has tried to raise Taiwan's relations with the United States back to the position of a full nation, a condition eradicated by President Jimmy Carter's decision to shift recognition from Taiwan to Beijing as the government of China on January 1, 1979. While the Taiwan Relations Act requires the United States to help Taiwan defend itself, that is a far cry from requiring the United States to defend Taiwan. In late 2006, Chen's wife and others in his entourage went on trial for corruption, seriously undermining his rule, but Chen appears likely to finish his second term before retiring from the political scene. His administration remains a target of multiple investigations but other politicians in Taiwan also face legal inquiries, indicating the vibrancy of "rule of law" in Taiwan, but appear highly unlikely to unseat the president before the March 2008 presidential vote.

Richard "Dick" Bruce Cheney (1941–)

Vice President Dick Cheney is the most powerful person in that position in the history of the nation. Born in Nebraska but raised in Casper, Wyoming, Cheney attended college at Yale University, but flunked out. After returning to Wyoming, he enrolled in the University of Wyoming, where he graduated. He enrolled in graduate school in the mid-1960s at the University of Wisconsin, which took him to Washington DC to do research. He was married by this point and had two daughters, exempting him from military service in Vietnam.

Beginning in the late 1960s, Cheney held a long series of increasingly more important jobs in the executive and legislative branches. Cheney met Donald Rumsfeld in the late 1960s, a former congressman from northern Illinois, who took him to the Gerald Ford White House in 1974, where Cheney became the youngest chief of staff ever in the job. Subsequent to that, Cheney returned to Wyoming, where he won election as the state's single representative in the House. In 1987, Cheney sat on the joint congressional committee to investigate the Iran-Contra scandal.

In 1989, Cheney was appointed secretary of defense after President George H. W. Bush's initial nominee, former Texas senator John Tower, was rejected by the Senate. Cheney served in this role through the administration, which included the first Gulf War. Cheney's tenure was marked with a notable controversy over the policy paper written by an aide advocating that the United States did not want to see the rise of any sort of peer competitor, riling U.S. allies.

In the mid-1990s, Cheney considered a presidential run, but decided against it, in part, because of his history of four heart attacks. Instead, Cheney became the head of Halliburton, a multinational corporation that became a crucial contractor in the reconstruction efforts in Iraq. In 2000, Cheney had the task of helping presidential candidate George W. Bush consider vice presidential candidates; Cheney's search resulted in his own choice. The Bush-Cheney ticket won the closest electoral victory in U.S. history after a six-week challenge to the results in the Florida electorate, which was ultimately settled in their favor by a split U.S. Supreme Court decision.

Eight months after assuming office, the September 11 terrorist attacks occurred while Cheney was at the White House and Bush was in Florida visiting a school. Already seen as a powerful vice president in his first months in office, the post–September 11 White House gave Cheney an unprecedented role in decision making. By all accounts, Cheney's positions were more hard line than those of the president, recalling the moves by the legislative branch, in Cheney's view, to usurp presidential power. Cheney was also one of the first to be concerned about Iraq's potential role in the September 11 attacks. Subsequent repeated analyses have never found any ties, but Cheney continued to worry that a connection between Saddam Hussein and the terrorists had existed.

Cheney became an increasingly controversial figure in the Bush administration: He aggressively voiced the need to remove weapons of mass destruction from Iraq while also taking the hardest possible moves against the prisoners held at Guantánamo Bay in preparation for military tribunals. Others have argued that the vice president pushed to have intelligence produce certain outcomes that buttressed the administration's position, but Cheney and the White House have adamantly rejected this charge.

In 2005, Cheney's aide, I. Lewis "Scooter" Libby, was indicted (and convicted in 2007) in a scandal about leaking the name of a covert Central Intelligence Agency officer whose husband had publicly disagreed with evidence the administration put forth in preparing the public for the Iraq invasion. Some of Cheney's strongest critics believe he was the source of this classified information, but this was never proven. Cheney remains an extraordinarily powerful but reclusive figure in the administration, but one who has steadfastly retained a hard-line view on what best suits U.S. national security.

Hillary Rodham Clinton (1947–)

An extraordinarily polarizing figure, although her critics and supporters alike acknowledge her capabilities, Hillary Rodham Clinton is the junior senator from New York even though she had never lived in the state before her 2000 election. Born into a Chicago-area Republican family, Clinton attended Wellesley College, where she embraced a more liberal philosophy, which was reflected in her 1969 graduation remarks advocating changes in the nation's power structure as well as a greater role for new generations.

Clinton met her future husband, Bill Clinton, while both studied law at Yale. Hillary served as a lawyer on the Watergate investigative staff in 1974, and then moved to Arkansas in 1975 to marry Bill Clinton and teach law. When her new spouse entered the Arkansas governor's office beginning in 1978, Hillary began practicing law at the Rose Law Firm in Little Rock. Upon Bill Clinton's defeat for reelection to the governorship in 1980, Hillary took his name and became a somewhat more traditional political spouse. She was controversial during the 1992 presidential campaign when many traditionalists feared she would be too powerful and would act as an unofficial member of Clinton's government. During Bill Clinton's administration, Hillary endured public attacks over her role in developing a national health care plan, questions about her role in financing for Whitewater and the associated investigation, and finally the humiliation of public discussion of an extramarital affair the president had with a young intern.

After Bill Clinton left office in 2000, the Clintons relocated their formal residence to New York, where she ran to fill the senatorial seat of retired Democrat Daniel Patrick Moynihan. Elected handily in 2000, Clinton took a relatively centrist position through much of the first Bush administration, including voting to authorize his decision to invade Iraq in 2003. Among her accomplishments as senator, she worked diligently to gain reconstruction funding after the September 11 terrorist attacks. Clinton also began laying the groundwork for a presidential run of her own. And despite the fact that she ran for reelection to the Senate in 2006 with no formal intention of abandoning that seat for the White House, in 2007 she declared her intention to run in the 2008 presidential election and has become a sharp critic of President Bush's war in Iraq.

Karl Eikenberry (1951–)

An erudite graduate of the U.S. Miltary Academy who holds a translator's certificate in Mandarin, Lieutenant General Eikenberry commanded the U.S. forces in Afghanistan supporting the government of Hamid Karzai. Eikenberry earned a graduate degree in east Asian studies from Harvard as well as a graduate degree in political science from Stanford. He has served as a foreign area officer in the Army and was posted multiple times to the embassy in Beijing before holding the job as senior country director for China, Taiwan, Hong Kong, and Mongolia in the Office of the Secretary of Defense. Eikenberry also served in Army positions in Hawaii, Germany, Korea, and Afghanistan. Eikenberry took charge of Combined Forces Command in Afghanistan in 2005, but conditions have been more challenging after the resurgence of the Taliban in 2006. He completed his Afghan command tour in early 2007 before being reassigned to the North Atlantic Treaty Organization headquarters.

Tommy Franks (1945–)

Franks was the combatant commander for U.S. Central Command in Tampa, Florida, when the Afghanistan and Iraq invasions occurred in 2001 and 2003, respectively. Franks is an Oklahoma-born Army officer who grew up in Midland, Texas, before entering the service in the late 1960s. He assumed leadership of the

Central Command from Marine General Anthony Zinni before the September 11 attacks. When asked to provide an invasion plan for Afghanistan, and then one for Iraq eighteen months later, Franks answered with ambitious phase-one war plans. His subsequent planning for peace operations proved less successful in both places. President George W. Bush awarded Franks the Medal of Freedom, the highest civilian award, a year after his retirement in mid-2003, along with Ambassador Jerry Bremer, former CIA Director George Tenet, and others who were seen as architects of the Iraq War. Frank's lack of post-conflict planning mystified some.

Peter W. Galbraith (1950–)

One of the children of the late ambassador and renowned economist John Kenneth Galbraith, Peter Galbraith was a long-time Senate staffer on foreign policy issues before President Bill Clinton named him envoy to Croatia in the 1990s. Educated at Harvard and Oxford before entering Georgetown University Law School, Galbraith grew up in decision-making circles. Dating to his time on Capitol Hill, Galbraith had an abiding interest in the Kurdish minority of the Middle East and the brutal and repressive behavior of Saddam Hussein's regime. After the 1991 ouster of Iraqi troops from Kuwait, the Shiite minority of southern Iraq led an ultimately unsuccessful revolt against the dictator, which Galbraith documented through personal travel through the country. After serving in Croatia during the period of Slobodan Milošević's cruelties in the disintegrating former Yugoslavia, Galbraith taught for several years at the National War College in Washington DC. During that period, Galbraith went to serve as de facto foreign minister of the newly independent East Timor. In the aftermath of the U.S. invasion of Iraq, Galbraith left the War College to serve as an observer and advisor to the Kurdish section of northern Iraq. In 2006, he wrote a highly critical assessment of U.S. policy in Iraq in the first three years of the occupation.

Jay Garner (1938–)

Army Lieutenant General Jay Garner was tapped by President George W. Bush to conduct the reconstruction efforts of Iraq after Saddam Hussein's ouster in April 2003. After graduating from

Florida State University, Garner served in the Florida National Guard and Marine Corps before taking his Army commission in 1962. Garner served in Vietnam, Germany, and Washington DC as he rose through the ranks. In 1991, Garner attracted attention in his capacity as commanding officer for the efforts to provide humanitarian assistance to Kurdish refugees in northern Iraq, which became known as Operation PROVIDE COMFORT. This work received much praise and led to Garner's appointment by the second Bush administration to provide rebuilding efforts in post-Saddam Iraq. Garner's position was as head of the Office of Reconstruction and Humanitarian Assistance, beginning in January 2003, less than three months before the invasion. Many subsequent reports indicate that Garner's work received short shrift among Pentagon planners who believed the reconstruction efforts would prove unnecessary in the light of anticipated welcome on the part of Iraqis. Garner arrived in Iraq in April 2003, but conditions were significantly worse than anticipated in Baghdad. Because of considerable confusion and an inability to provide the resources necessary to address the problems, President Bush replaced Garner with former diplomat L. Paul "Jerry" Bremer in mid-May, less than six weeks after Garner got on the ground in country.

William "Bill" Henry Gates III (1955–)

One of the world's richest persons, Bill Gates is the chairman of the computer software company Microsoft Corporation. Gates was one of three children born to a Seattle attorney and his wife, who was involved in the United Way. Gates attended Harvard, where he became interested in computer software and made friends with another computer aficionado, Steve Ballmer, down the hall . Gates dropped out of Harvard in the mid-1970s before completing his degree.

Gates returned to the Pacific Northwest, where he and a childhood friend, Paul Allen, began a small company working on the code material that makes a computer run, calling it Microsoft. IBM had first released personal computers (PCs) in the early 1980s, followed by Apple in 1984, and Microsoft began producing software to run on PCs, basing its philosophy on the belief that eventually computers would be on everyone's desks, making the world a more productive place. By the 1990s, Microsoft reached the position of global superiority in software, a state of affairs that made a number of regulators around the world, particularly in Europe, uncomfortable that the company was engaging in anti-competitive, if not predatory, practices.

By the time of his marriage to Melinda French in 1994, Gates's personal worth was in the multimillions. His wealth ultimately reached more than $100 billion, although Microsoft's stock value has declined since that high. The Gateses have three children but after founding the Bill and Melinda Gates Foundation, they decided they would not leave all of their money to their children. Instead, the Gates Foundation is altering the approach to answering health security around the world. The couple has donated billions of dollars to HIV/AIDS, malaria, and other research needs. In mid-2006, Gates announced his personal withdrawal from day-to-day operations at Microsoft to work increasingly on Foundation activities. Within weeks, Omaha investment magnate Warren Buffett announced he would donate 85 percent of his roughly $40 billion wealth to the Bill and Melinda Gates Foundation to help eradicate illnesses that the Gateses and Buffett believe can be ended. The work of the Gates Foundation, and by extension Bill Gates, has the possibility of altering the course of human health and security in large sections of the world.

Albert Gore, Jr. (1947–)

Son of a Democratic senator from Tennessee who lost his seat because of the turmoil of the Vietnam War, Gore also served as a congressman and senator from Tennessee before serving two terms as Clinton's vice president from 1993 to 2001. An Army veteran who served in Vietnam as a military journalist, Gore spent most of his early professional career in Congress representing Tennessee. Gore served Clinton loyally through the tumultuous years of his presidency, and then ran for president on his own in 2000, where he lost to George W. Bush by the thinnest margin in U.S. history. The election outcome was in doubt for several weeks but Gore was ultimately defeated. In the immediate aftermath, Gore withdrew to reconsider his options but came out in the middle of the first decade of the century as a harsh critic of U.S. policies in Iraq and abroad.

Over his years in office, Gore developed an abiding interest in the environment, arguing that it is a growing national security issue confronting the entire nation. In 2006, Gore's crusade about climate deterioration was the focus of a movie, *An Inconvenient Truth*, challenging President Bush's decision to abandon the Kyoto Protocol on global warming. Coming the year after serious questions about the harsh effects of Hurricane Katrina in 2005, Gore's concerns led to passionate support and disputation about the movie's goals and proof of the former vice president's aspirations and national security credentials. The film won an Academy Award in 2007, giving it and Gore much greater visibility, and sparking a revival of the public debate about global warming.

Alan C. Greenspan (1927–)

During his long tenure as chairman of the Federal Reserve Bank ("the Fed") Board of Governors, many people labeled Alan Greenspan "the second most powerful man in the world" because of the power his word had over global stock markets. Born to a Jewish family in New York, Greenspan attended Julliard before earning bachelor's and master's degrees in economics from New York University. Although Greenspan studied for a doctorate in the 1950s, he never completed a dissertation; however, the university awarded him the degree in 1977. Greenspan worked for the Conference Board for five years in the late 1940s and early 1950s before serving as a partner in an economic consulting company in New York. He held that position until he became the Federal Reserve chairman in 1987. Greenspan served in the Ford administration as chairman of the Council of Economic Advisors, but was otherwise a private-sector economist.

When Greenspan took over the Fed in 1987, he succeeded "inflation slayer" Paul Volcker, Fed chairman in the early 1980s, who managed to wring inflation out of the economy after the "stagflation" era of the 1970s. Greenspan took over the year that the New York Stock Exchange suffered a major correction during the Reagan administration. It took significant time to rebuild confidence in the market, but Greenspan's cool behavior helped settle the markets at home and abroad. Greenspan was also chairman during the late 1990s and early months of 2000 when the stock market went through what Greenspan himself labeled "irrational exuberance" to describe the inexplicable rise in stock prices. This situation produced unreasonable expectations and a market bubble. During this time, economists and politicians around the world listened carefully and entirely to Greenspan's observations on global expansion, which is what led to the belief that he had become the second most important man in the world behind the president of the United States. In particular, Greenspan warned of a property price bubble that had already begun to deflate when the September 11 attacks closed Wall Street for several days. Greenspan lowered interest rates to historic levels to stimulate the economy after the attacks but steadily raised those rates before his January 2006 retirement. After his retirement, critics have begun challenging the glowing interpretation of his rule at the Fed, as he did nothing to discourage federal spending but only addressed monetary policy. Without a doubt, however, Greenspan's tenure at the Fed reinforced the view that the national security of the United States is intimately linked to economic security and conditions in the world. In an autobiography, Greenspan was highly critical of Bush-era spending, but the former chairman himself has come under fire for loose credit in the early 2000s.

Hu Jintao (1942–)

A native of Anhui province in central China, Hu Jintao is considered the fourth-generation leadership in the People's Republic of China. A career bureaucrat who trained as an engineer, Hu served the Communist Party in many jobs after achieving membership in 1964. Initially, his work was in the field of engineering but he increasingly became a Communist Party figure, not an insignificant accomplishment during the height of the Great Proletarian People's Revolution (1966–1976) when all ties were dangerous in China. Hu served in Tibet before climbing to the top levels of the Communist Party in the late 1990s and early 2000s.

In 2003, Hu assumed the presidency of China but also became the general secretary of the Communist Party (his primary base of power) and chairman of the Central Military Commission. During his presidency, China's startling economic growth has continued, along with a tremendous amount of military modernization. Similarly, during his tenure as president, China has shown an increased willingness to engage in overseas ventures, both diplomatic and economic. A culminating moment will likely be the August 2008 opening of the Beijing Olympic games in the nation's capital. Presidents Hu and George W. Bush share relatively strong relations, although there are differences between the two on human rights, religious freedoms, and others issues.

Hamid Karzai (1957–)

Hamid Karzai, the U.S.-educated president of Afghanistan, hopes to transform his society and remains an anchor for U.S. efforts at democratization around the world. Karzai returned to his native country before the 2001 invasion but was a minor figure in the panoply of Afghan factions. A relatively secular figure in a society with strong religious zeal, Karzai became the first president of post-Taliban Afghanistan once that group fled in late 2001. He received many promises from the international community for financial support to sustain the efforts to rebuild the society along Western lines. Karzai walks a fine line between appearing to be a Western puppet and a genuine Afghan leader. A Pashtun in a society of many tribal groups, he is a minority president in many senses. Karzai is seen as a legitimate democrat by some but others believe he is practically a prisoner in Kabul, the nation's capital, and fear that he would be assassinated if he ventured far without his foreign bodyguards.

Zalmay Khalilzad (1951–)

A crucial player in the arc of crisis since 2001, Zalmay Khalilzad is an Afghan-born, University of Chicago–educated academic who has served in high levels of the George W. Bush administration. Khalilzad worked at the Rand Corporation through the 1980s and took a position on the National Security Council staff in the George H. W. Bush administration. After George H. W. Bush left office, Khalilzad returned to the private sector but was called upon by President George W. Bush after the invasions of Afghanistan and Iraq. Khalilzad became ambassador to Afghanistan and then to Baghdad after these states had more pro-U.S. regimes. In 2007, President Bush moved Khalilzad to the UN in an overall shift of personnel in the Iraq decision-making scheme.

Kim Jong Il (1942–)

Son of the first president of the Democratic People's Republic of North Korea, Kim assumed the office upon his father's death in 1994. Even after almost fifteen years in power, the details of his life are quite elusive. Leader of what has been long considered the "hermit kingdom," he ruled with the support of the North Korean military through a period of severe famine and drought. At roughly the time of his accession, U.S. negotiators tried to talk the North Koreans out of a nuclear weapons program. North Korea responded by withdrawing from the Nuclear Non-Proliferation Treaty (1970) but proved unwilling to abide by the "Agreed Framework" between the signatories of the Korean talks. In 1999, North Korea discomfited the Japanese and South Koreans by firing medium-range ballistic missiles in the area. In 2002, the Bush administration publicly accused North Korea of producing nuclear weapons. In July 2006, the North Koreans announced that they had detonated a nuclear device, although many were skeptical of its success. After more than four years of stopping and starting talks, the North Koreans again agreed stop making nuclear weapons in exchange for humanitarian and energy assistance. As late as March 2007, Kim's regime kept offering reasons why it might have to renege on its promise.

William Kristol (1952–)

Son of the prominent neoconservative writers Irving Kristol and Gertrude Himmelfarb, Bill Kristol is seen by many as the archetypical neoconservative power broker in the United States and a driving force for a strong national security posture. Educated at Harvard, Kristol first came to prominence in the 1980s when he worked first for Secretary of Education William Bennett, then as Vice President Dan Quayle's chief of staff. Kristol became the editor for the *Weekly Standard* in the 1990s and cofounder of the Project for a New American Century, a think tank advocating a strong national security position along with a democratic push that the United States alone could provide the world. In the late 1990s, the Project publicly urged President Bill Clinton to overthrow Saddam Hussein's government in Iraq because of the threat it posed to the world and to Israel, a key U.S. ally in the Middle East. With the advent of the Bush administration in 2000, Kristol pushed even harder. An avowed supporter of the invasion. Kristol also became a critic of the size of the armed forces, arguing they were being stretched too thinly. Kristol continued to argue that the United States, with its unique democratic values and power, had to project its willingness to lead for the world. In 2005, the Project closed its doors but Kristol remains a major thinker on national security issues.

Robert Mugabe (1927–)

The first head of an independent Zimbabwe after white Rhodesia collapsed in the late 1970s, Robert Mugabe has become the epitome of a dictator unwilling to bend to the international community. Initially hailed as a reformer who would lead the new state forward after the Lancaster House accord of 1980, Mugabe began amassing power and shutting down his adversaries. In the 1990s, land owned by whites came under confiscation rules, and the economy, already fragile, deteriorated further. In the 2000s, Mugabe's dictatorial steps became even greater as all opponents were exiled or jailed. International sanctions made no difference to Mugabe, who continued to rule with an iron hand and spit in the face of his critics, at home and abroad. In a show of efforts to reach out to resource-rich places, regardless of their political orientation, Mugabe became a client state of China in its growing African efforts.

Peter Pace (1946–)

One of the final chairmen of the Joint Chiefs of Staff to have served in Vietnam, Marine Corps General Peter Pace took over as the chairman of the Joint Chiefs of Staff in 2005 after having been vice chairman for the prior four years. A graduate of the National War College, Pace also served in Somalia, as director of the Joint Staff, and in various other jobs. He was vice chairman of the Joint Chiefs during the Afghanistan and Iraq invasions but took over the top job during the period of serious deterioration of the U.S. position in both places. Pace became a visible face as the press wondered about the Abu Ghraib scandal, detentions at Guantánamo, recruiting and retention issues for the armed forces, and the overall campaign in Iraq. In 2007, Pace and others were thought to have disagreed with the president's decision for a "surge" of 21,000 troops into Iraq. He also attracted public attention for his condemnation of homosexuality in March 2007. The chairmen of the Joint Chiefs of Staff often serve two-year terms as Pace was expected to do. In June 2007, Secretary of Defense Bob Gates announced that he recognized Pace's reappointment for a second term would be highly contentious; therefore, he was naming Admiral Michael Mullen, Chief of Naval Operations, to the position instead of renominating Pace for the second term.

David H. Petraeus (1952–)

The commander in Iraq as of 2007, General David Petraeus is a graduate of the Military Academy and Princeton University. Well-regarded by his soldiers, Petraeus studied counterinsurgency for his doctoral dissertation, making him the ideal person to go into Iraq after the 2003 invasion. His previous tours included training Iraqi military forces and working with the 82nd Airborne in northern Iraq. Petraeus served as the primary author of the Army and Marine Corps' new counterinsurgency manual, FM 3–24, which was issued in 2006 and highlighted the importance of direct contact with personnel on the ground in a possible insurgency. Petraeus returned to Iraq after conditions on the ground had deteriorated significantly by late 2006. He is charged with improving the security conditions on the ground while making strategic improvements for the country. Petraeus, in early statements during his command, indicates that he believes U.S. troops will have to stay in country far longer than many politicians and voters appear willing to endorse, saying he anticipates withdrawal no earlier than mid-2008 at the very earliest. By the end of the summer in 2007, Petraeus has become the centerpiece of U.S. strategy to achieve U.S. goals in Iraq. Politicians of all political stripes mention his assessments of successes and failures, problems and opportunities in Iraq as the measures of whether the United States is doing what it hopes to in the region.

Colin Luther Powell (1938–)

The first African American chairman of the Joint Chiefs of Staff and secretary of state, Powell personified the American dream. This son of Jamaican immigrants attended local college and rose through the ranks of the military to its leadership. An officer of junior rank during the Vietnam War, Powell recognized the broken condition that confronted the force as it left Southeast Asia. Powell became a consummate Washington insider after his positions as a White House Fellow and graduate of the National War College. He served as Secretary of Defense Casper Weinberger's aide and on Ronald Reagan's national security council staff before assuming the position of national security adviser toward the end of the latter's administration.

President George H. W. Bush named him the chairman of the Joint Chiefs of Staff even though he was a relatively young four-star general. Under Powell's tenure as chairman, the United States began adjusting to the end of the Cold War but also faced the new threats of Islamic militancy and the expansionist Saddam Hussein. Powell oversaw the U.S. military effort when the latter invaded Kuwait in 2000 and was one of the nation's most respected figures when he retired as chairman in September 1993. Many people enthusiastically encouraged Powell to run for president in 1996 but he demurred. In late 2000, he became a visible face for foreign policy in the aftermath of the contentious presidential election. General Powell was far more respected on foreign affairs than was the president-elect, George W. Bush, allowing many to wonder if the retired soldier would dominate the new Bush administration. As a result of other appointments, Powell's role as secretary of state became somewhat circumscribed. With the 2001 attacks and U.S. responses in Afghanistan and Iraq, Powell took center state as a highly respected, credible figure speaking for the United States. His February 5, 2003 speech at the United Nations assured some on the nature of the threat Saddam Hussein's regime posed to the international community. With the progress of the war after its inception in March 2003, Powell began to show discomfort with the policies. Over the months, Powell's disagreements with Secretary of Defense Donald Rumsfeld became well known. At the end of George W. Bush's first term, Powell tendered his resignation, which was accepted. Since his retirement from government, Powell has been relatively quiet on foreign affairs but has occasionally criticized the administration for its actions around the globe.

Vladimir Putin (1952–)

The first president of an entirely post-Soviet Russia, Vladimir Putin assumed the presidency of Russia in 2000 when serving as Boris Yeltsin's deputy. Earlier in his career Putin served in the KGB, and much of his time during the 1980s was spent in Germany. Putin then returned to the Russian Federation and became a confidant of President Boris Yeltsin as the latter's deteriorating health became public knowledge. When Yeltsin resigned in late 1999, he named Putin his successor; Putin later won election on his own. In 2001, President Bush spoke highly of Putin, noting that he "had seen into the [Russian] President's soul" and forged a strong relationship with him, but those ties soured as Russia regained much of its international prestige as it benefited from rising oil prices in the 2000s. Putin also proved unwilling to help with the invasion of Iraq, the desired sanctions against Iran, and other proposals for which President Bush sought Putin's assistance. In February 2007, Putin gave a scathing speech where he attacked the United States for overstepping its bounds in the international system. This speech coincided with Putin's consolidation of power and elimination of critics—a former KGB agent died of thallium poisoning in London and journalists in Moscow who had criticized the Putin government were assassinated. Putin has declared he will not run again for president in 2008, but many fear he will retain power behind the scenes because of his former KGB ties.

Condoleezza Rice (1954–)

Rice was the first African American woman to serve as the national security adviser and secretary of state. Born in the period of racial segregation in her hometown of Birmingham, Alabama, Rice was a single child who grew up as a concert pianist, ice skater, and academic prodigy. Rice studied international relations at the University of Denver with Josef Korbel, the father of Democratic Secretary of State Madeleine Korbel Albright. Rice also studied at the University of Notre Dame before returning to the University of Denver to complete her doctoral work in Soviet studies. Rice then joined the faculty at Stanford University, where she gained much attention within the Republican Party as an African American Soviet scholar. Rice served on the National Security Council staff under President George H. W. Bush before returning to Stanford as the university provost in 1993.

In early 2000, as Texas governor George W. Bush made his early moves toward the presidential primaries, Rice published what became an important article in *Foreign Affairs* magazine advocating his positions on national security, such as arguing strongly that U.S. military forces ought not engage in nation-building activities. For many, this was an indicator that Rice would likely have a prominent role in an administration of the younger Bush. And indeed, the president-elect named Rice as his national security adviser, a position that made her a crucial arbitrator between secretaries Donald Rumsfeld and Colin Powell, each of whom had a strong personality. Rice continued in this role through the first administration, keeping important public attention on the president's aims at going to war in Iraq and working toward acceptance of the concept of preemptive war. Rice was also the chief person to coordinate the administration's role in the Arab-Israeli conflict in October 2003. Rice's role in the intelligence evaluation that went to Bush became important as repeated questions arose about what was known about weapons of mass destruction in the lead-up to the 2003 invasion. Partially because Bush had such faith in her and partially because Secretary of State Powell had become expendable, Rice became the secretary of state upon the president's inauguration for his second term. Rice has promoted the democracy agenda forcefully throughout the world, ensuring that Middle Eastern states, east Asian states, and all others to understand how serious the United States is about this goal.

Donald Rumsfeld (1932–)

Donald Rumsfeld is the only man to serve as secretary of defense under two U.S. presidents, in tenures a quarter of a century apart. A Princeton student boxer and naval aviator, Rumsfeld was the congressional representative for a suburban Chicago district until the late 1960s, when he joined the Nixon administration and started a lifelong professional and personal friendship with Dick Cheney. In the Ford administration, Rumsfeld served first as chief of staff, then as secretary of defense in the mid-1970s while Cheney stepped up behind Rumsfeld as chief of staff in the White House. When the Ford administration ended in 1977, Rumsfeld went into the private sector as head of the pharmaceutical company Searle, but kept his hand in government as a possible presidential candidate and as head of a blue ribbon commission on national missile defense.

When George W. Bush assumed the presidency, he chose Rumsfeld to take over the largely unwieldy Defense Department. Rumsfeld took on the task with zeal and announced his intention to transform the national security community of the United States. After the September 11 attacks, Rumsfeld became a magnet for the press as he discussed U.S. options in Afghanistan in great detail. He locked horns with anyone not committed to transformation, including the Army Chief of Staff General Eric Shinseki, who Rumsfeld viewed as an obstacle to changing a service badly in need of major renovation. As the war in Iraq began to drag,

Rumsfeld became a more divisive figure in the administration. He refused to acknowledge that mistakes had been made in planning or to admit that things were not going well. His seeming lack of concern about the Abu Ghraib prison scandal led to an offer to resign in 2006. Many critics lay the blame for the Republican failure to hold the House of Representatives and Senate in 2006 at Rumsfeld's feet for misjudging the mood of the country on Iraq and beginning to institute changes in policy. Former CIA Director Robert Gates replaced Rumsfeld at the helm of the Department of Defense in 2007. Since his retirement, Rumsfeld has appeared rarely in public but remains the target of many critics who disagree with the Bush administration decisions on war in Iraq.

6

Data and Documents

This chapter is organized chronologically. The documents begin with the oldest, based on the date of release, and all the speeches are available as public documents. So much of the Bush administration has been focused on national security that this represents only a sample of the thousands of words on this vital issue.

Taiwan Relations Act of 1979, Public Law 96-8, 96th Congress

The Taiwan Relations Act serves as the basis of the U.S. relationship with Taiwan, but it is only one of a number of complicated pieces of the relationship with the People's Republic of China. At present, this appears to be the only issue that could bring the United States into war with that nuclear-armed state.

To help maintain peace, security, and stability in the Western Pacific and to promote the foreign policy of the United States by authorizing the continuation of commercial, cultural, and other relations between the people of the United States and the people on Taiwan, and for other purposes.

Be it enacted by the Senate and House of Representatives of the United States of America in Congress assembled . . .

This Act may be cited as the "Taiwan Relations Act" . . .

The President—having terminated governmental relations between the United States and the governing authorities on Taiwan recognized by the United States as the Republic of China prior to January 1, 1979, the Congress finds that the enactment of this Act is necessary—

    (1) to help maintain peace, security, and stability in the Western Pacific; and

    (2) to promote the foreign policy of the United States by authorizing the continuation of commercial, cultural, and other relations between the people of the United States and the people on Taiwan.

    (b) It is the policy of the United States—

    (1) to preserve and promote extensive, close, and friendly commercial, cultural, and other relations between the people of the United States and the people on Taiwan, as well as the people on the China mainland and all other peoples of the Western Pacific area;

    (2) to declare that peace and stability in the area are in the political, security, and economic interests of the United States, and are matters of international concern;

    (3) to make clear that the United States decision to establish diplomatic relations with the People's Republic of China rests upon the expectation that the future of Taiwan will be determined by peaceful means;

    (4) to consider any effort to determine the future of Taiwan by other than peaceful means, including by boycotts or embargoes, a threat to the peace and security of the Western Pacific area and of grave concern to the United States;

    (5) to provide Taiwan with arms of a defensive character; and

    (6) to maintain the capacity of the United States to resist any resort to force or other forms of coercion that would jeopardize the security, or the social or economic system, of the people on Taiwan.

    (c) Nothing contained in this Act shall contravene the interest of the United States in human rights, especially with respect to the human rights of all the approximately eighteen million inhabitants of Taiwan. The preservation and enhancement of the human rights of all the people on Taiwan are hereby reaffirmed as objectives of the United States.

IMPLEMENTATION OF UNITED STATES POLICY
WITH REGARD TO TAIWAN

    SEC. 3. (a) In furtherance of the policy set forth in section 2 of this Act, the United States will make available to Taiwan such defense articles and defense services in such quantity as may be necessary to enable Taiwan to maintain a sufficient self-defense capability.

    (b) The President and the Congress shall determine the nature and quantity of such defense articles and services based solely upon their judgment of the needs of Taiwan, in accordance with procedures established by law. Such determination of Taiwan's defense needs shall include review by United States military authorities in connection with recommendations to the President and the Congress.

(c) The President is directed to inform the Congress promptly of any threat to the security or the social or economic system of the people on Taiwan and any danger to the interests of the United States arising therefrom. The President and the Congress shall determine, in accordance with constitutional processes, appropriate action by the United States in response to any such danger.

APPLICATION OF LAWS; INTERNATIONAL AGREEMENTS
SEC. 4. (a) The absence of diplomatic relations or recognition shall not affect the application of the laws of the United States with respect to Taiwan, and the laws of the United States shall apply with respect to Taiwan in the manner that the laws of the United States applied with respect to Taiwan prior to January 1, 1979. . . .
(5) Nothing in this Act, nor the facts of the President's action in extending diplomatic recognition to the People's Republic of China, the absence of diplomatic relations between the people on Taiwan and the United States, or the lack of recognition by the United States, and attendant circumstances thereto, shall be construed in any administrative or judicial proceeding as a basis for any United States Government agency, commission, or department to make a finding of fact or determination of law, under the Atomic Energy Act of 1954 and the Nuclear Non-Proliferation Act of 1978, to deny an export license application or to revoke an existing export license for nuclear exports to Taiwan. . . .

(d) Nothing in this Act may be construed as a basis for supporting the exclusion or expulsion of Taiwan from continued membership in any international financial institution or any other international organization . . .

George W. Bush's State of the Union Address, January 29, 2002

President Bush's 2002 State of the Union address was a marker for how his administration views the future threats against the United States. His use of the term "axis of evil" gives clear evidence of future U.S. moves against three perceived threats.

Thank you very much. Mr. Speaker, Vice President Cheney, members of Congress, distinguished guests, fellow citizens: As we gather tonight, our nation is at war, our economy is in recession, and the civilized world faces unprecedented dangers. Yet the state of our Union has never been stronger.

We last met in an hour of shock and suffering. In four short months, our nation has comforted the victims, begun to rebuild New York and the Pentagon, rallied a great coalition, captured, arrested, and rid the world of thousands of terrorists, destroyed Afghanistan's terrorist training camps, saved a people from starvation, and freed a country from brutal oppression.

The American flag flies again over our embassy in Kabul. Terrorists who once occupied Afghanistan now occupy cells at Guantanamo Bay. And terrorist leaders who urged followers to sacrifice their lives are running for their own.

America and Afghanistan are now allies against terror. We'll be partners in rebuilding that country. And this evening we welcome the distinguished interim leader of a liberated Afghanistan: Chairman Hamid Karzai.

The last time we met in this chamber, the mothers and daughters of Afghanistan were captives in their own homes, forbidden from working or going to school. Today women are free, and are part of Afghanistan's new government. And we welcome the new Minister of Women's Affairs, Doctor Sima Samar.

Our progress is a tribute to the spirit of the Afghan people, to the resolve of our coalition, and to the might of the United States military. When I called our troops into action, I did so with complete confidence in their courage and skill. And tonight, thanks to them, we are winning the war on terror. The men and women of our Armed Forces have delivered a message now clear to every enemy of the United States: Even 7,000 miles away, across oceans and continents, on mountaintops and in caves—you will not escape the justice of this nation. . . .

Our cause is just, and it continues. Our discoveries in Afghanistan confirmed our worst fears, and showed us the true scope of the task ahead. We have seen the depth of our enemies' hatred in videos, where they laugh about the loss of innocent life. And the depth of their hatred is equaled by the madness of the destruction they design. We have found diagrams of American nuclear power plants and public water facilities, detailed instructions for making chemical weapons, surveillance maps of American cities, and thorough descriptions of landmarks in America and throughout the world.

What we have found in Afghanistan confirms that, far from ending there, our war against terror is only beginning. Most of the 19 men who hijacked planes on September the 11th were trained in Afghanistan's camps, and so were tens of thousands of others. Thousands of dangerous killers, schooled in the methods of murder, often supported by outlaw regimes, are now spread throughout the world like ticking time bombs, set to go off without warning.

Thanks to the work of our law enforcement officials and coalition partners, hundreds of terrorists have been arrested. Yet, tens of thousands of trained terrorists are still at large. These enemies view the entire world as a battlefield, and we must pursue them wherever they are. So long as training camps operate, so long as nations harbor terrorists, freedom is at risk. And America and our allies must not, and will not, allow it.

Our nation will continue to be steadfast and patient and persistent in the pursuit of two great objectives. First, we will shut down terrorist camps, disrupt terrorist plans, and bring terrorists to justice. And, second, we must prevent the terrorists and regimes who seek chemical, biological or nuclear weapons from threatening the United States and the world.

Our military has put the terror training camps of Afghanistan out of business, yet camps still exist in at least a dozen countries. A terrorist underworld—including groups like Hamas, Hezbollah, Islamic Jihad, Jaish-i-Mohammed—operates in remote jungles and deserts, and hides in the centers of large cities.

While the most visible military action is in Afghanistan, America is acting elsewhere. We now have troops in the Philippines, helping to train that country's armed forces to go after terrorist cells that have executed an American, and still hold hostages. Our soldiers, working with the Bosnian government, seized terrorists who were plotting to bomb our embassy. Our Navy is patrolling the coast of Africa to block the shipment of weapons and the establishment of terrorist camps in Somalia.

My hope is that all nations will heed our call, and eliminate the terrorist parasites who threaten their countries and our own. Many nations are acting forcefully. Pakistan is now cracking down on terror, and I admire the strong leadership of President Musharraf.

But some governments will be timid in the face of terror. And make no mistake about it: If they do not act, America will.

Our second goal is to prevent regimes that sponsor terror from threatening America or our friends and allies with weapons of mass destruction. Some of these regimes have been pretty quiet since September the 11th. But we know their true nature. North Korea is a regime arming with missiles and weapons of mass destruction, while starving its citizens.

Iran aggressively pursues these weapons and exports terror, while an unelected few repress the Iranian people's hope for freedom.

Iraq continues to flaunt its hostility toward America and to support terror. The Iraqi regime has plotted to develop anthrax, and nerve gas, and nuclear weapons for over a decade. This is a regime that has already used poison gas to murder thousands of its own citizens—leaving the bodies of mothers huddled over their dead children. This is a regime that agreed to international inspections—then kicked out the inspectors. This is a regime that has something to hide from the civilized world.

States like these, and their terrorist allies, constitute an axis of evil, arming to threaten the peace of the world. By seeking weapons of mass destruction, these regimes pose a grave and growing danger. They could provide these arms to terrorists, giving them the means to match their hatred. They could attack our allies or attempt to blackmail the United States. In any of these cases, the price of indifference would be catastrophic.

We will work closely with our coalition to deny terrorists and their state sponsors the materials, technology, and expertise to make and deliver weapons of mass destruction. We will develop and deploy effective missile defenses to protect America and our allies from sudden attack. And all nations should know: America will do what is necessary to ensure our nation's security.

We'll be deliberate, yet time is not on our side. I will not wait on events, while dangers gather. I will not stand by, as peril draws closer and closer. The United States of America will not permit the world's most dangerous regimes to threaten us with the world's most destructive weapons.

Our war on terror is well begun, but it is only begun. This campaign may not be finished on our watch—yet it must be and it will be waged on our watch.

We can't stop short. If we stop now—leaving terror camps intact and terror states unchecked—our sense of security would be false and temporary. History has called America and our allies to action, and it is both our responsibility and our privilege to fight freedom's fight. . . .

It costs a lot to fight this war. We have spent more than a billion dollars a month—over $30 million a day—and we must be prepared for future operations. Afghanistan proved that expensive precision weapons defeat the enemy and spare innocent lives, and we need more of them. We need to replace aging aircraft and make our military more agile, to put our troops anywhere in the world quickly and safely. Our men and women in uniform deserve the best weapons, the best equipment, the best training—and they also deserve another pay raise.

My budget includes the largest increase in defense spending in two decades—because while the price of freedom and security is high, it is never too high. Whatever it costs to defend our country, we will pay. . . .

George W. Bush's Graduation Speech at West Point, June 1, 2002

This speech featured the idea that the United States was acting on a pre-emption rather than a prevention basis. Many international leaders have questioned how the United States would implement this policy shift, but the Bush administration does not believe it is a shift but rather a continuation of existing, long-term U.S. policy.

Thank you very much, General Lennox. Mr. Secretary, Governor Pataki, members of the United States Congress, Academy staff and faculty, distinguished guests, proud family members, and graduates: I want to thank you for your welcome. Laura and I are especially honored to visit this great institution in your bicentennial year.

In every corner of America, the words "West Point" command immediate respect. This place where the Hudson River bends is more than a fine institution of learning. The United States Military Academy is the guardian of values that have shaped the soldiers who have shaped the history of the world.

A few of you have followed in the path of the perfect West Point graduate, Robert E. Lee, who never received a single demerit in four years. Some of you followed in the path of the imperfect graduate, Ulysses S. Grant, who had his fair share of demerits, and said the happiest day of his life was "the day I left West Point." During my college years I guess you could say I was . . . a Grant man.

You walk in the tradition of Eisenhower and MacArthur, Patton and Bradley—the commanders who saved a civilization. And you walk in the tradition of second lieutenants who did the same, by fighting and dying on distant battlefields.

Graduates of this academy have brought creativity and courage to every field of endeavor. West Point produced the chief engineer of the Panama Canal, the mind behind the Manhattan Project, the first American to walk in space. This fine institution gave us the man they say invented baseball, and other young men over the years who perfected the game of football.

You know this, but many in America don't—George C. Marshall, a VMI [Virginia Military Institute] graduate, is said to have given this order: "I want an officer for a secret and dangerous mission. I want a West Point football player."

As you leave here today, I know there's one thing you'll never miss about this place: Being a plebe. But even a plebe at West Point is made to feel he or she has some standing in the world. I'm told that plebes, when asked whom they outrank, are required to answer this: "Sir, the Superintendent's dog—the Commandant's cat, and all the admirals in the whole damn Navy." I probably won't be sharing that with the Secretary of the Navy.

West Point is guided by tradition, and in honor of the "Golden Children of the Corps," I will observe one of the traditions you cherish most. As the Commander-in-Chief, I hereby grant amnesty to all cadets who are on restriction for minor conduct offenses. Those of you in the end zone might have cheered a little early. Because, you see, I'm going to let General Lennox define exactly what "minor" means.

Every West Point class is commissioned to the Armed Forces. Some West Point classes are also commissioned by history, to take part in a great new calling for their country. Speaking here to the class of 1942—six months after Pearl Harbor—General Marshall said, "We're determined that before the sun sets on this terrible struggle, our flag will be recognized throughout the world as a symbol of freedom on the one hand, and of overwhelming power on the other."

Officers graduating that year helped fulfill that mission, defeating Japan and Germany, and then reconstructing those nations as allies. West Point graduates of the 1940s saw the rise of a deadly new challenge—the challenge of imperial communism—and opposed it from Korea to Berlin, to Vietnam, and in the Cold War, from beginning to end. And as the sun set on their struggle, many of those West Point officers lived to see a world transformed.

History has also issued its call to your generation. In your last year, America was attacked by a ruthless and resourceful enemy. You graduate from this Academy in a time of war, taking your place in an American military that is powerful and is honorable. Our war on terror is only begun, but in Afghanistan it was begun well.

I am proud of the men and women who have fought on my orders. America is profoundly grateful for all who serve the cause of freedom, and for all who have given their lives in its defense. This nation respects and trusts our military, and we are confident in your victories to come.

This war will take many turns we cannot predict. Yet I am certain of this: Wherever we carry it, the American flag will stand not only for our power, but for freedom. Our nation's cause has always been larger than our nation's defense. We fight, as we always fight, for a just peace—a peace that favors human liberty. We will defend the peace against threats from terrorists and tyrants. We will preserve the peace by building good relations among the great powers. And we will extend the peace by encouraging free and open societies on every continent.

Building this just peace is America's opportunity, and America's duty. From this day forward, it is your challenge, as well, and we will meet this challenge together. You will wear the uniform of a great and unique country. America has no empire to extend or utopia to establish. We wish for others only what we wish for ourselves—safety from violence, the rewards of liberty, and the hope for a better life.

In defending the peace, we face a threat with no precedent. Enemies in the past needed great armies and great industrial capabilities to endanger the American people and our nation. The attacks of September the 11th required a few hundred thousand dollars in the hands of a few dozen evil and deluded men. All of the chaos and suffering they caused came at much less than the cost of a single tank. The dangers have not passed. This government and the American people are on watch, we are ready, because we know the terrorists have more money and more men and more plans.

The gravest danger to freedom lies at the perilous crossroads of radicalism and technology. When the spread of chemical and biological and nuclear weapons, along with ballistic missile technology—when that occurs, even weak states and small groups could attain a catastrophic power to strike great nations. Our enemies have declared this very intention, and have been caught seeking these terrible weapons. They want the capability to blackmail us, or to harm us, or to harm our friends—and we will oppose them with all our power.

For much of the last century, America's defense relied on the Cold War doctrines of deterrence and containment. In some cases, those strategies still apply. But new threats also require new thinking. Deterrence—the promise of massive retaliation against nations—means nothing against shadowy terrorist networks with no nation or citizens to defend. Containment is not possible when unbalanced dictators with weapons of mass destruction can deliver those weapons on missiles or secretly provide them to terrorist allies.

We cannot defend America and our friends by hoping for the best. We cannot put our faith in the word of tyrants, who solemnly sign nonproliferation treaties, and then systemically break them. If we wait for threats to fully materialize, we will have waited too long.

Homeland defense and missile defense are part of stronger security, and they're essential priorities for America. Yet the war on terror will not be won on the defensive. We must take the battle to the enemy, disrupt his plans, and confront the worst threats before they emerge. In the world we have entered, the only path to safety is the path of action. And this nation will act.

Our security will require the best intelligence, to reveal threats hidden in caves and growing in laboratories. Our security will require modernizing domestic agencies such as the FBI, so they're prepared to act, and act quickly, against danger. Our security will require transforming the military you will lead—a military that must be ready to strike at a moment's notice in any dark corner of the world. And our security will require all Americans to be forward-looking and resolute, to be ready for preemptive action when necessary to defend our liberty and to defend our lives.

The work ahead is difficult. The choices we will face are complex. We must uncover terror cells in 60 or more countries, using every tool of finance, intelligence and law enforcement. Along with our friends and allies, we must oppose proliferation and confront regimes that sponsor terror, as each case requires. Some nations need military training to fight terror, and we'll provide it. Other nations oppose terror, but tolerate the hatred that leads to terror—and that must change. We will send diplomats where they are needed, and we will send you, our soldiers, where you're needed.

All nations that decide for aggression and terror will pay a price. We will not leave the safety of America and the peace of the planet at the mercy of a few mad terrorists and tyrants. We will lift this dark threat from our country and from the world.

Because the war on terror will require resolve and patience, it will also require firm moral purpose. In this way our struggle is similar to the Cold War. Now, as then, our enemies are totalitarians, holding a creed of power with no place for human dignity. Now, as then, they seek to impose a joyless conformity, to control every life and all of life.

America confronted imperial communism in many different ways—diplomatic, economic, and military. Yet moral clarity was essential to our victory in the Cold War. When leaders like John F. Kennedy and Ronald Reagan refused to gloss over the brutality of tyrants, they gave hope to prisoners and dissidents and exiles, and rallied free nations to a great cause.

Some worry that it is somehow undiplomatic or impolite to speak the language of right and wrong. I disagree. Different circumstances require different methods, but not different moralities. Moral truth is the same in every culture, in every time, and in every place. Targeting innocent civilians for murder is always and everywhere wrong. Brutality against women is always and everywhere wrong. There can be no neutrality between justice and cruelty, between the innocent and the guilty. We are in a conflict between good and evil, and America will call evil by its name. By confronting evil and lawless regimes, we do not create a problem, we reveal a problem. And we will lead the world in opposing it.

As we defend the peace, we also have an historic opportunity to preserve the peace. We have our best chance since the rise of the nation state in the 17th century to build a world where the great powers compete in peace instead of prepare for war. The history of the last century, in particular, was dominated by a series of destructive national rivalries that left battlefields and graveyards across the Earth. Germany fought France, the Axis fought the Allies, and then the East fought the West, in proxy wars and tense standoffs, against a backdrop of nuclear Armageddon.

Competition between great nations is inevitable, but armed conflict in our world is not. More and more, civilized nations find ourselves on the same side—united by common dangers of terrorist violence and chaos. America has, and intends to keep, military strengths beyond challenge—thereby, making the destabilizing arms races of other eras pointless, and limiting rivalries to trade and other pursuits of peace.

Today the great powers are also increasingly united by common values, instead of divided by conflicting ideologies. The United States, Japan and our Pacific friends, and now all of Europe, share a deep commitment to human freedom, embodied in strong alliances such as NATO. And the tide of liberty is rising in many other nations.

Generations of West Point officers planned and practiced for battles with Soviet Russia. I've just returned from a new Russia, now a country reaching toward democracy, and our partner in the war against terror. Even in China, leaders are discovering that economic freedom is the only lasting source of national wealth. In time, they will find that social and political freedom is the only true source of national greatness.

When the great powers share common values, we are better able to confront serious regional conflicts together, better able to cooperate in preventing the spread of violence or economic chaos. In the past, great power rivals took sides in difficult regional problems, making divisions deeper and more complicated. Today, from the Middle East to South Asia, we are gathering broad international coalitions to increase the pressure for peace. We must build strong and great power relations when times are good; to help manage crisis when times are bad. America needs partners to preserve the peace, and we will work with every nation that shares this noble goal.

And finally, America stands for more than the absence of war. We have a great opportunity to extend a just peace, by replacing poverty, repression, and resentment around the world with hope of a better day. Through most of history, poverty was persistent, inescapable, and almost universal. In the last few decades, we've seen nations from Chile to South Korea build modern economies and freer societies, lifting millions of people out of despair and want. And there's no mystery to this achievement.

The 20th century ended with a single surviving model of human progress, based on non-negotiable demands of human dignity, the rule of law, limits on the power of the state, respect for women and private property and free speech and equal justice and religious tolerance. America cannot impose this vision—yet we can support and reward governments that make the right choices for their own people. In our development aid, in our diplomatic efforts, in our international broadcasting, and in our educational assistance, the United States will promote moderation and tolerance and human rights. And we will defend the peace that makes all progress possible.

When it comes to the common rights and needs of men and women, there is no clash of civilizations. The requirements of freedom apply fully to Africa and Latin America and the entire Islamic world. The peoples of the Islamic nations want and deserve the same freedoms and opportunities as people in every nation. And their governments should listen to their hopes.

A truly strong nation will permit legal avenues of dissent for all groups that pursue their aspirations without violence. An advancing nation will pursue economic reform, to unleash the great entrepreneurial energy of its people. A thriving nation will respect the rights of women, because no society can prosper while denying opportunity to half its citizens. Mothers and fathers and children across the Islamic world, and all the world, share the same fears and aspirations. In poverty, they struggle. In tyranny, they suffer. And as we saw in Afghanistan, in liberation they celebrate.

America has a greater objective than controlling threats and containing resentment. We will work for a just and peaceful world beyond the war on terror.

The bicentennial class of West Point now enters this drama. With all in the United States Army, you will stand between your fellow citizens and grave danger. You will help establish a peace that allows millions around the world to live in liberty and to grow in prosperity. You will face times of calm, and times of crisis. And every test will find you prepared—because you're the men and women of West Point. You leave here marked by the character of this Academy, carrying with you the highest ideals of our nation.

Toward the end of his life, Dwight Eisenhower recalled the first day he stood on the plain at West Point. "The feeling came over me," he said, "that the expression 'the United States of America' would now and henceforth mean something different than it had ever before. From here on, it would be the nation I would be serving, not myself."

Today, your last day at West Point, you begin a life of service in a career unlike any other. You've answered a calling to hardship and purpose, to risk and honor. At the end of every day you will know that you have faithfully done your duty. May you always bring to that duty the high standards of this great American institution. May you always be worthy of the long gray line that stretches two centuries behind you.

On behalf of the nation, I congratulate each one of you for the commission you've earned and for the credit you bring to the United States of America. May God bless you all.

George W. Bush's Remarks at the United Nations General Assembly, September 12, 2002

The United Nations (UN) speech gave the president the opportunity to lay out his views on why Iraq was such a threat to the United States under Saddam Hussein.

Mr. Secretary General, Mr. President, distinguished delegates, and ladies and gentlemen: We meet one year and one day after a terrorist attack brought grief to my country, and brought grief to many citizens of our world. Yesterday, we remembered the innocent lives taken that terrible morning. Today, we turn to the urgent duty of protecting other lives, without illusion and without fear.

We've accomplished much in the last year—in Afghanistan and beyond. We have much yet to do—in Afghanistan and beyond. Many nations represented here have joined in the fight against global terror, and the people of the United States are grateful.

The United Nations was born in the hope that survived a world war—the hope of a world moving toward justice, escaping old patterns of conflict and fear. The founding members resolved that the peace of the world must never again be destroyed by the will and wickedness of any man. We created the United Nations Security Council, so that, unlike the League of Nations, our deliberations would be more than talk, our resolutions would be more than wishes. After generations of deceitful dictators and broken treaties and squandered lives, we dedicated ourselves to standards of human dignity shared by all, and to a system of security defended by all.

Today, these standards, and this security, are challenged. Our commitment to human dignity is challenged by persistent poverty and raging disease. The suffering is great, and our responsibilities are clear. The United States is joining with the world to supply aid where it reaches people and lifts up lives, to extend trade and the prosperity it brings, and to bring medical care where it is desperately needed. . . .

Our common security is challenged by regional conflicts—ethnic and religious strife that is ancient, but not inevitable. In the Middle East, there can be no peace for either side without freedom for both sides. America stands committed to an independent and democratic Palestine, living side by side with Israel in peace and security. Like all other people, Palestinians deserve a government that serves their interests and listens to their voices. My nation will continue to encourage all parties to step up to their responsibilities as we seek a just and comprehensive settlement to the conflict.

Above all, our principles and our security are challenged today by outlaw groups and regimes that accept no law of morality and have no limit to their violent ambitions. In the attacks on America a year ago, we saw the destructive intentions of our enemies. This threat hides within many nations, including my own. In cells and camps, terrorists are plotting further destruction, and building new bases for their war against civilization. And our greatest fear is that terrorists will find a shortcut to their mad ambitions when an outlaw regime supplies them with the technologies to kill on a massive scale.

In one place—in one regime—we find all these dangers, in their most lethal and aggressive forms, exactly the kind of aggressive threat the United Nations was born to confront.

Twelve years ago, Iraq invaded Kuwait without provocation. And the regime's forces were poised to continue their march to seize other countries and their resources. Had Saddam Hussein been appeased instead of stopped, he would have endangered the peace and stability of the world. Yet this aggression was stopped—by the might of coalition forces and the will of the United Nations.

To suspend hostilities, to spare himself, Iraq's dictator accepted a series of commitments. The terms were clear, to him and to all. And he agreed to prove he is complying with every one of those obligations.

He has proven instead only his contempt for the United Nations, and for all his pledges. By breaking every pledge—by his deceptions, and by his cruelties—Saddam Hussein has made the case against himself.

In 1991, Security Council Resolution 688 demanded that the Iraqi regime cease at once the repression of its own people, including the systematic repression of minorities—which the Council said, threatened international peace and security in the region. This demand goes ignored.

Last year, the U.N. Commission on Human Rights found that Iraq continues to commit extremely grave violations of human rights, and that the regime's repression is all pervasive. Tens of thousands of political opponents and ordinary citizens have been subjected to arbitrary arrest and imprisonment, summary execution, and torture by beating and burning, electric shock, starvation, mutilation, and rape. Wives are tortured in front of their husbands, children in the presence of their parents—and all of these horrors concealed from the world by the apparatus of a totalitarian state.

In 1991, the U.N. Security Council, through Resolutions 686 and 687, demanded that Iraq return all prisoners from Kuwait and other lands. Iraq's regime agreed. It broke its promise. Last year the Secretary General's high-level coordinator for this issue reported that Kuwait, Saudi, Indian, Syrian, Lebanese, Iranian, Egyptian, Bahraini, and Omani nationals remain unaccounted for—more than 600 people. One American pilot is among them.

In 1991, the U.N. Security Council, through Resolution 687, demanded that Iraq renounce all involvement with terrorism, and permit no terrorist organizations to operate in Iraq. Iraq's regime agreed. It broke this promise. In violation of Security Council Resolution 1373, Iraq continues to shelter and support terrorist organizations that direct violence against Iran, Israel, and Western governments. Iraqi dissidents abroad are targeted for murder. In 1993, Iraq attempted to assassinate the Emir of Kuwait and a former American President. Iraq's government openly praised the attacks of September the 11th. And al Qaeda terrorists escaped from Afghanistan and are known to be in Iraq.

In 1991, the Iraqi regime agreed to destroy and stop developing all weapons of mass destruction and long-range missiles, and to prove to the world it has done so by complying with rigorous inspections. Iraq has broken every aspect of this fundamental pledge.

From 1991 to 1995, the Iraqi regime said it had no biological weapons. After a senior official in its weapons program defected and exposed this lie, the regime admitted to producing tens of thousands of liters of anthrax and other deadly biological agents for use with Scud warheads, aerial bombs, and aircraft spray tanks. U.N. inspectors believe Iraq has produced two to four times the amount of biological agents it declared, and has failed to account for more than three metric tons of material that could be used to produce biological weapons. Right now, Iraq is expanding and improving facilities that were used for the production of biological weapons. . . .

Today, Iraq continues to withhold important information about its nuclear program—weapons design, procurement logs, experiment data, an accounting of nuclear materials and documentation of foreign assistance. Iraq employs capable nuclear scientists and technicians. It retains physical infrastructure needed to build a nuclear weapon. Iraq has made several attempts to buy high-strength aluminum tubes used to enrich uranium for a nuclear weapon. Should Iraq acquire fissile material, it would be able to build a nuclear weapon within a year. And Iraq's state-controlled media has reported numerous meetings between Saddam Hussein and his nuclear scientists, leaving little doubt about his continued appetite for these weapons.

Iraq also possesses a force of Scud-type missiles with ranges beyond the 150 kilometers permitted by the U.N. Work at testing and production facilities shows that Iraq is building more long-range missiles that it can inflict mass death throughout the region.

In 1990, after Iraq's invasion of Kuwait, the world imposed economic sanctions on Iraq. Those sanctions were maintained after the war to compel the regime's compliance with Security Council resolutions. In time, Iraq was allowed to use oil revenues to buy food. Saddam Hussein has subverted this program, working around the sanctions to buy missile technology and military materials. He blames the suffering of Iraq's people on the United Nations, even as he uses his oil wealth to build lavish palaces for himself, and to buy arms for his country. By refusing to comply with his own agreements, he bears full guilt for the hunger and misery of innocent Iraqi citizens.

In 1991, Iraq promised U.N. inspectors immediate and unrestricted access to verify Iraq's commitment to rid itself of weapons of mass destruction and long-range missiles. Iraq broke this promise, spending seven years deceiving, evading, and harassing U.N. inspectors before ceasing cooperation entirely. Just months after the 1991 cease-fire, the Security Council twice renewed its demand that the Iraqi regime cooperate fully with inspectors, condemning Iraq's serious violations of its obligations. The Security Council again renewed that demand in 1994, and twice more in 1996, deploring Iraq's clear violations of its obligations. The Security Council renewed its demand three more times in 1997, citing flagrant violations; and three more times in 1998, calling Iraq's behavior totally unacceptable. And in 1999, the demand was renewed yet again. . . .

Delegates to the General Assembly, we have been more than patient. We've tried sanctions. We've tried the carrot of oil for food, and the stick of coalition military strikes. But Saddam Hussein has defied all these efforts and continues to develop weapons of mass destruction. The first time we may be completely certain he has nuclear weapons is when, God forbid, he uses one. We owe it to all our citizens to do everything in our power to prevent that day from coming.

The conduct of the Iraqi regime is a threat to the authority of the United Nations, and a threat to peace. Iraq has answered a decade of U.N. demands with a decade of defiance. All the world now faces a test, and the United Nations a difficult and defining moment. Are Security Council resolutions to be honored and enforced, or cast aside without consequence? Will the United Nations serve the purpose of its founding, or will it be irrelevant?

The United States helped found the United Nations. We want the United Nations to be effective, and respectful, and successful. We want the resolutions of the world's most important multilateral body to be enforced. And right now those resolutions are being unilaterally subverted by the Iraqi regime. Our partnership of nations can meet the test before us, by making clear what we now expect of the Iraqi regime.

If the Iraqi regime wishes peace, it will immediately and unconditionally forswear, disclose, and remove or destroy all weapons of mass destruction, long-range missiles, and all related material.

If the Iraqi regime wishes peace, it will immediately end all support for terrorism and act to suppress it, as all states are required to do by U.N. Security Council resolutions.

If the Iraqi regime wishes peace, it will cease persecution of its civilian population, including Shi'a, Sunnis, Kurds, Turkomans, and others, again as required by Security Council resolutions.

If the Iraqi regime wishes peace, it will release or account for all Gulf War personnel whose fate is still unknown. It will return the remains of any who are deceased, return stolen property, accept liability for losses resulting from the invasion of Kuwait, and fully cooperate with international efforts to resolve these issues, as required by Security Council resolutions. . . .

The United States has no quarrel with the Iraqi people; they've suffered too long in silent captivity. Liberty for the Iraqi people is a great moral cause, and a great strategic goal. The people of Iraq deserve it; the security of all nations requires it. Free societies do not intimidate through cruelty and conquest, and open societies do not threaten the world with mass murder. The United States supports political and economic liberty in a unified Iraq.

We can harbor no illusions—and that's important today to remember. Saddam Hussein attacked Iran in 1980 and Kuwait in 1990. He's fired ballistic missiles at Iran and Saudi Arabia, Bahrain, and Israel. His regime once ordered the killing of every person between the ages of 15 and 70 in certain Kurdish villages in northern Iraq. He has gassed many Iranians, and 40 Iraqi villages.

My nation will work with the U.N. Security Council to meet our common challenge. If Iraq's regime defies us again, the world must move deliberately, decisively to hold Iraq to account. We will work with the U.N. Security Council for the necessary resolutions. But the purposes of the United States should not be doubted. The Security Council resolutions will be enforced—the just demands of peace and security will be met—or action will be unavoidable. And a regime that has lost its legitimacy will also lose its power.

Events can turn in one of two ways: If we fail to act in the face of danger, the people of Iraq will continue to live in brutal submission. The regime will have new power to bully and dominate and conquer its neighbors, condemning the Middle East to more years of bloodshed and fear. The regime will remain unstable—the region will remain unstable, with little hope of freedom, and isolated from the progress of our times. With every step the Iraqi regime takes toward gaining and deploying the most terrible weapons, our own options to confront that regime will narrow. And if an emboldened regime were to supply these weapons to terrorist allies, then the attacks of September the 11th would be a prelude to far greater horrors.

If we meet our responsibilities, if we overcome this danger, we can arrive at a very different future. The people of Iraq can shake off their captivity. They can one day join a democratic Afghanistan and a democratic Palestine, inspiring reforms throughout the Muslim world. These nations can show by their example that honest government, and respect for women, and the great Islamic tradition of learning can triumph in the Middle East and beyond. And we will show that the promise of the United Nations can be fulfilled in our time.

Neither of these outcomes is certain. Both have been set before us. We must choose between a world of fear and a world of progress. We cannot stand by and do nothing while dangers gather. We must stand up for our security, and for the permanent rights and the hopes of mankind. By heritage and by choice, the United States of America will make that stand. And, delegates to the United Nations, you have the power to make that stand, as well.

George W. Bush's State of the Union Address, January 28, 2003

The president's second State of the Union address, in the weeks immediately before the invasion of Iraq, further showed the administration's position on the weapons of mass destruction some believed were there. Subsequently, major questions have arisen about the quality of the intelligence used in this speech.

Mr. Speaker, Vice President Cheney, members of Congress, distinguished citizens and fellow citizens: Every year, by law and by custom, we meet here to consider the state of the union. This year, we gather in this chamber deeply aware of decisive days that lie ahead.

You and I serve our country in a time of great consequence. During this session of Congress, we have the duty to reform domestic programs vital to our country; we have the opportunity to save millions of lives abroad from a terrible disease. We will work for a prosperity that is broadly shared, and we will answer every danger and every enemy that threatens the American people.

In all these days of promise and days of reckoning, we can be confident. In a whirlwind of change and hope and peril, our faith is sure, our resolve is firm, and our union is strong. . . .

During the last two years, we have seen what can be accomplished when we work together. To lift the standards of our public schools, we achieved historic education reform—which must now be carried out in every school and in every classroom, so that every child in America can read and learn and succeed in life. To protect our country, we reorganized our government and created the Department of Homeland Security, which is mobilizing against the threats of a new era. To bring our economy out of recession, we delivered the largest tax relief in a generation. To insist on integrity in American business we passed tough reforms, and we are holding corporate criminals to account. . . .

The qualities of courage and compassion that we strive for in America also determine our conduct abroad. The American flag stands for more than our power and our interests. Our founders dedicated this country to the cause of human dignity, the rights of every person, and the possibilities of every life. This conviction leads us into the world to help the afflicted, and defend the peace, and confound the designs of evil men.

In Afghanistan, we helped liberate an oppressed people. And we will continue helping them secure their country, rebuild their society, and educate all their children—boys and girls. In the Middle East, we will continue to seek peace between a secure Israel and a democratic Palestine. Across the Earth, America is feeding the hungry—more than 60 percent of international food aid comes as a gift from the people of the United States. As our nation moves troops and builds alliances to make our world safer, we must also remember our calling as a blessed country is to make this world better . . .

There are days when our fellow citizens do not hear news about the war on terror. There's never a day when I do not learn of another threat, or receive reports of operations in progress, or give an order in this global war against a scattered network of killers. The war goes on, and we are winning.

To date, we've arrested or otherwise dealt with many key commanders of al Qaeda. They include a man who directed logistics and funding for the September the 11th attacks; the chief of al Qaeda operations in the Persian Gulf, who planned the bombings of our embassies in East Africa and the USS *Cole*; an al Qaeda operations chief from Southeast Asia; a former director of al Qaeda's training camps in Afghanistan; a key al Qaeda operative in Europe; a major al Qaeda leader in Yemen. All told, more than 3,000 suspected terrorists have been arrested in many countries. Many others have met a different fate. Let's put it this way—they are no longer a problem to the United States and our friends and allies.

We are working closely with other nations to prevent further attacks. America and coalition countries have uncovered and stopped terrorist conspiracies targeting the American embassy in Yemen, the American embassy in Singapore, a Saudi military base, ships in the Straits of Hormuz and the Straits the Gibraltar. We've broken al Qaeda cells in Hamburg, Milan, Madrid, London, Paris, as well as, Buffalo, New York.

We have the terrorists on the run. We're keeping them on the run. One by one, the terrorists are learning the meaning of American justice. . . .

Our war against terror is a contest of will in which perseverance is power. In the ruins of two towers, at the western wall of the Pentagon, on a field in Pennsylvania, this nation made a pledge, and we renew that pledge tonight: Whatever the duration of this struggle, and whatever the difficulties, we will not permit the triumph of violence in the affairs of men—free people will set the course of history.

Today, the gravest danger in the war on terror, the gravest danger facing America and the world, is outlaw regimes that seek and possess nuclear, chemical, and biological weapons. These regimes could use such weapons for blackmail, terror, and mass murder. They could also give or sell those weapons to terrorist allies, who would use them without the least hesitation. . . .

Different threats require different strategies. In Iran, we continue to see a government that represses its people, pursues weapons of mass destruction, and supports terror. We also see Iranian citizens risking intimidation and death as they speak out for liberty and human rights and democracy. Iranians, like all people, have a right to choose their own government and determine their own destiny—and the United States supports their aspirations to live in freedom.

On the Korean Peninsula, an oppressive regime rules a people living in fear and starvation. Throughout the 1990s, the United States relied on a negotiated framework to keep North Korea from gaining nuclear weapons. We now know that that regime was deceiving the world, and developing those weapons all along. And today the North Korean regime is using its nuclear program to incite fear and seek concessions. America and the world will not be blackmailed.

America is working with the countries of the region—South Korea, Japan, China, and Russia—to find a peaceful solution, and to show the North Korean government that nuclear weapons will bring only isolation, economic stagnation, and continued hardship. The North Korean regime will find respect in the world and revival for its people only when it turns away from its nuclear ambitions.

Our nation and the world must learn the lessons of the Korean Peninsula and not allow an even greater threat to rise up in Iraq. A brutal dictator, with a history of reckless aggression, with ties to terrorism, with great potential wealth, will not be permitted to dominate a vital region and threaten the United States.

Twelve years ago, Saddam Hussein faced the prospect of being the last casualty in a war he had started and lost. To spare himself, he agreed to disarm of all weapons of mass destruction. For the next 12 years, he systematically violated that agreement. He pursued chemical, biological, and nuclear weapons, even while inspectors were in his country. Nothing to date has restrained him from his pursuit of these weapons—not economic sanctions, not isolation from the civilized world, not even cruise missile strikes on his military facilities.

Almost three months ago, the United Nations Security Council gave Saddam Hussein his final chance to disarm. He has shown instead utter contempt for the United Nations, and for the opinion of the world. The 108 U.N. inspectors were . . . not sent to conduct a scavenger hunt for hidden materials across a country the size of California. The job of the inspectors is to verify that Iraq's regime is disarming. It is up to Iraq to show exactly where it is hiding its banned weapons, lay those weapons out for the world to see, and destroy them as directed. Nothing like this has happened.

The United Nations concluded in 1999 that Saddam Hussein had biological weapons sufficient to produce over 25,000 liters of anthrax—enough doses to kill several million people. He hasn't accounted for that material. He's given no evidence that he has destroyed it.

The United Nations concluded that Saddam Hussein had materials sufficient to produce more than 38,000 liters of botulinum toxin—enough to subject millions of people to death by respiratory failure. He hasn't accounted for that material. He's given no evidence that he has destroyed it.

Our intelligence officials estimate that Saddam Hussein had the materials to produce as much as 500 tons of sarin, mustard and VX nerve agent. In such quantities, these chemical agents could also kill untold thousands. He's not accounted for these materials. He has given no evidence that he has destroyed them.

U.S. intelligence indicates that Saddam Hussein had upwards of 30,000 munitions capable of delivering chemical agents. Inspectors recently turned up 16 of them—despite Iraq's recent declaration denying their existence. Saddam Hussein has not accounted for the remaining 29,984 of these prohibited munitions. He's given no evidence that he has destroyed them.

From three Iraqi defectors we know that Iraq, in the late 1990s, had several mobile biological weapons labs. These are designed to produce germ warfare agents, and can be moved from place to a place to evade inspectors. Saddam Hussein has not disclosed these facilities. He's given no evidence that he has destroyed them.

The International Atomic Energy Agency confirmed in the 1990s that Saddam Hussein had an advanced nuclear weapons development program, had a design for a nuclear weapon and was working on five different methods of enriching uranium for a bomb. The British government has learned that Saddam Hussein recently sought significant quantities of uranium from Africa. Our intelligence sources tell us that he has attempted to purchase high-strength aluminum tubes suitable for nuclear weapons production. Saddam Hussein has not credibly explained these activities. He clearly has much to hide.

The dictator of Iraq is not disarming. To the contrary; he is deceiving. From intelligence sources we know, for instance, that thousands of Iraqi security personnel are at work hiding documents and materials from the U.N. inspectors, sanitizing inspection sites and monitoring the inspectors themselves. Iraqi officials accompany the inspectors in order to intimidate witnesses.

Iraq is blocking U-2 surveillance flights requested by the United Nations. Iraqi intelligence officers are posing as the scientists inspectors are supposed to interview. Real scientists have been coached by Iraqi officials on what to say. Intelligence sources indicate that Saddam Hussein has ordered that scientists who cooperate with U.N. inspectors in disarming Iraq will be killed, along with their families.

Year after year, Saddam Hussein has gone to elaborate lengths, spent enormous sums, taken great risks to build and keep weapons of mass destruction. But why? The only possible explanation, the only possible use he could have for those weapons, is to dominate, intimidate, or attack.

With nuclear arms or a full arsenal of chemical and biological weapons, Saddam Hussein could resume his ambitions of conquest in the Middle East and create deadly havoc in that region. And this Congress and the America people must recognize another threat. Evidence from intelligence sources, secret communications, and statements by people now in custody reveal that Saddam Hussein aids and protects terrorists, including members of al Qaeda. Secretly, and without fingerprints, he could provide one of his hidden weapons to terrorists, or help them develop their own.

Before September the 11th, many in the world believed that Saddam Hussein could be contained. But chemical agents, lethal viruses and shadowy terrorist networks are not easily contained. Imagine those 19 hijackers with other weapons and other plans—this time armed by Saddam Hussein. It would take one vial, one canister, one crate slipped into this country to bring a day of horror like none we have ever known. We will do everything in our power to make sure that that day never comes.

Some have said we must not act until the threat is imminent. Since when have terrorists and tyrants announced their intentions, politely putting us on notice before they strike? If this threat is permitted to fully and suddenly emerge, all actions, all words, and all recriminations would come too late. Trusting in the sanity and restraint of Saddam Hussein is not a strategy, and it is not an option.

The dictator who is assembling the world's most dangerous weapons has already used them on whole villages—leaving thousands of his own citizens dead, blind, or disfigured. Iraqi refugees tell us how forced confessions are obtained—by torturing children while their parents are made to watch. International human rights groups have catalogued other methods used in the torture chambers of Iraq: electric shock, burning with hot irons, dripping acid on the skin, mutilation with electric drills, cutting out tongues, and rape. If this is not evil, then evil has no meaning.

And tonight I have a message for the brave and oppressed people of Iraq: Your enemy is not surrounding your country—your enemy is ruling your country. And the day he and his regime are removed from power will be the day of your liberation.

The world has waited 12 years for Iraq to disarm. America will not accept a serious and mounting threat to our country, and our friends and our allies. The United States will ask the U.N. Security Council to convene on February the 5th to consider the facts of Iraq's ongoing defiance of the world. Secretary of State Powell will present information and intelligence about Iraqi's legal—Iraq's illegal weapons programs, its attempt to hide those weapons from inspectors, and its links to terrorist groups.

We will consult. But let there be no misunderstanding: If Saddam Hussein does not fully disarm, for the safety of our people and for the peace of the world, we will lead a coalition to disarm him.

Tonight I have a message for the men and women who will keep the peace, members of the American Armed Forces: Many of you are assembling in or near the Middle East, and some crucial hours may lay [sic] ahead. In those hours, the success of our cause will depend on you. Your training has prepared you. Your honor will guide you. You believe in America, and America believes in you. . . .

We seek peace. We strive for peace. And sometimes peace must be defended. A future lived at the mercy of terrible threats is no peace at all. If war is forced upon us, we will fight in a just cause and by just means—sparing, in every way we can, the innocent. And if war is forced upon us, we will fight with the full force and might of the United States military—and we will prevail.

And as we and our coalition partners are doing in Afghanistan, we will bring to the Iraqi people food and medicines and supplies—and freedom. . . .

Americans are a free people, who know that freedom is the right of every person and the future of every nation. The liberty we prize is not America's gift to the world, it is God's gift to humanity. . . .

Secretary of State Colin L. Powell Addresses the UN Security Council, February 5, 2003

Secretary of State Colin Powell's remarks were viewed with seriousness because of his personal stature as a retired chairman of the Joint Chiefs of Staff and an international statesman. Subsequent debate about the sources of the intelligence used as the basis for his assertions has been heated.

Thank you, Mr. President. Mr. President, Mr. Secretary General, distinguished colleagues, I would like to begin by expressing my thanks for the special effort that each of you made to be here today.

This is [an] important day for us all as we review the situation with respect to Iraq and its disarmament obligations under U.N. Security Council Resolution 1441.

Last November 8, this council passed Resolution 1441 by a unanimous vote. The purpose of that resolution was to disarm Iraq of its weapons of mass destruction. Iraq had already been found guilty of material breach of its obligations, stretching back over 16 previous resolutions and 12 years.

Resolution 1441 was not dealing with an innocent party, but a regime this council has repeatedly convicted over the years. Resolution 1441 gave Iraq one last chance, one last chance to come into compliance or to face serious consequences. No council member present in voting on that day had any illusions about the nature and intent of the resolution or what serious consequences meant if Iraq did not comply. . . .

We laid down tough standards for Iraq to meet to allow the inspectors to do their job. . . .

I asked for this session today for two purposes: First, to support the core assessments made by Dr. Blix and Dr. ElBaradei. As Dr. Blix reported to this council on January 27th . . . "Iraq appears not to have come to a genuine acceptance, not even today, of the disarmament which was demanded of it." . . .

My second purpose today is to provide you with additional information, to share with you what the United States knows about

Iraq's weapons of mass destruction as well as Iraq's involvement in terrorism, which is also the subject of Resolution 1441 and other earlier resolutions. . . .

The material I will present to you comes from a variety of sources. Some are U.S. sources. And some are those of other countries. Some of the sources are technical, such as intercepted telephone conversations and photos taken by satellites. Other sources are people who have risked their lives to let the world know what Saddam Hussein is really up to.

I cannot tell you everything that we know. But what I can share with you, when combined with what all of us have learned over the years, is deeply troubling.

What you will see is an accumulation of facts and disturbing patterns of behavior. The facts on Iraqis' behavior . . . demonstrate that Saddam Hussein and his regime have made no effort—no effort—to disarm as required by the international community. Indeed, the facts and Iraq's behavior show that Saddam Hussein and his regime are concealing their efforts to produce more weapons of mass destruction. . . .

This effort to hide things from the inspectors is not one or two isolated events, quite the contrary. This is part and parcel of a policy of evasion and deception that goes back 12 years, a policy set at the highest levels of the Iraqi regime.

We know that Saddam Hussein has what is called . . . "a higher committee for monitoring the inspections teams." . . . Think about that. Iraq has a high-level committee to monitor the inspectors who were sent in to monitor Iraq's disarmament. . . .

Everything we have seen and heard indicates that, instead of cooperating actively with the inspectors to ensure the success of their mission, Saddam Hussein and his regime are busy doing all they possibly can to ensure that inspectors succeed in finding absolutely nothing.

My colleagues, every statement I make today is backed up by sources, solid sources. These are not assertions. What we're giving you are facts and conclusions based on solid intelligence. I will cite some examples, and these are from human sources. . . .

While we were here in this council chamber debating Resolution 1441 last fall, we know . . . from sources that a missile brigade outside Baghdad was disbursing rocket launchers and warheads containing biological warfare agents to various locations, distributing them to various locations in western Iraq. Most of the launchers and warheads have been hidden in large groves of palm trees and were to be moved every one to four weeks to escape detection.

We also have satellite photos that indicate that banned materials have recently been moved from a number of Iraqi weapons of mass destruction facilities. . . .

Iraq did not meet its obligations under 1441 to provide a comprehensive list of scientists associated with its weapons of mass destruction programs. Iraq's list was out of date and contained only about 500 names, despite the fact that UNSCOM [United Nations Special Commission] had earlier put together a list of about 3,500 names. . . .

Ladies and gentlemen, these are not assertions. These are facts, corroborated by many sources, some of them sources of the intelligence services of other countries.

For example, in mid-December weapons experts at one facility were replaced by Iraqi intelligence agents who were to deceive inspectors about the work that was being done there.

As the examples I have just presented show, the information and intelligence we have gathered point to an active and systematic effort on the part of the Iraqi regime to keep key materials and people from the inspectors in direct violation of Resolution 1441. The pattern is not just one of reluctant cooperation, nor is it merely a lack of cooperation. What we see is a deliberate campaign to prevent any meaningful inspection work. . . .

Iraq has now placed itself in danger of the serious consequences called for in U.N. Resolution 1441. And this body places itself in danger of irrelevance if it allows Iraq to continue to defy its will without responding effectively and immediately. . . .

Iraq declared 8,500 liters of anthrax, but UNSCOM estimates that Saddam Hussein could have produced 25,000 liters. If concentrated into this dry form, this amount would be enough to fill tens upon tens upon tens of thousands of teaspoons. And Saddam Hussein has not verifiably accounted for even one teaspoon-full of this deadly material.

And that is my third point. And it is key. The Iraqis have never accounted for all of the biological weapons they admitted they had and we know they had. They have never accounted for all the organic material used to make them. And they have not accounted for many of the weapons filled with these agents such as there are 400 bombs. This is evidence, not conjecture. This is true. This is all well-documented. . . .

Ladies and gentlemen, these are sophisticated facilities. For example, they can produce anthrax and botulinum toxin. In fact, they can produce enough dry biological agent in a single month to kill thousands upon thousands of people. And dry agent of this type is the most lethal form for human beings. . . .

We know from Iraq's past admissions that it has successfully weaponized not only anthrax, but also other biological agents, including botulinum toxin, aflatoxin and ricin.

But Iraq's research efforts did not stop there. Saddam Hussein has investigated dozens of biological agents causing diseases such as gas gangrene, plague, typhus, tetanus, cholera, camelpox and hemorrhagic fever, and he also has the wherewithal to develop smallpox. . . .

There can be no doubt that Saddam Hussein has biological weapons and the capability to rapidly produce more, many more. And he has the ability to dispense these lethal poisons and diseases in ways that can cause massive death and destruction. If biological weapons seem too terrible to contemplate, chemical weapons are equally chilling. . . . First, Saddam Hussein has used these horrific weapons on another country and on his own people. In fact, in the history of chemical warfare, no country has had more battlefield experience with chemical weapons since World War I than Saddam Hussein's Iraq.

Second, as with biological weapons, Saddam Hussein has never accounted for vast amounts of chemical weaponry: 550 artillery shells with mustard, 30,000 empty munitions and enough precursors to increase his stockpile to as much as 500 tons of chemical agents. If we consider just one category of missing weaponry—6,500 bombs from the Iran-Iraq war—UNMOVIC [United Nations Monitoring, Verification and Inspection Commission] says the amount of chemical agent in them would be in the order of 1,000 tons. These quantities of chemical weapons are now unaccounted for. . . .

Third point, Iraq's record on chemical weapons is replete with lies. It took years for Iraq to finally admit that it had produced four tons of the deadly nerve agent, VX. A single drop of VX on the skin will kill in minutes. . . .

We know that Iraq has embedded key portions of its illicit chemical weapons infrastructure within its legitimate civilian industry. To all outward appearances, even to experts, the infrastructure looks like an ordinary civilian operation. Illicit and legitimate production can go on simultaneously; or, on a dime, this dual-use infrastructure can turn from clandestine to commercial and then back again. . . .

Under the guise of dual-use infrastructure, Iraq has undertaken an effort to reconstitute facilities that were closely associated with its past program to develop and produce chemical weapons. . . .

To support its deadly biological and chemical weapons programs, Iraq procures needed items from around the world using an extensive clandestine network. What we know comes largely from intercepted communications and human sources who are in a position to know the facts.

Iraq's procurement efforts include equipment that can filter and separate micro-organisms and toxins involved in biological weapons, equipment that can be used to concentrate the agent, growth media that can be used to continue producing anthrax and botulinum toxin, sterilization equipment for laboratories, glass-lined reactors and specialty pumps that can handle corrosive chemical weapons agents and precursors, large amounts of vinyl chloride, a precursor for nerve and blister agents, and other chemicals such as sodium sulfide, an important mustard agent precursor.

Now, of course, Iraq will argue that these items can also be used for legitimate purposes. But if that is true, why do we have to learn about them by intercepting communications and risking the lives of human agents? With Iraq's well documented history on biological and chemical weapons, why should any of us give Iraq the benefit of the doubt? I don't, and I don't think you will either after you hear this next intercept. . . .

Saddam Hussein has chemical weapons. Saddam Hussein has used such weapons. And Saddam Hussein has no compunction about using them again, against his neighbors and against his own people. . . .

Let me turn now to nuclear weapons. We have no indication that Saddam Hussein has ever abandoned his nuclear weapons program. On the contrary, we have more than a decade of proof that he remains determined to acquire nuclear weapons. . . .

Nonetheless, Iraq continued to tell the IAEA [International Atomic Energy Agency] that it had no nuclear weapons program. If Saddam had not been stopped, Iraq could have produced a nuclear bomb by 1993, years earlier than most worse-case assessments that had been made before the war.

In 1995, as a result of another defector, we find out that, after his invasion of Kuwait, Saddam Hussein had initiated a crash program to build a crude nuclear weapon in violation of Iraq's U.N. obligations.

Saddam Hussein already possesses two out of the three key components needed to build a nuclear bomb. He has a cadre of nuclear scientists with the expertise, and he has a bomb design.

Since 1998, his efforts to reconstitute his nuclear program have been focused on acquiring the third and last component, sufficient fissile material to produce a nuclear explosion. To make the fissile material, he needs to develop an ability to enrich uranium.

Saddam Hussein is determined to get his hands on a nuclear bomb. He is so determined that he has made repeated covert attempts to acquire high-specification aluminum tubes from 11 different countries, even after inspections resumed.

These tubes are controlled by the Nuclear Suppliers Group precisely because they can be used as centrifuges for enriching uranium. By now, just about everyone has heard of these tubes, and we all know that there are differences of opinion. There is controversy about what these tubes are for.

Most U.S. experts think they are intended to serve as rotors in centrifuges used to enrich uranium. Other experts, and the Iraqis themselves, argue that they are really to produce the rocket bodies for a conventional weapon, a multiple rocket launcher.

Let me tell you what is not controversial about these tubes. First, all the experts who have analyzed the tubes in our possession agree that they can be adapted for centrifuge use. Second, Iraq had no business buying them for any purpose. They are banned for Iraq.

I am no expert on centrifuge tubes, but just as an old Army trooper, I can tell you a couple of things: First, it strikes me as quite odd that these tubes are manufactured to a tolerance that far exceeds U.S. requirements for comparable rockets.

Maybe Iraqis just manufacture their conventional weapons to a higher standard than we do, but I don't think so. . . .

The high tolerance aluminum tubes are only part of the story. We also have intelligence from multiple sources that Iraq is attempting to acquire magnets and high-speed balancing machines; both items can be used in a gas centrifuge program to enrich uranium.

In 1999 and 2000, Iraqi officials negotiated with firms in Romania, India, Russia and Slovenia for the purchase of a magnet production plant. Iraq wanted the plant to produce magnets weighing 20 to 30 grams. That's the same weight as the magnets used in Iraq's gas centrifuge program before the Gulf War. This incident linked with the tubes is another indicator of Iraq's attempt to reconstitute its nuclear weapons program.

Intercepted communications from mid-2000 through last summer show that Iraq front companies sought to buy machines that can be used to balance gas centrifuge rotors. One of these companies also had been involved in a failed effort in 2001 to smuggle aluminum tubes into Iraq.

People will continue to debate this issue, but there is no doubt in my mind, these elicit procurement efforts show that Saddam Hussein is very much focused on putting in place the key missing piece from his nuclear weapons program, the ability to produce fissile material. He also has been busy trying to maintain the other key parts of his nuclear program, particularly his cadre of key nuclear scientists.

It is noteworthy that, over the last 18 months, Saddam Hussein has paid increasing personal attention to Iraqi's top nuclear scientists, a group that the governmental-controlled press calls openly, his nuclear mujahedeen. He regularly exhorts them and praises their progress. Progress toward what end? . . .

Saddam Hussein's intentions have never changed. He is not developing the missiles for self-defense. These are missiles that Iraq wants in order to project power, to threaten, and to deliver chemical, biological and, if we let him, nuclear warheads. . . .

But what I want to bring to your attention today is the potentially much more sinister nexus between Iraq and the Al Qaida terrorist network, a nexus that combines classic terrorist organizations and modern methods of murder. Iraq today harbors a deadly terrorist network headed by Abu Musab Al-Zarqawi, an associated collaborator of Osama bin Laden and his Al Qaida lieutenants.

Zarqawi, a Palestinian born in Jordan, fought in the Afghan war more than a decade ago. Returning to Afghanistan in 2000, he oversaw a terrorist training camp. One of his specialities and one of the specialities of this camp is poisons. When our coalition ousted the Taliban, the Zarqaqi network helped establish another poison and explosive training center camp. And this camp is located in northeastern Iraq. . . .

We, in the United States, all of us at the State Department, and the Agency for International Development—we all lost a dear friend with the cold-blooded murder of Mr. Lawrence Foley in Amman, Jordan, last October—a despicable act was committed that day. The assassination of an individual whose sole mission was to assist the people of Jordan. The captured assassin says his cell received money and weapons from Zarqawi for that murder. . . .

And now let me add one other fact. We asked a friendly security service to approach Baghdad about extraditing Zarqawi and providing information about him and his close associates. This service contacted Iraqi officials twice, and we passed details that should have made it easy to find Zarqawi. The network remains in Baghdad. Zarqawi still remains at large to come and go. . . .

Going back to the early and mid-1990s, when bin Laden was based in Sudan, an Al Qaida source tells us that Saddam and bin Laden reached an understanding that Al Qaida would no longer support activities against Baghdad. Early Al Qaida ties were forged by secret, high-level intelligence service contacts with Al Qaida, secret Iraqi intelligence high-level contacts with Al Qaida.

We know members of both organizations met repeatedly and have met at least eight times at very senior levels since the early 1990s. In 1996, a foreign security service tells us, that bin Laden met with a senior Iraqi intelligence official in Khartoum, and later met the director of the Iraqi intelligence service.

Saddam became more interested as he saw Al Qaida's appalling attacks. A detained Al Qaida member tells us that Saddam was more willing to assist Al Qaida after the 1998 bombings of our embassies in Kenya and Tanzania. Saddam was also impressed by Al Qaida's attacks on the USS *Cole* in Yemen in October 2000.

Iraqis continued to visit bin Laden in his new home in Afghanistan. A senior defector, one of Saddam's former intelligence chiefs in Europe, says Saddam sent his agents to Afghanistan sometime in the mid-1990s to provide training to Al Qaida members on document forgery.

From the late 1990s until 2001, the Iraqi embassy in Pakistan played the role of liaison to the Al Qaida organization.

Some believe, some claim these contacts do not amount to much. They say Saddam Hussein's secular tyranny and Al Qaida's religious tyranny do not mix. I am not comforted by this thought. Ambition and hatred are enough to bring Iraq and Al Qaida together, enough so Al Qaida could learn how to build more sophisticated bombs and learn how to forge documents, and enough so that Al Qaida could turn to Iraq for help in acquiring expertise on weapons of mass destruction.

And the record of Saddam Hussein's cooperation with other Islamist terrorist organizations is clear. Hamas, for example, opened an office in Baghdad in 1999, and Iraq has hosted conferences attended by Palestine Islamic Jihad. These groups are at the forefront of sponsoring suicide attacks against Israel.

Al Qaida continues to have a deep interest in acquiring weapons of mass destruction. As with the story of Zarqawi and his network, I can trace the story of a senior terrorist operative telling how Iraq provided training in these weapons to Al Qaida. . . .

[Saddam's] campaign against the Kurds from 1987 to '89 included mass summary executions, disappearances, arbitrary jailing, ethnic cleansing and the destruction of some 2,000 villages. He has also conducted ethnic cleansing against the Shi'a Iraqis and the Marsh Arabs whose culture has flourished for more than a millennium. Saddam Hussein's police state ruthlessly eliminates anyone who dares to dissent. Iraq has more forced disappearance cases than any other country, tens of thousands of people reported missing in the past decade.

Nothing points more clearly to Saddam Hussein's dangerous intentions and the threat he poses to all of us than his calculated cruelty to his own citizens and to his neighbors. Clearly, Saddam Hussein and his regime will stop at nothing until something stops him. . . .

We know that Saddam Hussein is determined to keep his weapons of mass destruction; he's determined to make more. Given Saddam Hussein's history of aggression, given what we know of his grandiose plans, given what we know of his terrorist associations and given his determination to exact revenge on those who oppose him, should we take the risk that he will not some day use these weapons at a time and the place and in the manner of his choosing at a time when the world is in a much weaker position to respond?

The United States will not and cannot run that risk to the American people. Leaving Saddam Hussein in possession of weapons of mass destruction for a few more months or years is not an option, not in a post-September 11th world.

My colleagues, over three months ago this council recognized that Iraq continued to pose a threat to international peace and security, and that Iraq had been and remained in material breach of its disarmament obligations. Today Iraq still poses a threat and Iraq still remains in material breach.

Indeed, by its failure to seize on its one last opportunity to come clean and disarm, Iraq has put itself in deeper material breach and closer to the day when it will face serious consequences for its continued defiance of this council.

My colleagues, we have an obligation to our citizens, we have an obligation to this body to see that our resolutions are complied with. We wrote 1441 not in order to go to war[;] we wrote 1441 to try to preserve the peace. We wrote 1441 to give Iraq one last chance. Iraq is not so far taking that one last chance.

We must not shrink from whatever is ahead of us. We must not fail in our duty and our responsibility to the citizens of the countries that are represented by this body.

George W. Bush's Address to the Nation about the Iraq Invasion, March 19, 2003

This is the notification message the president gave to the public on the night the invasion of Iraq began. His goal was to establish why the invasion was essential to U.S. national security.

My fellow citizens, at this hour, American and coalition forces are in the early stages of military operations to disarm Iraq, to free its people and to defend the world from grave danger.

On my orders, coalition forces have begun striking selected targets of military importance to undermine Saddam Hussein's ability to wage war. These are opening stages of what will be a broad and concerted campaign. More than 35 countries are giving crucial support—from the use of naval and air bases, to help with intelligence and logistics, to the deployment of combat units. Every nation in this coalition has chosen to bear the duty and share the honor of serving in our common defense.

To all the men and women of the United States Armed Forces now in the Middle East, the peace of a troubled world and the hopes of an oppressed people now depend on you. That trust is well placed.

The enemies you confront will come to know your skill and bravery. The people you liberate will witness the honorable and decent spirit of the American military. In this conflict, America faces an enemy who has no regard for conventions of war or rules of morality. Saddam Hussein has placed Iraqi troops and equipment in civilian areas, attempting to use innocent men, women and children as shields for his own military—a final atrocity against his people.

I want Americans and all the world to know that coalition forces will make every effort to spare innocent civilians from harm. A campaign on the harsh terrain of a nation as large as California could be longer and more difficult than some predict. And helping Iraqis achieve a united, stable and free country will require our sustained commitment.

We come to Iraq with respect for its citizens, for their great civilization and for the religious faiths they practice. We have no ambition in Iraq, except to remove a threat and restore control of that country to its own people.

I know that the families of our military are praying that all those who serve will return safely and soon. Millions of Americans are praying with you for the safety of your loved ones and for the protection of the innocent. For your sacrifice, you have the gratitude and respect of the American people. And you can know that our forces will be coming home as soon as their work is done.

Our nation enters this conflict reluctantly—yet, our purpose is sure. The people of the United States and our friends and allies will not live at the mercy of an outlaw regime that threatens the peace with weapons of mass murder. We will meet that threat now, with our Army, Air Force, Navy, Coast Guard and Marines, so that we do not have to meet it later with armies of fire fighters and police and doctors on the streets of our cities.

Now that conflict has come, the only way to limit its duration is to apply decisive force. And I assure you, this will not be a campaign of half measures, and we will accept no outcome but victory.

My fellow citizens, the dangers to our country and the world will be overcome. We will pass through this time of peril and carry on the work of peace. We will defend our freedom. We will bring freedom to others and we will prevail.

May God bless our country and all who defend her.

George W. Bush Announces that Major Combat Operations in Iraq Have Ended, May 1, 2003

President Bush flew to the aircraft carrier USS Abraham Lincoln *to celebrate the end of the major combat operations. In hindsight, however, the speech appears somewhat premature.*

Thank you all very much. Admiral Kelly, Captain Card, officers and sailors of the USS *Abraham Lincoln*, my fellow Americans: Major combat operations in Iraq have ended. In the battle of Iraq, the United States and our allies have prevailed. And now our coalition is engaged in securing and reconstructing that country. . . .

Operation Iraqi Freedom was carried out with a combination of precision and speed and boldness the enemy did not expect, and the world had not seen before. From distant bases or ships at sea, we sent planes and missiles that could destroy an enemy division, or strike a single bunker. Marines and soldiers charged to Baghdad across 350 miles of hostile ground, in one of the swiftest advances of heavy arms in history. You have shown the world the skill and the might of the American Armed Forces.

This nation thanks all the members of our coalition who joined in a noble cause. We thank the Armed Forces of the United Kingdom, Australia, and Poland, who shared in the hardships of war. We thank all the citizens of Iraq who welcomed our troops and joined in the liberation of their own country. And tonight, I have a special word for Secretary Rumsfeld, for General Franks, and for all the men and women who wear the uniform of the United States: America is grateful for a job well done.

The character of our military through history—the daring of Normandy, the fierce courage of Iwo Jima, the decency and idealism that turned enemies into allies—is fully present in this generation. When Iraqi civilians looked into the faces of our servicemen and women, they saw strength and kindness and goodwill. When I look at the members of the United States military, I see the best of our country, and I'm honored to be your Commander-in-Chief.

In the images of falling statues, we have witnessed the arrival of a new era. For a hundred of years of war, culminating in the nuclear age, military technology was designed and deployed to inflict casualties on an ever-growing scale. In defeating Nazi Germany and Imperial Japan, Allied forces destroyed entire cities, while enemy leaders who started the conflict were safe until the final days. Military power was used to end a regime by breaking a nation.

Today, we have the greater power to free a nation by breaking a dangerous and aggressive regime. With new tactics and precision weapons, we can achieve military objectives without directing violence against civilians. No device of man can remove the tragedy from war; yet it is a great moral advance when the guilty have far more to fear from war than the innocent.

In the images of celebrating Iraqis, we have also seen the ageless appeal of human freedom. Decades of lies and intimidation could not make the Iraqi people love their oppressors or desire their own enslavement. Men and women in every culture need liberty like they need food and water and air. Everywhere that freedom arrives, humanity rejoices; and everywhere that freedom stirs, let tyrants fear.

We have difficult work to do in Iraq. We're bringing order to parts of that country that remain dangerous. We're pursuing and finding leaders of the old regime, who will be held to account for their crimes. We've begun the search for hidden chemical and biological weapons and already know of hundreds of sites that will be investigated. We're helping to rebuild Iraq, where the dictator built palaces for himself, instead of hospitals and schools. And we will stand with the new leaders of Iraq as they establish a government of, by, and for the Iraqi people.

The transition from dictatorship to democracy will take time, but it is worth every effort. Our coalition will stay until our work is done. Then we will leave, and we will leave behind a free Iraq.

The battle of Iraq is one victory in a war on terror that began on September the 11, 2001—and still goes on. That terrible morning, 19 evil men—the shock troops of a hateful ideology—gave America and the civilized world a glimpse of their ambitions. They imagined, in the words of one terrorist, that September the 11th would be the "beginning of the end of America." By seeking to turn our cities into killing fields, terrorists and their allies believed that they could destroy this nation's resolve, and force our retreat from the world. They have failed.

In the battle of Afghanistan, we destroyed the Taliban, many terrorists, and the camps where they trained. We continue to help the Afghan people lay roads, restore hospitals, and educate all of their children. Yet we also have dangerous work to complete. As I speak, a Special Operations task force, led by the 82nd Airborne, is on the trail of the terrorists and those who seek to undermine the free government of Afghanistan. America and our coalition will finish what we have begun.

From Pakistan to the Philippines to the Horn of Africa, we are hunting down al Qaeda killers. Nineteen months ago, I pledged that the terrorists would not escape the patient justice of the United States. And as of tonight, nearly one-half of al Qaeda's senior operatives have been captured or killed.

The liberation of Iraq is a crucial advance in the campaign against terror. We've removed an ally of al Qaeda, and cut off a source of terrorist funding. And this much is certain: No terrorist network will gain weapons of mass destruction from the Iraqi regime, because the regime is no more. . . .

Any person, organization, or government that supports, protects, or harbors terrorists is complicit in the murder of the innocent, and equally guilty of terrorist crimes.

Any outlaw regime that has ties to terrorist groups and seeks or possesses weapons of mass destruction is a grave danger to the civilized world—and will be confronted.

And anyone in the world, including the Arab world, who works and sacrifices for freedom has a loyal friend in the United States of America.

Our commitment to liberty is America's tradition—declared at our founding; affirmed in Franklin Roosevelt's Four Freedoms; asserted in the Truman Doctrine and in Ronald Reagan's challenge to an evil empire. We are committed to freedom in Afghanistan, in Iraq, and in a peaceful Palestine. The advance of freedom is the surest strategy to undermine the appeal of terror in the world. Where freedom takes hold, hatred gives way to hope. When freedom takes hold, men and women turn to the peaceful pursuit of a better life. American values and American interests lead in the same direction: We stand for human liberty. . . .

Our mission continues. Al Qaeda is wounded, not destroyed. The scattered cells of the terrorist network still operate in many nations, and we know from daily intelligence that they continue to plot against free people. The proliferation of deadly weapons remains a serious danger. The enemies of freedom are not idle, and neither are we. Our government has taken unprecedented measures to defend the homeland. And we will continue to hunt down the enemy before he can strike.

The war on terror is not over; yet it is not endless. We do not know the day of final victory, but we have seen the turning of the tide. No act of the terrorists will change our purpose, or weaken our resolve, or alter their fate. Their cause is lost. Free nations will press on to victory.

Other nations in history have fought in foreign lands and remained to occupy and exploit. Americans, following a battle, want nothing more than to return home. And that is your direction tonight. After service in the Afghan—and Iraqi theaters of war—after 100,000 miles, on the longest carrier deployment in recent history, you are homeward bound. Some of you will see new family members for the first time—150 babies were born while their fathers were on the *Lincoln*. Your families are proud of you, and your nation will welcome you. . . .

Thank you for serving our country and our cause. May God bless you all, and may God continue to bless America.

Military Support for Stability, Security, Transition, and Reconstruction Operations, November 28, 2005

The military arm of the national security community of the United States has always prided itself on its expertise in conventional conflict. The 2005 Department of Defense (DoD) directive elevates the more controversial aspects of military operations to an equal footing with conventional conflict: security, stability, transition, and reconstruction (SSTR) operations.

1. *PURPOSE*
This Directive:
1.1 Provides guidance on stability operations that will evolve over time as joint operating concepts, mission sets, and lessons learned develop. Future DoD policy will address these areas and provide guidance on the security, transition, and reconstruction operations components of SSTR operations and DoD's role in each.

1.2 Establishes DoD policy and assigns responsibilities within the Department of Defense for planning, training, and preparing to conduct and support stability operations pursuant to the authority vested in the Secretary of Defense under reference (a) and the guidance and responsibilities assigned in reference (b). . . .

2. *APPLICABILITY AND SCOPE*

This Directive applies to the Office of the Secretary of Defense, the Military Departments, the Chairman of the Joint Chiefs of Staff, the Combatant Commands, the Office of the Inspector General of the Department of Defense, the Defense Agencies, the DoD Field Activities, and all other organizational entities in the Department of Defense (hereafter referred to collectively as the "DoD Components").

3. *DEFINITIONS*

3.1. *Stability Operations.* Military and civilian activities conducted across the spectrum from peace to conflict to establish or maintain order in States and regions.

3.2 *Military support to Stability, Security, Transition and Reconstruction (SSTR).* Department of Defense activities that support U.S. Government plans for stabilization, security, reconstruction and transition operations, which lead to sustainable peace while advancing U.S. interests.

4. *POLICY*

It is DoD policy that:

4.1. Stability operations are a core U.S. military mission that the Department of Defense shall be prepared to conduct and support. They shall be given priority comparable to combat operations and be explicitly addressed and integrated across all DoD activities including doctrine, organizations, training, education, exercises, materiel, leadership, personnel, facilities, and planning.

4.2. Stability operations are conducted to help establish order that advances U.S. interests and values. The immediate goal often is to provide the local populace with security, restore essential services, and meet humanitarian needs. The long-term goal is to help develop indigenous capacity for securing essential services, a viable market economy, rule of law, democratic institutions, and a robust civil society.

4.3. Many stability operations tasks are best performed by indigenous, foreign, or U.S. civilian professionals. Nonetheless, U.S. military forces shall be prepared to perform all tasks necessary to establish or maintain order when civilians cannot do so. Successfully performing such tasks can help secure a lasting peace and facilitate the timely withdrawal of U.S. and foreign forces. Stability operations tasks include helping:

4.3.1. Rebuild indigenous institutions including various types of security forces, correctional facilities, and judicial systems necessary to secure and stabilize the environment;

4.3.2. Revive or build the private sector, including encouraging citizen-driven, bottom-up economic activity and constructing necessary infrastructure; and

4.3.3. Develop representative governmental institutions.

4.4. Integrated civilian and military efforts are key to successful stability operations. Whether conducting or supporting stability operations, the Department of Defense shall be prepared to work closely with relevant U.S. Departments and Agencies, foreign governments and security forces, global and regional international organizations (hereafter referred to as "International Organizations"), U.S. and foreign nongovernmental organizations (hereafter referred to as "NGOs"), and private sector individuals and for-profit companies (hereafter referred to as "Private Sector").

4.5. Military-civilian teams are a critical U.S. Government stability operations tool. The Department of Defense shall continue to lead and support the development of military-civilian teams.

4.5.1. Their functions shall include ensuring security, developing local governance structures, promoting bottom-up economic activity, rebuilding infrastructure, and building indigenous capacity for such tasks.

4.5.2. Participation in such teams shall be open to representatives from other U.S. Departments and Agencies, foreign governments and security forces, International Organizations, NGOs, and members of the Private Sector with relevant skills and expertise.

4.6. Assistance and advice shall be provided to and sought from the Department of State and other U.S. Departments and Agencies, as appropriate, for developing stability operations capabilities.

4.7. The Department of Defense shall develop greater means to help build other countries' security capacity quickly to ensure security in their own lands or to contribute forces to stability operations elsewhere. . . .

4.9. The Department of Defense shall support indigenous persons or groups—political, religious, educational, and media—promoting freedom, the rule of law, and an entrepreneurial economy, who oppose extremism and the murder of civilians.

4.10. DoD intelligence efforts shall be designed to provide the optimal mix of capabilities to meet stability operations requirements, taking into account other priorities.

4.11. Stability operations skills, such as foreign language capabilities, regional area expertise, and experience with foreign governments and International Organizations, shall be developed and incorporated into Professional Military Education at all levels. . . .

5.1.6. Develop a list of countries and areas with the potential for U.S. military engagement in stability operations in consultation with relevant DoD Components and U.S. Departments and Agencies. This list shall be submitted semiannually to the Secretary of Defense and the Chairman of the Joint Chiefs of Staff.

George W. Bush's State of the Union Address, January 31, 2006

President Bush's 2006 State of the Union comments indicate the radical shift in national security concerns that have occurred since the end of the Cold War and the September 11, 2001, terrorist attacks in the United States.

. . . Abroad, our nation is committed to an historic, long-term goal—we seek the end of tyranny in our world. Some dismiss that goal as misguided idealism. In reality, the future security of America depends on it. On September the 11th, 2001, we found that problems originating in a failed and oppressive state 7,000 miles away could bring murder and destruction to our country. Dictatorships shelter terrorists, and feed resentment and radicalism, and seek weapons of mass destruction. Democracies replace resentment with hope, respect the rights of their citizens and their neighbors, and join the fight against terror. Every step toward freedom in the world makes our country safer—so we will act boldly in freedom's cause.

Far from being a hopeless dream, the advance of freedom is the great story of our time. In 1945, there were about two dozen lonely democracies in the world. Today, there are 122. And we're writing a new chapter in the story of self-government—with women lining up to vote in Afghanistan, and millions of Iraqis marking their liberty with purple ink, and men and women from Lebanon to Egypt debating the rights of individuals and the necessity of freedom. At the start of 2006, more than half the people of our world live in democratic nations. And we do not forget the other half—in places like Syria and Burma, Zimbabwe, North Korea, and Iran—because the demands of justice, and the peace of this world, require their freedom, as well.

No one can deny the success of freedom, but some men rage and fight against it. And one of the main sources of reaction and opposition is radical Islam—the perversion by a few of a noble faith into an ideology of terror and death. Terrorists like bin Laden are serious about mass murder—and all of us must take their declared intentions seriously. They seek to impose a heartless system of totalitarian control throughout the Middle East, and arm themselves with weapons of mass murder.

Their aim is to seize power in Iraq, and use it as a safe haven to launch attacks against America and the world. Lacking the military strength to challenge us directly, the terrorists have chosen the weapon of fear. When they murder children at a school in Beslan, or blow up commuters in London, or behead a bound captive, the terrorists hope these horrors will break our will, allowing the violent to inherit the Earth. But they have miscalculated: We love our freedom, and we will fight to keep it.

In a time of testing, we cannot find security by abandoning our commitments and retreating within our borders. If we were to leave these vicious attackers alone, they would not leave us alone. They would simply move the battlefield to our own shores. There is no peace in retreat. And there is no honor in retreat. By allowing radical Islam to work its will—by leaving an assaulted world to fend for itself—we would signal to all that we no longer believe in our own ideals, or even in our own courage. But our enemies and our friends can be certain: The United States will not retreat from the world, and we will never surrender to evil.

America rejects the false comfort of isolationism. We are the nation that saved liberty in Europe, and liberated death camps, and helped raise up democracies, and faced down an evil empire. Once again, we accept the call of history to deliver the oppressed and move this world toward peace. We remain on the offensive against terror networks. We have killed or captured many of their leaders—and for the others, their day will come.

We remain on the offensive in Afghanistan, where a fine President and a National Assembly are fighting terror while building the institutions of a new democracy. We're on the offensive in Iraq, with a clear plan for victory. First, we're helping Iraqis build an inclusive government, so that old resentments will be eased and the insurgency will be marginalized.

Second, we're continuing reconstruction efforts, and helping the Iraqi government to fight corruption and build a modern economy, so all Iraqis can experience the benefits of freedom. And, third, we're striking terrorist targets while we train Iraqi forces that are increasingly capable of defeating the enemy. Iraqis are showing their courage every day, and we are proud to be their allies in the cause of freedom.

Our work in Iraq is difficult because our enemy is brutal. But that brutality has not stopped the dramatic progress of a new democracy. In less than three years, the nation has gone from dictatorship to liberation, to sovereignty, to a constitution, to national elections. At the same time, our coalition has been relentless in shutting off terrorist infiltration, clearing out insurgent strongholds, and turning over territory to Iraqi security forces. I am confident in our plan for victory; I am confident in the will of the Iraqi people; I am confident in the skill and spirit of our military. Fellow citizens, we are in this fight to win, and we are winning.

The road of victory is the road that will take our troops home. As we make progress on the ground, and Iraqi forces increasingly take the lead, we should be able to further decrease our troop levels—but those decisions will be made by our military commanders, not by politicians in Washington, D.C.

Our coalition has learned from our experience in Iraq. We've adjusted our military tactics and changed our approach to reconstruction. Along the way, we have benefited from responsible criticism and counsel offered by members of Congress of both parties. In the coming year, I will continue to reach out and seek your good advice. Yet, there is a difference between responsible criticism that aims for success, and defeatism that refuses to acknowledge anything but failure. Hindsight alone is not wisdom, and second-guessing is not a strategy.

With so much in the balance, those of us in public office have a duty to speak with candor. A sudden withdrawal of our forces from Iraq would abandon our Iraqi allies to death and prison, would put men like bin Laden and Zarqawi in charge of a strategic country, and show that a pledge from America means little. Members of Congress, however we feel about the decisions and debates of the past, our nation has only one option: We must keep our word, defeat our enemies, and stand behind the American military in this vital mission. . . .

Our offensive against terror involves more than military action. Ultimately, the only way to defeat the terrorists is to defeat their dark vision of hatred and fear by offering the hopeful alternative of political freedom and peaceful change. So the United States of America supports democratic reform across the broader Middle East. Elections are vital, but they are only the beginning. Raising up a democracy requires the rule of law, and protection of minorities, and strong, accountable institutions that last longer than a single vote.

The great people of Egypt have voted in a multi-party presidential election—and now their government should open paths of peaceful opposition that will reduce the appeal of radicalism. The Palestinian people have voted in elections. And now the leaders of Hamas must recognize Israel, disarm, reject terrorism, and work for lasting peace. Saudi Arabia has taken the first steps of reform—now it can offer its people a better future by pressing forward with those efforts. Democracies in the Middle East will not look like our own, because they will reflect the traditions of their own citizens. Yet liberty is the future of every nation in the Middle East, because liberty is the right and hope of all humanity.

The same is true of Iran, a nation now held hostage by a small clerical elite that is isolating and repressing its people. The regime in that country sponsors terrorists in the Palestinian territories and in Lebanon—and that must come to an end. The Iranian government is defying the world with its nuclear ambitions, and the nations of the world must not permit the Iranian regime to gain nuclear weapons. America will continue to rally the world to confront these threats.

Tonight, let me speak directly to the citizens of Iran: America respects you, and we respect your country. We respect your right to choose your own future and win your own freedom. And our nation hopes one day to be the closest of friends with a free and democratic Iran.

2006 Quadrennial Defense Review Report of the United States, February 6, 2005

The Quadrennial Defense Review resulted from a congressional mandate. Although the document is detailed, the chapter titles give a superb understanding of the topics the report considers in detail. The entire Review appears at www.defenselink.mil/qdr/report/Report20060203.pdf online.

According to the document's preface, "the United States is engaged in what will be a long war." The following topics are covered in the full report:

Fighting the Long War
Operationalizing the Strategy
Reorienting Capabilities and Forces
Reshaping the Defense Enterprise
Developing a 21st Century Total Force
Achieving Unity of Effort

The National Security Strategy of the United States, March 16, 2006

The federal government periodically publishes its national strategy. Excerpted below is the president's strategy, as it appeared in March 2006, almost five years after the September 11, 2001, terrorist attacks.

I. Overview of America's National Security Strategy

It is the policy of the United States to seek and support democratic movements and institutions in every nation and culture, with the ultimate goal of ending tyranny in our world. In the world today, the fundamental character of regimes matters as much as the distribution of power among them. The goal of our statecraft is to help create a world of democratic, well-governed states that can meet the needs of their citizens and conduct themselves responsibly in the international system. This is the best way to provide enduring security for the American people.

Achieving this goal is the work of generations. The United States is in the early years of a long struggle, similar to what our country faced in the early years of the Cold War. The 20th century witnessed the triumph of freedom over the threats of fascism and communism. Yet a new totalitarian ideology now threatens, an ideology grounded not in secular philosophy but in the perversion of a proud religion. Its content may be different from the ideologies of the last century, but its means are similar: intolerance, murder, terror, enslavement, and repression.

Like those who came before us, we must lay the foundations and build the institutions that our country needs to meet the challenges we face. The chapters that follow will focus on several essential tasks. The United States must:

Champion aspirations for human dignity;

Strengthen alliances to defeat global terrorism and work to prevent attacks against us and our friends;

Work with others to defuse regional conflicts;

Prevent our enemies from threatening us, our allies, and our friends with weapons of mass destruction (WMD);

Ignite a new era of global economic growth through free markets and free trade;

Expand the circle of development by opening societies and building the infrastructure of democracy;

Develop agendas for cooperative action with other main centers of global power;

Transform America's national security institutions to meet the challenges and opportunities of the 21st century; and

Engage the opportunities and confront the challenges of globalization.

George W. Bush's State of the Union Address, January 23, 2007

(excerpted)

President Bush has offered his most trenchant ideas on national security frequently through his State of the Union messages. With public support for the war declining, the president has a number of concerns more than five years after the attacks.

. . . With the distance of time, we find ourselves debating the causes of conflict and the course we have followed. Such debates are essential when a great democracy faces great questions. Yet one question has surely been settled: that to win the war on terror we must take the fight to the enemy.

From the start, America and our allies have protected our people by staying on the offense. The enemy knows that the days of comfortable sanctuary, easy movement, steady financing, and free flowing communications are long over. For the terrorists, life since 9/11 has never been the same.

Our success in this war is often measured by the things that did not happen. We cannot know the full extent of the attacks that we and our allies have prevented, but here is some of what we do know: We stopped an al Qaeda plot to fly a hijacked airplane into the tallest building on the West Coast. We broke up a Southeast Asian terror cell grooming operatives for attacks inside the United States. We uncovered an al Qaeda cell developing anthrax to be used in attacks against America.

And just last August, British authorities uncovered a plot to blow up passenger planes bound for America over the Atlantic Ocean. For each life saved, we owe a debt of gratitude to the brave public servants who devote their lives to finding the terrorists and stopping them.

Every success against the terrorists is a reminder of the shoreless ambitions of this enemy. The evil that inspired and rejoiced in 9/11 is still at work in the world. And so long as that's the case, America is still a nation at war.

In the mind of the terrorist, this war began well before September the 11th, and will not end until their radical vision is fulfilled. And these past five years have given us a much clearer view of the nature of this enemy. Al Qaeda and its followers are Sunni extremists, possessed by hatred and commanded by a harsh and narrow ideology. Take almost any principle of civilization, and their goal is the opposite. They preach with threats, instruct with bullets and bombs, and promise paradise for the murder of the innocent.

Our enemies are quite explicit about their intentions. They want to overthrow moderate governments, and establish safe havens from which to plan and carry out new attacks on our country. By killing and terrorizing Americans, they want to force our country to retreat from the world and abandon the cause of liberty. They would then be free to impose their will and spread their totalitarian ideology. Listen to this warning from the late terrorist Zarqawi: "We will sacrifice our blood and bodies to put an end to your dreams, and what is coming is even worse." Usama bin Laden declared: "Death is better than living on this Earth with the unbelievers among us."

These men are not given to idle words, and they are just one camp in the Islamist radical movement. In recent times, it has also become clear that we face an escalating danger from Shia extremists who are just as hostile to America, and are also determined to dominate the Middle East. Many are known to take direction from the regime in Iran, which is funding and arming terrorists like Hezbollah—a group second only to al Qaeda in the American lives it has taken.

The Shia and Sunni extremists are different faces of the same totalitarian threat. Whatever slogans they chant, when they slaughter the innocent they have the same wicked purposes. They want to kill Americans, kill democracy in the Middle East, and gain the weapons to kill on an even more horrific scale.

In the sixth year since our nation was attacked, I wish I could report to you that the dangers had ended. They have not. And so it remains the policy of this government to use every lawful and proper tool of intelligence, diplomacy, law enforcement, and military action to do our duty, to find these enemies, and to protect the American people.

This war is more than a clash of arms—it is a decisive ideological struggle, and the security of our nation is in the balance. To prevail, we must remove the conditions that inspire blind hatred, and drove 19 men to get onto airplanes and to come and kill us. What every terrorist fears most is human freedom—societies where men and women make their own choices, answer to their own conscience, and live by their hopes instead of their resentments. Free people are not drawn to violent and malignant ideologies—and most will choose a better way when they're given a chance. So we advance our own security interests by helping moderates and reformers and brave voices for democracy. The great question of our day is whether America will help men and women in the Middle East to build free societies and share in the rights of all humanity. And I say, for the sake of our own security, we must.

In the last two years, we've seen the desire for liberty in the broader Middle East—and we have been sobered by the enemy's fierce reaction. In 2005, the world watched as the citizens of Lebanon raised the banner of the Cedar Revolution, they drove out the Syrian occupiers and chose new leaders in free elections. In 2005, the people of Afghanistan defied the terrorists and elected a democratic legislature. And in 2005, the Iraqi people held three national elections, choosing a transitional government, adopting the most progressive, democratic constitution in the Arab world, and then electing a government under that constitution. Despite endless threats from the killers in their midst, nearly 12 million Iraqi citizens came out to vote in a show of hope and solidarity that we should never forget.

A thinking enemy watched all of these scenes, adjusted their tactics, and in 2006 they struck back. In Lebanon, assassins took the life of Pierre Gemayel, a prominent participant in the Cedar Revolution. Hezbollah terrorists, with support from Syria and Iran, sowed conflict in the region and are seeking to undermine Lebanon's legitimately elected government. In Afghanistan, Taliban and al Qaeda fighters tried to regain power by regrouping and engaging Afghan and NATO forces. In Iraq, al Qaeda and other Sunni extremists blew up one of the most sacred places in Shia Islam—the Golden Mosque of Samarra. This atrocity, directed at a Muslim house of prayer, was designed to provoke retaliation from Iraqi Shia—and it succeeded. Radical Shia elements, some of whom receive support from Iran, formed death squads. The result was a tragic escalation of sectarian rage and reprisal that continues to this day.

This is not the fight we entered in Iraq, but it is the fight we're in. Every one of us wishes this war were over and won. Yet it would not be like us to leave our promises unkept, our friends abandoned, and our own security at risk. Ladies and gentlemen: On this day, at this hour, it is still within our power to shape the outcome of this battle. Let us find our resolve, and turn events toward victory.

We're carrying out a new strategy in Iraq—a plan that demands more from Iraq's elected government, and gives our forces in Iraq the reinforcements they need to complete their mission. Our goal is a democratic Iraq that upholds the rule of law, respects the rights of its people, provides them security, and is an ally in the war on terror.

In order to make progress toward this goal, the Iraqi government must stop the sectarian violence in its capital. But the Iraqis are not yet ready to do this on their own. So we're deploying reinforcements of more than 20,000 additional soldiers and Marines to Iraq. The vast majority will go to Baghdad, where they will help Iraqi forces to clear and secure neighborhoods, and serve as advisers embedded in Iraqi Army units. With Iraqis in the lead, our forces will help secure the city by chasing down the terrorists, insurgents, and the roaming death squads. And in Anbar Province, where al Qaeda terrorists have gathered and local forces have begun showing a willingness to fight them, we're sending an additional 4,000 United States Marines, with orders to find the terrorists and clear them out. We didn't drive al Qaeda out of their safe haven in Afghanistan only to let them set up a new safe haven in a free Iraq.

The people of Iraq want to live in peace, and now it's time for their government to act. Iraq's leaders know that our commitment is not open-ended. They have promised to deploy more of their own troops to secure Baghdad—and they must do so. They pledged that they will confront violent radicals of any faction or political party—and they need to follow through, and lift needless restrictions on Iraqi and coalition forces, so these troops can achieve their mission of bringing security to all of the people of Baghdad. Iraq's leaders have committed themselves to a series of benchmarks—to achieve reconciliation, to share oil revenues among all of Iraq's citizens, to put the wealth of Iraq into the rebuilding of Iraq, to allow more Iraqis to re-enter their nation's civic life, to hold local elections, and to take responsibility for security in every Iraqi province. But for all of this to happen, Baghdad must be secure. And our plan will help the Iraqi government take back its capital and make good on its commitments.

My fellow citizens, our military commanders and I have carefully weighed the options. We discussed every possible approach. In the end, I chose this course of action because it provides the best chance for success. Many in this chamber understand that America must not fail in Iraq, because you understand that the consequences of failure would be grievous and far-reaching.

If American forces step back before Baghdad is secure, the Iraqi government would be overrun by extremists on all sides. We could expect an epic battle between Shia extremists backed by Iran, and Sunni extremists aided by al Qaeda and supporters of the old regime. A contagion of violence could spill out across the country—and in time, the entire region could be drawn into the conflict.

For America, this is a nightmare scenario. For the enemy, this is the objective. Chaos is the greatest ally—their greatest ally in this struggle. And out of chaos in Iraq would emerge an emboldened enemy with new safe havens, new recruits, new resources, and an even greater determination to harm America. To allow this to happen would be to ignore the lessons of September the 11th and invite tragedy. Ladies and gentlemen, nothing is more important at this moment in our history than for America to succeed in the Middle East, to succeed in Iraq and to spare the American people from this danger.

This is where matters stand tonight, in the here and now. I have spoken with many of you in person. I respect you and the arguments you've made. We went into this largely united, in our assumptions and in our convictions. And whatever you voted for, you did not vote for failure. Our country is pursuing a new strategy in Iraq, and I ask you to give it a chance to work. And I ask you to support our troops in the field, and those on their way.

The war on terror we fight today is a generational struggle that will continue long after you and I have turned our duties over to others. And that's why it's important to work together so our nation can see this great effort through. Both parties and both branches should work in close consultation. It's why I propose to establish a special advisory council on the war on terror, made up of leaders in Congress from both political parties. We will share ideas for how to position America to meet every challenge that confronts us. We'll show our enemies abroad that we are united in the goal of victory.

And one of the first steps we can take together is to add to the ranks of our military so that the American Armed Forces are ready for all the challenges ahead. Tonight I ask the Congress to authorize an increase in the size of our active Army and Marine Corps by 92,000 in the next five years. A second task we can take on together is to design and establish a volunteer Civilian Reserve Corps. Such a corps would function much like our military reserve. It would ease the burden on the Armed Forces by allowing us to hire civilians with critical skills to serve on missions abroad when America needs them. It would give people across America who do not wear the uniform a chance to serve in the defining struggle of our time.

7

Organizations

This chapter is divided into several categories. The most important criterion for inclusion is direct linkage to national security, not merely foreign policy questions. The nongovernmental sector includes organizations qualifying as such under the U.S. Tax Code as 501 (c)(3) groups, frequently known as not-for-profits. Among other conditions, the 501 (c)(3) cannot spend more than about 10 percent of its time on any overtly political decisions. Some of these groups have parallel lobbying activities but those primarily are listed as such. The nongovernmental sector also includes several prominent academic institutions but not each and every university center for foreign policy. Those included have a majority portion of their scholarship aimed at national security rather than simply foreign affairs. This section is more detailed than the federal sections because the nongovernmental organizations are less well known. Additionally, because of space limitations, only those organizations operating as of March 2007 appear so that highly influential groups, such as the Project for a New American Century, that no longer operate will not merit discussion.

The Federally Funded Research and Development Centers (FFRDCs) engage in research for various agencies of the U.S. government, most often under contract. For federal institutions, each and every single educational institution under the broad term "professional military education" is not listed because of space limitations but those with a strategic level of education are included because they produce policymakers who can influence national security. In a few instances, organizations asked by Congress to evaluate policy options are included because of the effect they can have on national security.

Nongovernmental Sector

American Enterprise Institute for Public Policy Research
E-mail: webmaster@aei.org
Website: www.aei.org

The American Enterprise Institute (AEI) is one of the oldest, widest-ranging think tanks in the nation, and a significant portion of its work is dedicated to national security issues. Vice President Richard B. Cheney, the late former United Nations Ambassador Jeane J. Kirkpatrick, former Speaker of the House Newt Gingrich, former Tennessee Senator and actor Fred Thompson, former Reagan administration Defense Department official Richard Perle, former Ambassador to the People's Republic of China and Republic of Korea James Lilley, and constitutional scholar John Woo have all operated as AEI specialists on defense and security concerns. AEI began during World War II in 1943 as a public policy center. The three foci of the Institute are economic policy studies, defense and foreign policy studies, and social and political studies. The AEI website has a detailed explanation of its operating policies, including its 501 (c)(3) status as a not-for-profit organization as well as an overview of AEI's efforts to avoid conflict of interest, a description of the outside activities of its fellows, and further information on the Institute's work. AEI hosts many meetings and occasional day-long conferences, often broadcasting the event in a webcast; the results of these sessions often appear on the AEI website as video and some are also posted as transcripts. AEI events cover vast subjects within the field of national security, ranging from military modernization questions on the People's Liberation Army to how the U.S. Navy should proceed in developing the next generation of warships. AEI asks questions about regional studies and specific public policy topics in the United States. The organization is large and is respected as a scholarly resource for national security concerns. The AEI Press publishes books, monographs, the *AEI Newsletter*, and numerous short publications and papers, including the AEI Policy Series and the AEI Working Paper Series. In addition, AEI often presents testimony on national security issues before Congress.

American Foreign Policy Council
E-mail: afpc@afpc.org
Website: www.afpc.org

Established in 1982, the American Foreign Policy Council (AFPC) is a not-for-profit organization with an intense interest in national security issues. AFPC has a relatively small staff but has four major, regionally based programs: China, Russia, Eurasia, and Iran. The Council publishes a number of bulletins, including *Russia Reform Monitor, China Reform Monitor, Eurasia Security Watch, Asia Security Monitor, Missile Defense Briefing Report,* and two others on foreign affairs. AFPC also encourages its staff to write op-ed pieces and articles and to be available to Congress as regional and thematic specialists.

Arms Control Association
E-mail: aca@armscontrol.org
Website: www.armscontrol.org

On its website, the Arms Control Association (ACA) touts its role in the national debate on security as "the authoritative source on arms control." The group dates to 1971 when it began working to lessen the use of nuclear weapons through verifiable arms control. The Association accomplishes its work through conferences and publications (including its journal, *Arms Control Today*) and by providing basic, verifiable expertise to the U.S. Congress and the media. ACA's staff of ten is headquartered in Washington, but the Association also has an office in Berlin, Germany. Although ACA receives individual donations, it receives most of its funding from major U.S. philanthropies, such as the John D. and Catherine T. MacArthur Foundation, the Ford Foundation, and the U.S. Institute for Peace. Many prominent arms control advocates, such as Randall Forsberg, Michael Klare, and John Steinbruner, serve on the ACA board of directors.

Atlantic Council of the United States
E-mail: info@acus.org
Website: www.acus.org

The Atlantic Council clearly reflects the shift that has occurred in the U.S. national security evaluation of the U.S. and the world in the past fifty years. Founded with an orientation toward Western Europe, the Atlantic Council began recognizing the importance of the Asia region in the 1990s and now describes itself as an organization to promote U.S. world leadership in international affairs. Created from the Atlantic Treaty Association of 1949, former secretaries of state Dean Acheson and Christian Herter and others recrafted the Treaty Association into the Atlantic Council in 1961. In the early 1990s, the Council began broadening its concerns beyond the trans-Atlantic environment. The Council has many "establishment" members, individuals retired from their high policy-making positions, such as the late General Andrew Goodpaster who had been General Dwight Eisenhower's aide as well as former commandant of the National War College, or Ambassador Rozanne Ridgway, formerly of the State Department. The staff is relatively small, a couple of people for each project the Council undertakes, and its National Councillors Program features a long list of impressive practitioners and scholars. The Council holds meetings and publishes studies on a range of topics, all at least indirectly aimed at the national security environment. The Council accepts donations from the public but also applies for grant money from philanthropies to accomplish its work. Upon his retirement as Supreme Allied Commander Europe, the Council elected Marine General James Jones as chairman of its board of directors, keeping the link between policy and study.

Brookings Institution
E-mail: inquiries@brookings.edu
Website: www.brookings.edu

The Brookings Institution, created immediately before World War I in 1916 as the Institute for Government Research, is one of the most established think tanks in the United States. Reconstituted in 1927 after a bequest by St. Louis native Robert Somer Brookings, the Institute for Government Research, the Brookings Graduate School, and the Institute of Economics were recast as the Brookings Institution in his honor. Brookings has been influential in public policy affairs since its inception. While often associated with the Democratic Party, Brookings is a not-for-profit, meaning it cannot have avowed political affiliation. Brookings has a dozen full research areas, including defense, global economics, U.S. economics, global politics, environment and energy, and governance. The Institution also has five research programs, including foreign policy studies, governance, and global economics. Within those are a number of specialized research centers and initiatives, such as the Northeast Asia Center, the China Initiative, the Saban Center for Middle East, and the Center on the United States and Europe. Brookings has an impressive array of scholars on national security and other topics, including Michael O'Hanlon, Kenneth Pollack,

Richard Bush, Robert Leiken, Cheng Li, Shaul Bakhash, Stephen Cohen, William Quandt, and many others. The Brookings Institution press publishes books, policy briefs, and periodic journals and encourages scholars to provide Congressional testimony and to write op-ed pieces and letters to the editor on national security issues. The Institution holds conferences and posts conference presentations on the Institution's website.

Carnegie Endowment for International Peace
E-mail: info@CarnegieEndowment.org
Website: www.carnegieendowment.org

Steel magnate Andrew Carnegie donated a substantial endowment to create the think tank that bears his name almost a century later. Carnegie has three major regional concentrations, the China Program, the Russian & Eurasian Program, and the Global Policy Program and established the nonprofit Group of Fifty for global business leaders. Carnegie is known for its long-standing commitment to nonproliferation questions, global governance, and issues relating to the U.S. role in the world. Its national security concerns are broad-ranging and feature the work of some of the most well-known scholars in the field, including Jessica Tuchman Matthews, currently the Endowment's president, Michael Swaine, Robert Kagan, Marina Ottaway, Martha Brill Olcott, Ashley Tellis, Rose Gottemoeller, and Minxin Pei. The Carnegie Endowment publishes books, reports, policy briefs, and Carnegie Papers, most of which are available for download or purchase from the website. The Endowment is particularly prominent in nuclear nonproliferation studies, an increasingly important topic in national security discussions. Additionally, the Carnegie Endowment has long published *Foreign Policy*, a bimonthly magazine on foreign affairs, including national security topics. The Endowment hosts many meetings, and presentations from the meetings are circulated on the Endowment website or in publications.

Cato Institute
E-mail: webmaster@cato.org
Website: www.cato.org

The Cato Institute, named after the Roman statesman, advocates individual liberty and responsibility and that the nation's security commitment should largely involve the defense of the continental United States. Created as a not-for-profit think institution in 1977,

Cato prefers a national security policy of limited engagements around the world instead of wide-ranging involvement in places Cato deems of only tangential interest to the nation. Ted Galen Carpenter, Cato's vice president for foreign policy and defense studies, is perhaps the most prominent national security scholar on staff but is far from the only person in the field. Cato covers a range of public policy concerns, and its efforts on national security are current and fairly encompassing, including the global war on terror (about which it held a September 2006 reconsideration on the five-year anniversary of the September 11 terrorist attacks), effects of the wars in Iraq and Afghanistan on the United States, and the use of the U.S. military around the world. Cato holds frequent conferences with speakers from across the political spectrum. These events are broadcast live on the web via RSS feeds or can be accessed from the Cato archive online. Cato also publishes conference transcripts, books, studies, and the *Cato Journal* and sends out a daily update of policy questions under consideration by the staff as well as e-updates of recent publications. Cato is one of the rare Washington institutions to offer its publications in Spanish on www.elcato.org, in Arabic at www.misbahalhurriyya. org, and in Russian on cato.ru. A fourth website reaching out to the world, including material on national security, is www.lampofliberty.org.

Center for American Progress
E-mail: progress@americanprogress.org
Website: www.americanprogress.org

The Center for American Progress is the inspiration of John D. Podesta, the chief of staff to former President Bill Clinton. The center's intent is to provide "progressive ideas for a strong, just, and free America." Its website almost appears to be that of either a "shadow cabinet" or a blue print for a post-Bush administration. The Center for American Progress is a not-for-profit organization, which requires it to be nonpartisan. One of its three basic areas of concern is national security, specifically Iraq, intelligence, human rights, strategy, international alliances, regions, homeland security, nuclear and biological weapons, global terrorism, and the U.S. military. Four of the organization's many projects focus on the national security field: Defense Review, Strategic Redeployment, Security and Peace, and Americas Project. The Center has a long list of specialists, including Morton Halperin (who served in the Nixon administration; his nomination for the position of assistant secretary of defense in the Clinton administration was not confirmed), Lawrence Korb (who served in Reagan's Defense Department), and nonproliferation specialist Joseph Cirincione. The Center holds events on topics of interest and circulates its ideas through press releases, media packets, speeches, testimony, and other outlets. The Center reaches out to students, and its website has a long list of campus coordinators and internship opportunities.

Center for Defense Information
E-mail: info@cdi.org
Website: www.cdi.org

The Center for Defense Information (CDI) dates to the Nixon administration, when it began trying to provide a less militarized approach to national security. CDI is a member of the World Security Institute, along with several other groups that are opposed to an overemphasis on a single tool of statecraft for policy. The CDI mission is somewhat different from any others in that it has never accepted federal funding to ensure that its conclusions are not affected by funding sources. As a result, it is highly reliant upon foundation grants and public donations. The CDI website provides hyperlinks to information in about two dozen research topic areas and has projects in nine specific "hot spots": the Middle East, space security, children and armed conflict, the arms trade, terrorism, nuclear proliferation, missile defense, the Straus military reform project, and small arms and light weapons. CDI publishes half a dozen newsletters, including the long-running *The Defense Monitor,* which updates readers on military programs and germane international security issues.

Center for International Policy
E-mail: cip@ciponline.org
Website: www.ciponline.org

The Center for International Policy (CIP) seeks to move the national security debate toward the demilitarized side of the spectrum. Its staff and membership include a number of former government analysts who are highly critical of the use of intelligence in a political manner to skew public perceptions, such as former Ambassador Robert White and former Central Intelligence Agency Soviet specialist and National War College professor Melvin A. Goodman. The Center is a not-for-profit organization that has programs in the areas of Asia, Colombia, Central America, Cuba, national security, and global financial integrity, and it participates in several joint programs with other organizations, including "Just the Facts," which is a database of U.S. security assistance to Latin America and the Caribbean. Hard copies of CIP's international policy reports may be purchased or downloaded from the Center's website.

Center for the National Security Interest
E-mail: info@national-security.org
Website: www.national-security.org/

The Center for the National Security Interest (CNSI) is an avowedly pro-defense think tank that supports all steps to enhance national security while acknowledging that the nation ought only engage in wars that are just. CNSI strongly supports the war on terrorism and the war in Iraq while seeking to maintain the goals of the Monroe Doctrine in the Western hemisphere. The Center also supports an antimissile defense system. CNSI has published a number of op-ed pieces and reports and position papers to buttress its positions. The CNSI has an interesting web page link to national security organizations across the country.

Center for Security Policy
E-mail: info@centerforsecuritypolicy.org
Website: www.centerforsecuritypolicy.org

The Center for Security Policy, which was created in 1988, is one of the most vigilant in the nation's capital about the need to protect U.S. national security against threats new and old. Frank Gaffney, a figure in President Reagan's Department of Defense in the 1980s, is head of the Center, which he uses aggressively to remind the public of dangers that some of the world pursues to our detriment. Gaffney and the Center are keenly aware of growing Chinese power around the world, the dangers posed by nuclear nonproliferation failures in places like North Korea and Iran, and the possible spread of terrorism against U.S. assets. The Center holds meetings and publishes its materials on its website and through electronic mailings. The Center for Security Policy is a 501 (c)(3) not-for-profit organization that accepts donations from the public.

Center for Strategic and Budgetary Assessments
E-mail: info@csbaonline.org
Website: www.csbaonline.org

The Center for Strategic and Budgetary Assessment (CSBA) website notes that the organization seeks "thinking smarter about defense" and actively reaches out to do so. CSBA divides its work into two primary areas: strategic studies and defense studies. It is a nonpartisan, not-for-profit 501 (c)(3) organization seeking to enhance national debate and participation on defense issues. Its board of directors includes former Congressman Dave McCurdy, an Oklahoma Democrat, and former Senator Dan Coats, an Indiana Republican. The Center has about eight staffers, providing written publications as well as appearing at conferences around the nation's capital. These staffers include well-respected transformation and counterinsurgency specialist and former Army officer Andrew Krepinevich, the Center's president, and board of directors member General Jack Keane, a retired Army Vice Chief of Staff who comments frequently in the media on national security issues. The Center is frequently cited in the media and offers internships to younger scholars interested in getting into the field.

Center for Strategic and International Studies
E-mail: aschwartz@csis.org
Website: www.csis.org

The Center for Strategic and International Studies (CSIS) is perhaps the most frequently cited think tank in the national security field today. Founded by Admiral Arleigh Burke, USN, and Ambassador David Abshire in 1962 as an outgrowth of Georgetown University, the Center became an independent entity twenty-five years later. With Burke and Abshire's natural interest in the issues of Cold War security, CSIS made its mark as an institution with a firm commitment to studying national security concerns. Today its efforts are broader; it is a genuine public policy institution studying a panoply of subjects: defense and security policy, global challenges, and regional transformation. CSIS currently has more than two dozen programs, many of which are national security driven, such as the Freeman Program on China and the International Security Program. CSIS has a dazzling array of trustees, councillors, advisers, corporate officers, and international affiliates, such as former

Secretary of State Henry Kissinger, former Senator Sam Nunn, former Ambassador Anne Armstrong, and many more. The distinguished researchers and scholars at CSIS cover the areas of national security, global trends, regions of the world, and global strategy, and are among the most cited analysts in the world on national security. The long and distinguished list of CSIS researchers has included Anthony Cordesman, an expert on the Iraq conflict; former Clinton official Kurt Campbell; the former Freeman Chair on China, Dr. Bates Gill; former diplomat Peter DeShazio on Latin America; and Theresita Schaffer, a South Asian scholar. CSIS also has a range of international advisers and a long list of significant business councillors from across the country. CSIS runs a long list of events, often several in a single day, ranging from small meetings to conferences for hundreds of participants. The CSIS invitation receives attention when it arrives because of the strong networking opportunities that CSIS events provide. The events transpire in Washington, for the most part, but CSIS also has affiliations with organizations around the world. CSIS publishes a vast range of newsletters (electronically and in hard copy), the prestigious *Washington Quarterly* journal, conference reports, policy papers, and books. In addition, CSIS maintains a superb press office to answer media requests. In the mid-1980s, a senior CSIS representative noted that the organization guaranteed that it would present a specialist on any national security issue within an hour of receiving a press inquiry. CSIS scholars are frequent talk show guests and are frequently called on to present congressional testimony. CSIS has a multimillion dollar budget but remains a not-for-profit 501(c)(3) and accepts public contributions for its research.

Council on Foreign Relations
E-mail: communications@cfr.org
Website: www.cfr.org

The Council on Foreign Relations (CFR), founded in 1921, has long been known in the United States as the "establishment" organization in national security and foreign affairs. Located in New York, CFR also hosts many meetings in Washington DC. The Council grew out of the aftermath of World War I as prominent citizens interested in national security decided they could make a difference if they rallied together under on institutional banner. CFR prides itself on being a focus for national debate and learning on relevant issues. The membership is quite limited but considered quite prestigious. To ensure a wide range of influential thinkers, the Council welcomes senior active-duty military officers, former policymakers, and traditional academics to its midst. The Council publishes the oft-cited journal *Foreign Affairs*, a bimonthly publication that has played an occasional role in serious national security debates over the years. The journal has published highly influential articles, such as the famous 1947 "Mr. X" article, which first used the term "containment" to characterize U.S. policy toward the Soviet Union until the end of the Cold War. The Council also forms task forces on such issues as Chinese military power, and each task force publishes a final report with policy recommendations. The CFR website has many links to current research within the organization. In addition, CFR hosts myriad luncheons, dinners, speeches, and other public discussions on topics of current and future interest, such as avian flu, postconflict Iraq, Darfur, and Indonesia after the terrorist bombings in 2002 and 2005.

Federation of American Scientists
E-mail: webmaster@fas.org
Website: www.fas.org

The Federation of American Scientists (FAS) was founded in 1945 by former participants in the Manhattan Project, the government's effort to find the technology to build an atomic bomb. These scientists also included a group who believed they had an ethical responsibility to bring the implications of this work to the public and to warn them of the possibilities that lie ahead with these new weapons. The FAS has been one of the leading organizations to focus on explaining the science as well as public policy implications of the national security field. The FAS holds many conferences, press conferences, and media events on public policy questions. The staff includes many Nobel laureates and persons who have worked in scientific laboratories, and the board of directors includes some of the most prominent scientists in the nation's history. One of the most popular parts of the Federation's outreach is the Strategic Security Project, which has a goal of reducing the threats to the nation and world. A 501 (c)(3) not-for-profit group that offers individual memberships and accepts donations, the Federation has a long list of major projects that receive funding from some of the most prominent philanthropic groups in the

United States; these projects run the gamut of national security issues such as government secrecy, security studies, information warfare, and energy and the environment. Security studies includes more than a dozen fields, such as arms control, chain of command, weapons programs, intelligence, and terrorism. The FAS publishes an Occasional Paper Series on individual issues such as Chinese military modernization or space security. It also publishes the *Public Interest Report* and *Secrecy News*.

Foreign Policy Association
E-mail: info@fpa.org
Website: www.fpa.org

The Foreign Policy Association (FPA) is heavily involved with trying to educate the public on the range of public policy questions relating to foreign affairs; thus, there is a logical emphasis on national security within the Association's agenda. The FPA, which was created in 1918, fosters public policy discussions in its individual chapters in a number of large and small U.S. cities; these local chapters often go by the name "Council on Foreign Relations," even though they are not run by the New York–based Council. These local chapters hold frequent meetings at the local level to educate the public, particularly public school teachers, about the basics of national security. The FPA publishes books, pamphlets, and the like on overarching national security questions the United States is pondering, such as the role of the United Nations, the future of arms control, and the role the United States ought play in the international scene. The FPA's best-known series is "Great Decisions," which highlights the national security concerns in various areas of the world.

Foreign Policy Research Institute
E-mail: fpri@fpri.org
Website: www.fpri.org

In 1955, the Foreign Policy Research Institute (FPRI) started as a mechanism for applying scholarship on national security to the creation of national security strategy. The Institute, located in Philadelphia, conducts research and engages in massive outreach through its quarterly journal, *Orbis*, which reaches the academic community around the world. Both the journal and the other online publicaitons of FPRI reach a considerable number of interested people outside of the traditional decision-making circles. FPRI has six primary research programs: Asia Program; Think Tanks and Civil Societies; Project on Democratic Transitions; Program on National Security; Center on Terrorism, Counter-Terrorism, and Homeland Security; and Center for the Study of America and the West. Regarding education, FPRI operates the Marvin Wachman Fund for International Education and the History Institute for Teachers. FPRI also hosts six lecture series on questions of national security. One of the Institute's major goals is to foster enhanced teaching in the security field. In addition to *Orbis*, FPRI publishes *E-notes*, *FPRI Wire*, *Peacefacts*, and *Watch on the West* online. The Institute hosts a significant number of conferences on security questions, and the proceedings are subsequently posted online.

Friends Committee on National Legislation
Website: www.fcnl.org

The Friends Committee on National Legislation (FCNL), which was created in 1943 during World War II, has always been affiliated with the Religious Society of Friends, known as the Quakers, and considers itself the largest peace organization in the nation's capital. The FCNL organizes for the range of peace and social justice under the representation of the oldest religious lobbying group in the United States. Unlike many other organizations in the national security field, the FCNL is not a 501 (c)(3) not-for-profit organization because it engages in lobbying, although the FCNL Education Fund does have not-for-profit status. Historically, the FCNL has campaigned to change the international distribution of justice by lobbying for the creation of the Peace Corps in the early 1960s and the Arms Control Agency in the 1970s. More recently, the FCNL has been involved in trying to prevent genocide in Darfur and orchestrate withdrawal from Iraq, and its eight primary issue areas for 2007 are Iraq, disarmament, civil liberties, conventional weapons, the federal budget, the environment, torture, and Native Americans. Although the Committee prepares publications on issues of interest, a significant portion of its efforts go to getting citizens involved in the public policy debate and pressuring officials. Iran has been an enduring concern for the FCNL since the United States has been in a position of conflict with the Middle Eastern state for almost three decades. Committee members often go to parts of the earth where the U.S. government is not welcome to make it clear that the U.S. people often differ from their political leaders on individual issues; for example, Committee members met with Iranian officials in early 2007. The FCNL's overarching, enduring goal is to create a more demilitarized U.S. national security policy, and the group works assiduously to influence congressional representatives to ensure that occurs.

Globalsecurity.org
E-mail: info@globalsecurity.org
Website: www.globalsecurity.org

GlobalSecurity.org started in 2000 to provide information on the threats of the new millennium, focusing on military issues, intelligence, weapons of mass destruction, space, and homeland security. Its primary vehicle for reaching the public is its website, which is the first online destination for security data for many. GlobalSecurity.org's website has both visual and text data on the questions most commonly arising on the world security scene today as well as hyperlinks to more information. The website is extremely up-to-date with materials directly out of the Pentagon and other government agencies on items such as current government defense contracts or reports from agencies or Congress. The founder of GlobalSecurity.org, John Pike, appears frequently in media interviews to comment on the nature of threats in the organization's fields. Pike was a staffer at the Federation of American Scientists for many years and had a serious following on the topic of defense in space. The organization has a small staff and about half a dozen senior fellows pursuing work in GlobalSecurity.org's key areas of focus; a few internships are available. GlobalSecurity. org has an interesting approach to raising money: it sells space to advertisers on its website.

Greenpeace, USA
E-mail: info@wdc.greenpeace.org
Website: www.greenpeace.org

Greenpeace, which dates to 1971, is the world's best-known environmental organization that has a distinctly antinuclear goal for national security. Greenpeace, with 250,000 members in the United States and 2.5 million worldwide, is an active organization around the world, often known as the owner of the *Rainbow Warrior*, a ship that toured the world on an antinuclear campaign until the French intelligence service blew it up in Auckland, New Zealand, in 1985. Greenpeace works to raise consciousness about the environment and to motivate citizenry to work against environmentally destructive policies in areas such as toxins, global warming, nuclear issues, forests, oceans, and genetic engineering. Greenpeace solicits public contributions and does not accept government or corporate funding.

Henry L. Stimson Center
E-mail: info@stimson.org
Website: www.stimson.org

The Henry L. Stimson Center, named after the former Secretary of State Henry L. Stimson, is a think tank dedicated to international security issues. Founded in 1989, the Stimson Center is active in nonproliferation, regional issues, and international cooperation concerns, among others. Its researchers are divided into three tiers (senior fellows, fellows, and researchers) and often have significant practical service, frequently in government service. They focus on building bridges with academic, government, think tank, and international actors. The Center publishes proceedings from its many conferences (in hard copy and electronic versions). The Center is nonpartisan and not-for-profit, accepting donations under its 501 (c)(3) tax status. Stimson is particularly strong on East Asian and nuclear nonproliferation concerns within the security field.

Heritage Foundation
E-mail: info@heritage.org
Website: www.heritage.org

The Heritage Foundation resulted from the conservatives' desire to counter what they believed was disproportionate liberal power in think tanks in Washington. Founded by Dr. Edwin Feulner and endowed with significant support from the Coors family of Colorado, Heritage began in 1973. With the advent of Ronald Reagan's conservative revolution in the 1980s, Heritage became a prominent institution, offering many rapid analyses of pressing public policy issues and publishing newsletters, reports, policy studies, and books. Because so much of the Reagan period saw discussion center on national security concerns, Heritage built a formidable group of scholars advocating a strong national defense and a sensible national security path. Heritage scholars have long supported strengthening defense through developing ballistic missiles, building stronger ties with certain allies such as Taiwan, and reinforcing steps to prevent states like North Korea from becoming powers. Heritage receives considerable corporate funding but also welcomes individual contributions. Heritage scholars past and present include a number of former and current government appointees, such as Kim Holmes and Peter Brookes. Heritage is an active organization, hosting many meetings and book launches, for example. In many cases, attendance is open to the public as well as broadcast online so that those outside the nation's capital can hear the discussion as it occurs. Heritage also maintains an extensive website with a bookstore for its publications and links to other websites covering national security issue. Heritage regularly publishes a range of other materials such as backgrounders, Heritage Memoranda, Heritage Reports, and Heritage Lectures.

Hoover Institution on War, Revolution and Peace,
Stanford University
Email: horaney@hoover.stanford.edu
Website: www.hoover.org

The Hoover Institution on War, Revolution and Peace began in 1919 shortly before its namesake, Herbert Hoover, became president. In the initial years, the Institution focused on writing papers and conducting studies about World War I. The brutal war in Europe had sparked revolution in a number of countries while destroying empires, which tied to the organization's primary goal of providing scholarship on revolution, peace, and war in the broad context of the international environment. Outsiders generally describe the Hoover Institution as conservative in orientation but the Institution says its interest is in "free societies" rather on a single ideology. Programmatic themes at Hoover include property rights and rule of law, individuals in societies, role of societies and cultures, economic growth and taxation, the role of governments in all aspects of society, and international rivalries and global cooperation. Hoover has about a hundred scholars and a large support staff that includes librarians. Some scholars, such as William Ratliff, are long term while others do a brief stint at the Stanford campus where the Institution is housed. Hoover is a 501 (c)(3) public charity but also has a significant endowment that finances about 45 percent of the Institution's activities; the remainder comes from foundation support. The organization has an extensive publishing and media operation that includes the Hoover Press; influential periodicals such as the quarterly *Hoover Digest*, the bimonthly *Policy Review,* and the online *China Leader-*

ship Monitor; and a television show targeted to those "outside the beltway," called *Uncommon Knowledge*. The Institution also hosts conferences for scholars on a wide array of topics in national security and associated fields.

Hudson Institute
Email: info@hudson.org
Website: www.hudson.org

The Hudson Institute is one of the longer enduring national security think tanks in the United States, holding not-for-profit, 501 (c)(3) status. Cofounded by one of the most prominent figures from the nuclear era, Herman Kahn, the Hudson Institute began operating in 1961 in Croton-upon-Hudson, New York, then moved to Indianapolis, Indiana, in the 1980s and 1990s, only to move to the nation's capital after the new millennium in an effort to effect policy more directly. The Hudson Institute has a primary focus on national security but has also broadened its work to domestic issues. Its fourteen policy centers feature dozens of policy research programs, some focusing on functional areas, such as foreign policy and human rights, and others focusing on specific regions, such as the Middle East, Korea, China, Eastern Europe, Africa, Western Europe, the former Soviet Union and Russia, and Japan. Today, Hudson hosts numerous meetings on contemporary questions such as the future of Iraq, the U.S. relationship with Russia, and how to address terrorism. Along with its conferences, Hudson researchers provide strategic analysis on national security issues, those confronting the nation today and those likely to be important in the future, through a range of traditional and online publications, including op-ed pieces, books, articles, and reports. The most prominent contemporary scholar associated with Hudson is retired Lieutenant General William Odom, former director of the National Security Agency.

Institute for Defense & Disarmament Studies
E-mail: info@idds.org
Website: www.idds.org

Begun by Randall C. Forsberg in 1980, at the beginning of the antinuclear wave, the Institute for Defense & Disarmament Studies (IDDS) encourages a national security policy based on fewer military arms, greater democratic institutions, and a different view of security in the future—and has held true to these policy alternatives for more than a quarter of a century. IDDS is a not-for-profit, 501 (c)(3) educational institution with board members from across the nation and the globe; it accepts individual donations. The IDDS holds conferences and publishes books and other materials (including some related to its vast database of arms) to encourage greater public debate about alternatives to militarization for conflict resolution. The Institute began its work with a decidedly antinuclear focus but has expanded to include the range of issues in conventional, nuclear, and space technologies that now appear in debates on national security. IDDS has several ongoing projects, such as the Global Action to Prevent War, which mobilizes people around the world to act against military solutions to crises, and Urgentcall.org, which encourages people to lobby the United States to stop its current nuclear policies for allied states. More explicitly than some groups, the IDDS works on public education to alter the grassroots views of national security policy, arms in space, missile technologies, and associated areas of concern.

Institute for Policy Studies
E-mail: scott@ips-dc.org
Website: www.ips-dc.org

Although the Institute for Policy Studies (IPS) is often considered a liberal national security think tank, its self-professed description is a "progressive think tank." IPS is a 501 (c)(3), not-for-profit group located in the nation's capital. The Institute originated in the civil rights era of 1963 and has long pursued national security openness and questions relating to surveillance and Latin American policy issues. The group still seeks to achieve peace, justice, and environmental sustainability. IPS studies a range of policy issues, but its national security concerns are the Middle East, drug policies, sustainable energy, nuclear policy, and foreign policy. In addition, IPS publishes many articles, op-ed piecess, and reports.

International Assessment and Strategy Center
E-mail: contact@strategycenter.net
Website: www.strategycenter.net

The International Assessment and Strategy Center (IASC) is a not-for-profit 501 (c)(3) organization based in Washington, which has a nonpartisan emphasis on protecting the nation against medium- and long-term national security threats. The IASC's general orientation is toward a robust national security posture, taking proper account of U.S. friends and foes. IASC has five distinct program areas: national security law and intelligence policy; Asian security and democracy; terrorism, homeland security, and government; the Eurasian sand table; and the military databases. The Center's scholars write on these topics and the organization hosts conferences on specific issues such as Chinese involvement in Latin America. Several IASC scholars are prominent supporters of a policy that balances U.S. relations with Taiwan differently from the post-1979 diplomatic alignment with the People's Republic of China. The scholars at IASC include Dr. Arthur Waldron of the University of Pennsylvania and Rick Fisher, both of whom specialize in security issues involving the People's Republic of China. The IASC accepts public donations and works on government contracts to enhanced understanding of national security threats ahead for the United States.

International Institute for Strategic Studies
Website: www.iiss.org

The International Institute for Strategic Studies (IISS) was founded in the United Kingdom in 1958; it has offices in London, Washington DC (opened in 2001), and Singapore. The Institute is one of the most respected research centers, and it focuses exclusively on broad national security concerns such as military and political conflict. The organization has a global membership; new members are nominated by existing members to participate in studying and discussing issues such as nonproliferation, ballistic missile defense, and global energy challenges. The IISS holds an annual Global Strategy Review in Geneva, Switzerland, in the autumn. At those sessions, IISS convenes its membership and an array of international policymakers who can speak to the difficulties and successes the international community sees in nations' efforts to enhance stability. IISS holds periodic meetings on other topics, including an annual May/June meeting in Singapore, known as the Shangri-La or Asian Dialogue, which frequently attracts statespersons from around the world to consider this burgeoning security environment. The Gulf Dialogue considers the significant issues confronting that region of the world. The flagship IISS publication is *Survival*, a quarterly published by Oxford University Press. In addition, the *Adelphi Papers* are short monographs pondering pressing security issues such as potential disputes in the

South China Sea or reorientation of information operations during the era of the global war on terror.

Jamestown Foundation
E-mail: pubs@jamestown.org
Website: www.jamestown.org

The Jamestown Foundation shows the role of a leader in determining shifts in an organization's orientation. Since its founding in 1984, Jamestown has been one of the most conservative organizations on national security in the United States, but in the early 2000s, its leadership consciously decided to take a more centrist view to best understand global societal trends that could affect U.S. security. The 501 (c)(3) still has a focus on a traditional threat-based approach to national security analysis, but its publications have begun to include a broader array of views than those of traditional hawks. Instead, Jamestown created a focus on terrorism issues, Russia and the former Soviet Union, and China as potential threats against the United States. It also studies contemporary problems, such as Iraq. Jamestown holds a small number of conferences but is primarily known for its electronic newsletters and reports on its three foundational areas: terrorism, China, and Russia.

Jewish Institute for National Security Affairs
E-mail: info@jinsa.org
Website: www.jinsa.org

The Jewish Institute for National Security Affairs (JINSA) has reached out to educate people in the United States, regardless of their faith, about the threats to the United States from weak alliances around the world as well as the crucial part Israel plays in promoting democracy and stability, especially in the Middle East. A stalwart supporter of Israel and a strong U.S.-Israeli relationship, JINSA arranges visits to the region for retired U.S. military officers and policymakers. The Institute's board of advisers contains a significant number of retired senior U.S. military and governmental officers, many of whom are not Jewish but who are worried about national security. JINSA's programs offer clear-cut education about global threats to the United States, and its website gives further indication of the risks ahead. Programs include the flag and general officer visits; the Perry Military Institutes Program, which allows intensive exchanges between rising U.S.

military officers and their counterparts in Israel's defense establishment; the Nathan Golden Lectures in Middle East Security; law enforcement exchanges; and the Gottesman Lecture Series about events in Israel. The Institute also publishes the semiannual *Journal of International Security Affairs* and various other periodic reports, such as *Observer, Islamic Extremism Newswatch,* and *Profiles in Terror*. JINSA is a not-for-profit, 501 (c)(3) think tank.

The Lexington Institute
E-mail: mail@lexingtoninstitute.org
Website: www.lexingtoninstitute.org

The Lexington Institute specializes in educating the nation about the need for a limited government but one that promotes national security and other priorities that will protect the United States and benefit the world. Lexington promotes democracy and strong defense above anything else in the public policy realm. Lexington conducts studies and educates the public on a number of domestic concerns, but its focus lies primarily in defense, homeland security, military logistics, and the navy. The specialists at Lexington, such as the chairman, former New Jersey Representative James Courter; the chief operating officer Loren Thompson; and Dan Gouré, a well-cited military analyst, all write frequent op-ed pieces and appear at events. Lexington is a relatively small institute in staff size, but it has a notable presence in the discussion of national security issues.

National Institute for Public Policy
Email: amy.joseph@nipp.org
Website: www.nipp.org

Since 1981, the National Institute for Public Policy (NIPP) has educated the public about the range of international and national security concerns confronting the nation in the waning years and then the aftermath of the Cold War. NIPP is a not-for-profit 501 (c)(3) that receives donations, receives charity and corporate grants, and works for government contracts. The Institute has two dozen staff members, most of whom are specialists in national security concerns around the world. NIPP publishes *Comparative Strategy,* which covers pressing issues in the security community. Keith Payne, the head of the Institute, is a noted specialist in missile defense questions, and European director Colin Gray is one of the world's most cited specialists on strategy. Outside advisers to NIPP include William Van Cleave, a prominent member of the Reagan administration; Charles Kupperman, long a critic of underestimates of terrorism; and William Odom, former head of the National Security Agency. NIPP has its own press.

National Priorities Project
Email: info@nationalpriorities.org
Website: www.nationalpriorities.org

The National Priorities Project (NPP) seeks to help the public understand how spending and taxation choices affect society at the grassroots level. The NPP is a not-for-profit public policy institution that has no political orientation. The organization seeks to alter national security policy toward less military spending, greater port security, and broader use of instruments of national power beyond the armed forces. The NPP publishes a series of reports on how to shift the balance of spending on instruments of power toward a less militarized role. The website is full of graphics that provide basic information to the public at large. The NPP also considers economic policy, the budget, and associated issues that are set as national spending priorities and maintains an extensive database on spending and budgetary trade-offs. Its publications are available on the website.

National Security Network
E-mail: info@nationalsecurity.org
Website: www.nsnetwork.org

The National Security Network (NSN) is one of the more recent organizations analyzing national security and promoting "national security above partisan interests." The NSN, which includes practitioners of foreign policy and politicians among its thousand participants, has major projects: the Security Principles Project focuses on what is required to return the United States to balance the threats to the nation against its resources and priorities. Regional programs to promote public policy debate outside the Beltway cover national security basic training, rapid response, and community mapping and communications. The NSN also runs the Security Framework Project, a link from its website to recommended readings on several topics in the national security field. The topics include Iraq, Iran, reconstruction efforts, and defense and military policy among others. The NSN describes itself as trying to cross partisan lines, as of 2006, but many of the group's leadership had served in the Clinton administration. The organization's website, which is its major method of disseminating its views, lists half a dozen major national security concerns, such as Iraq, along with ideas it would pursue to change course on the issue. The Network accepts donations for its work.

National Strategy Forum
E-mail: nsf@nationalstrategy.com
Website: www.nationalstrategy.com

The National Strategy Forum (NSF), which is located in Chicago, is arguably the most influential U.S. organization outside the Washington–New York nexus involved in education on national security issues. Established in 1983 by the late Morris Liebman, a prominent Chicago lawyer with good connections to the national security community, the NSF has hosted a superb range of speakers, including President Ronald Reagan, who previewed the Moscow summit in 1987; retired General Anthony Zinni, who reflected on the war on terror in 2006; and former Secretary of State Madeleine Albright, who considered the role of religion in national security questions. A not-for-profit organization under Illinois tax registration, the NSF is nonpartisan in its efforts to raise important national security concerns to public attention. The NSF hosts conferences, often in conjunction with other like-minded groups, on national security concerns such as preparing for catastrophic incidents or using private security firms. Conference proceedings are then published online. The NSF hosts a monthly luncheon with speakers from around the world. The Forum publishes a quarterly journal, *National Strategy Forum Review*, on current concerns and has a regular assessment of the current hot spots around the world called "Strategy Watch."

Natural Resources Defense Council
E-mail: nrdcinfo@nrdc.org
Website: www.nrdc.org

The Natural Resources Defense Council (NRDC) seeks to educate the public about the centrality of the environment in national security and other parts of the contemporary lifestyle. In addition to its New York headquarters, the NRDC has four regional offices in the United States and one in Beijing, China. The organization focuses on a series of environmental issues ranging from clean water to clean air, global warming, and fish/wildlife. Prominent in its work is the issue of nuclear weapons, energy, and waste, which affects national security concerns. The section dedicated specifically to nuclear weapons, for example, includes a report on whether the U.S. government is overestimating Chinese capabilities, the role of nuclear material in Pakistan, and the role commercial nuclear sales play in international politics. NRDC staff marry science with public policy in discussing national security concerns. The Council publishes long and short policy papers and tries to promote policy change. NRDC is a not-for-profit 501 (c)(3) but has a parallel lobbying group called Earth Action Center.

New American Foundation
Website: www.newamerica.net
Email: Irvine@newamerica.net

Founded in 1999 by Ted Halstead, the New American Foundation (NAF) is a not-for-profit 501(c)(3) think tank with headquarters in Washington DC and an office in Sacramento, California. The NAF is proud of its commitment to new thinking, new voices, and new ideas in public discouse, and foreign policy and associated national security issues are key concerns.. The NAF uses the Internet to provide an almost instantaneous link with its members and potential members by alerting them to NAF events as well as to announce the frequent opinion pieces its staff has written. The Foundation's website notes its desire to engage with people through "a venture capital approach . . . [to invest] in outstanding individuals and policy solutions that transcend the conventional spectrum." Prominent NAF senior fellows in national security include Peter Bergen, who also appears on CNN as a specialist on terrorism and al Qaeda; Flynt Leverett, an analyst on Middle East strategy; Michael Lind, who studies broad national security strategy; and Anatol Lieven, who concentrates on Europe. The Foundation hosts almost daily events on a range of topics, many of which concern national security: Iran, Iraq, terrorism, and changes in strategy are some of the topics on the Foundation's event calendar. In September 2006, the NAF hosted a major event on policy toward Iran that featured *The Looming Tower* author Lawrence Wright, who engaged in an extended discussion of his research into al Qaeda. The NAF has launched a companion website, AmericasPurpose .org, which began as an outgrowth of a September 2005 conference and operates to galvanize people to promote a broader national debate on security. The NAF publishes policy papers under the Foundation's moniker and presents its views in op-ed pieces in a number of prominent newspapers in the United States and abroad. In the summer of 2007, the Foundation announced that Steve Coll, formerly of the *Washington Post* and *The New Yorker*, would replace Halstead at this bi-coastal think tank.

Nuclear Control Institute
E-mail: mail@nci.org
Website: www.nci.org

The Nuclear Control Institute (NCI) began in 1981 to address nuclear nonproliferation and nuclear terrorism. It is a not-for-profit under the U.S. Tax Code, accepting donations as a 501 (c)(3) to help educate the public about eradicating nuclear bombs and destroying nuclear materials. In 2003, the NCI took a novel step of abolishing its conferences and hard copies of material in favor of a web-based database and outreach to a greater number of people than would occur as a brick-and-mortar institution. The materials from the Institute's twenty years of operations in the nation's capital went to the National Security Archive. Today NCI concentrates on plutonium and reprocessing, India-Pakistan, nuclear terrorism, nuclear material shipped around the world by sea or air, U.S.-China trade, and the role of plutonium and enriched uranium in today's world.

Peace Action
Website: www.peace-action.org

Peace Action began in the late 1990s when two long-standing, antinuclear, grassroots organizations merged after the 1996 signing of the Comprehensive Nuclear Test Ban Treaty. Peace Action is a national organization seeking to free the world from violence and war while crafting a national security strategy that reduces the use of nuclear weapons, opposes preemption, and keeps U.S. forces out of places such as Iraq. Peace Action has 100 chapters and numerous state affiliates. Unlike the overwhelming majority of organizations in this category, Peace Action's lobbying prohibits it from not-for-profit status. Peace Action has a national network and a student network for its activities. Its publications are largely fact sheets on specific issues such as Iraq.

Security Policy Working Group
E-mail: dmerz@proteusfund.org
Website: www.proteusfund.org/spwg

The Security Policy Working Group is an amalgam, created in September 2002, of nine organizations that are working to "fundamentally reshape security policy in the United States and to broaden and deepen the public discourse on what constitutes true security in the aftermath of the September 11, 2001 terror attacks." In addition they strive to lessen the use of military force. The organizations include the Center for Defense Information; the Arms Trade Resource Center; the Center for War, Peace and the News Media; the Massachusetts Institute of Technology Security Studies Program; the Graduate Program in International Affairs at the New School University; the National Priorities Project (see a description of this organization elsewhere in the chapter); the Project on Defense Alternatives; Economists for Peace and Security; and the Center for Strategic and Budgetary Assessments. These nongovernmental organizations and individual members believed contributing to this bigger coalition will be more effective in changing security definitions. The Proteus Fund is an Amherst, Massachusetts–based philanthropy that was founded in 1994. The Proteus Fund focuses on democracy growing. The Security Policy Working Group has published a five-year appraisal of security after 9/11.

Union of Concerned Scientists
Website: www.ucsusa.org

The Union of Concerned Scientists (UCS) brings science and public policy together as it has done since its inception at the Massachusetts Institute of Technology in 1969. The UCS seeks to provide impartial, objective information to the public policy debate on such issues as nuclear weapons, nuclear power, global warming, and various other questions. The UCS's global security program focuses on missile defense, space weapons, and terrorism, among other topics. The Union publishes much of its work online, and its members, many of whom are Nobel Prize laureates, testify frequently before Congress. The Union is a not-for-profit organization but also has a parallel lobbying group that does not have tax-deductible status.

War Resisters League
E-mail: wrl@warresisters.org
Website: www.warresisters.org

The War Resisters League (WRL) is one of the oldest organizations seeking to keep the United States out of foreign wars; it has been promoting its goal of nonviolence since 1923. The League has chapters in several parts of the country and takes on a more active posture during times of major U.S. military involvements abroad such as the war in Iraq. The WRL organizes major rallies and events to communicate their view that grassroots support does not endorse these foreign involvements with arms. The WRL publishes several pamphlets and materials on nonviolent response to problems and how to avoid paying war taxes. The WRL is also part of the international peace movement through its membership in War Resisters International and affiliation with the International Peace Bureau. The WRL is able to engage in political lobbying because it is not a tax-deductible organization.

Washington Institute for Near East Policy
Website: www.washingtoninstitute.org

The Washington Institute for Near East Policy dates to 1985, when it embarked on a program of trying to provide balanced assessments of U.S. national interests in the Middle East and support meaningful alliances and partnerships while eschewing ties for convenience. The Institute has a staff of more than a dozen experts, all with long-standing ties to the region, to offer immediate analysis for the press and policy communities. The Institute has ties to both the Democratic and Republican leadership, including former Vice President Al Gore and Secretary of State Condoleezza Rice. Many consider the Institute's ties to Israel to be stronger than average. The Institute has programs on virtually each state between Iran and Morocco and on functional topics such as energy policy in the Gulf, terrorism, proliferation, the Israeli-Palestinian peace process, energy and economics, Arab and Islamic politics, and military and defense concerns. The Institute has two continuing publications, *Peace Watch* and *Policy Watch*.

Women in International Security
E-mail: wiisinfo@georgetown.edu
Website: wiis.georgetown.edu

Women in International Security (WIIS), now located at Georgetown University, began in 1987 through the efforts of a small number of women in the security studies field; its first home was at the
University of Maryland. WIIS not only holds meetings and sym-
posia for discussions of prominent topics across the security field
but it also reaches out to bring graduate women into the professional field. WIIS holds a major week-long international security
symposium where those in attendance (men and women) hear
some of the top people in the field discuss the aspects of the theme
for the year. WIIS is a 501 (c)(3) membership organization, and it
publishes an up-to-date database on jobs in the academic, private,
and not-for-profit sectors.

World Policy Institute
E-mail: wpi@newschool.edu
Website: www.worldpolicy.org

The New School of Social Research absorbed the World Policy
Institute (WPI) in 1991, but the Institute's history is a longer one.
Its traditional emphasis has always been on finding creative solutions to pressing and emerging world problems, particularly
those with security implications. The Institute conducts research
and advocates solutions to these problems, circulating their ideas
through a biannual membership letter. The Institute also publishes the quarterly *World Policy Journal*, which discusses a range
of security research. Areas of research at the WPI include arms
trade, counterterrorism, citizenship, Russia, Rwanda, post-9/11
strategy, and several other areas. Along with its research and publications, the WPI offers panels for public discussion.

World Security Institute
E-mail: info@worldsecurityinstitute.org
Website: www.worldsecurityinstitute.org

The World Security Institute (WSI) is a nonpartisan, not-for-profit
research organization seeking to promote news and policy discussion at home and abroad. Its major goal is to promote security
discussion globally. The Center for Defense Information is a division of the Institute. The WSI publishes newsletters, periodic letters, and other press accounts of security issues around the world.
Topics discussed by WSI include space weapons, terrorism, small
arms, nuclear weapons, and regional concerns such as Russia and

China. The Institute accepts public donations and receives grants from philanthropic groups.

Federally Funded Research and Development Centers

The descriptions of federally funded research and development centers (FFRDCs) are not as detailed as those for groups in the not-for-profit sector because many, if not all, of the organizations in this section have responsibilities in addition to security.

Center for Naval Analyses
E-mail: inquiries@cna.org
Website: www.cna.org

The Center for Naval Analyses (CNA) is a research institution with a strong naval heritage, headed by Dr. Christine Fox. Established in 1942 as concerns about German U-boats accelerated, the Center does much of its work on contract from the U.S. Navy and the other military services but also has the authority to engage in self-generated operations; some of its work is classified while the rest is not. With nineteen areas of expertise, the Center is an innovator for navy strategy and capabilities, and national security is one of its predominant concerns. CNA's major fields are advanced technology and systems analysis, operational research, the Center for Strategic Studies (including a highly active East Asia program), and resource analysis. CNA also conducts studies on specific past navy activities. The Center has an international arena group, including a particularly strong analytical capability on East Asia, an area of obvious interest to the Navy. It also runs many conferences and publishes research studies. The Center is nonpartisan but is not a not-for-profit think thank.

Institute for Defense Analyses
Website: www.ida.org

Run by retired senior military commanders, such as Combatant Commander Admiral Dennis C. Blair (2003–2006) and former Air Force Chief of Staff General Larry Welch, the Institute for Defense Analyses (IDA) has been involved in national security since its founding by former Defense Secretary James Forrestal in an earlier incarnation in 1947. The organization had ties to the Massachusetts Institute of Technology in the 1950s and opened as the Institute for Defense Analyses in 1958. The IDA works in three FFRDCs and in the widest array of national security concerns, studying the current and future questions at the center of the public policy debate. The studies are on technical issues, most often at the classified level, or on policy questions.

RAND Corporation
Website: www.rand.org

The RAND Corporation is probably the best known FFRDC in the country. Created in the late 1940s as a think tank for the newly created Department of the Air Force, the Research and Development Corporation (RAND) became involved in national security studies in the early years of the Cold War. Sixty years later, RAND still proudly notes its role in the cutting-edge analysis of a wide array of public policy questions ranging from drug abuse and health care coverage to military readiness, nuclear weapons, and China's role in Taiwan. RAND has a much more diverse field of study than security but security remains a primary focus. RAND has nine specific research divisions, including national security, which subdivides into acquisition and technology policy; forces and resources; intelligence policy; international security and defense policy; and international programs. The research divisions all produce a mammoth number of traditional and online publications. Additionally, much of RAND's work is contracted by the federal and state governments, and a portion of it is classified. RAND's work in national security is absolutely crucial and is often the benchmark by which policies are measured. RAND also operates two offices overseas, in Germany and Qatar.

Federal Institutions

This section is shorter than the not-for-profit section as many of these organization have other responsibilities besides security.

Air University
Website: www.au.af.mil/

The Air University is the center of the Air Force professional military education system. Begun in 1946, the Air University educates senior Air Force officers and noncommissioned officers about the use of airpower and space power in national security strategy at myriad military education facilities. Its work includes producing studies on national security. Each of the courses is designed to produce higher-quality air officers for national service and subsequent work beyond government service.

Central Intelligence Agency
Website: www.cia.gov

The Central Intelligence Agency (CIA) grew from the World War II organization called the Office of Special Services, a euphemism for a spy and associated action repository. The CIA resulted from the Defense Reform Act of 1947, which also created the Air Force and substituted the Department of Defense for the Department of War. The Agency's goals are to provide timely, solid resources about the plans and activities of U.S. adversaries, engage in covert action to promote national interests, and provide useful analysis to policymakers at the highest level of the U.S. government as well as in those areas where Agency personnel participate in public policy debate. Few portions of the U.S. government have evoked as much distress and suspicion as the CIA, particularly when intelligence failures occur, but its role remains important as intelligence in the post-9/11 world is more highly desired than ever. The overwhelming majority of the CIA's work is classified but it offers public assessments of its studies at various times. The Agency has long been the senior agency in the intelligence community but now the director of National Intelligence oversees all of the community after September 11.

Department of Defense
Website: www.defenselink.mil

The Pentagon, a vast complex on the banks of the Potomac River in Virginia overlooking the nation's capital, employs thousands of uniformed and civilian employees under the Department of Defense (DoD). The DoD resulted from the 1947 Department of Defense Reorganization, which also established the CIA and the Air Force. The DoD has a staggering list of divisions and activities, ranging from defending U.S. citizens overseas to waging war against terrorists around the world. The DoD, under the secretary of defense, operates the vast security community that is in uniformed service for the United States; other security organizations, such as Homeland Security, also operate in the nation. The DoD's organization is a challenge for all administrations because it is such a large but vital bureaucracy. One of the biggest changes in the post–Cold War era is the privatizing of defense as the U.S. government sought to cut back on spending and use private-sector efficiencies. As a result, in the Iraq conflict, for example, the DoD has combat and support troops in Iraq but it also pays contractors to accomplish many support missions.

Federal Bureau of Investigation
Website: www.fbi.gov

The Federal Bureau of Investigation (FBI) is the law enforcement agency charged with protecting the nation against national security threats that can be stopped through using the law. Its job is to protect the country against national security threats as well as common crime. The Bureau headquarters are in Washington, but it also has fifty-six field officers in other cities and maintains connections with civilian law enforcement and international bureaus. In recent years, the FBI has been the brunt of some concern as people have raised questions about intelligence failures in the lead up to the September 11, 2001, terrorist attacks as well as the FBI's role in domestic spying and infringing on domestic civil rights as it administers the provisions of the Patriot Act. The FBI has made a determined effort to maintain its overall goals in a rapidly changing security context.

Government Accountability Office
E-mail: webmaster@gao.gov
Website: www.gao.gov

Known as the government watchdog, the agency started as the General Accounting Office, but in July 2004, it became the Government Accountability Office (GAO). The GAO is the investigative arm of the legislature. Established as a result of the Budget and Accounting Act of 1921, the GAO is Congress's tool for checking the executive branch's operations. The GAO has the reputation and responsibility of being an independent, nonpartisan source of analysis that can conduct management or financial audits. The comptroller serves a single, fifteen-year term to ensure independence. The GAO audits any expenditures Congress authorizes and conducts mandated audits of various programs as well as audits requested by Congress. A significant portion of the GAO's work focuses on national security and/or defense issues. The GAO conducts its audits and then presents its findings as oral testimony and reports; all of the unclassified versions appear in open sources. The GAO maintains an extensive website with its publications.

Industrial College of the Armed Forces
Website: www.ndu.edu/icaf

The Industrial College of the Armed Forces (ICAF) is the federal institution that addresses how the United States would provide the resources for fighting its conflicts. Recently, it added the specific task of studying strategic acquisition within the context of the national security community. The ICAF, located at historic Fort Lesley J. McNair in southwest Washington DC, dates to the aftermath of World War I when the United States discovered it had several major logistical difficulties in providing the resources required in the European theater during World War I. The reforms that followed the conflict in the interwar period included a much greater emphasis on asking the military's logistics corps to ascertain how to get a comprehensive, strategic vision of the best way to provide adequate supplies and resources. The Army Industrial College, as it was originally known, began this process and made connections with one of the major industrialists of the twentieth century, Bernard Baruch. In the 1930s, a young Army officer, Dwight Eisenhower, served on the faculty as he learned about the logistical matters that would become so crucial to his work in Europe two decades later. The Industrial College took on its present, "joint" mission at the conclusion of World War II when generals George C. Marshall and Eisenhower decided to act on the lessons they had learned during World War II. In the 1940s, the Industrial College of the Armed Forces emerged from the Army Industrial College with a mission of educating logistics specialists from across the armed services and civilian sector of the government. The Industrial College joined the National Defense University at the latter's creation in 1976. The Industrial College educates students at the strategic level and is a senior service college in the professional U.S. military education system. It operates an accredited ten-month master's degree program in national resource strategy. In the 1990s, the Industrial College broadened some of its activities by adding civilians from the private sector as well as civilians from other nations to complement the military officers who first joined the ICAF classes in the mid-1980s at the invitation of the various chairmen of the Joint Chiefs of Staff. Army General John Vessey graduated from the Industrial College before his accession to the position of chairman of the Joint Chiefs of Staff in the 1980s.

Marine Corps University
Website: www.mcu.usmc.mil

The Marine Corps University (MCU) is located at Quantico Marine Base south of the nation's capital. The MCU has several components that provide the foundational courses in the Marine Corps' professional military education program. These include degree programs at the Marine War College, Marine Command and Staff College, and School of Advanced Warfighting, as well as schools such as the Lejeune Leadership Institute, the Expeditionary Warfare School, and others. Small in number of students and faculty, MCU teaches its students to grasp how the Marine Corps operates as an instrument of the military tool of statecraft and offers Marines the opportunity to understand how to better use statecraft in conjunction with its fellow military services. Curricula concentrate on leadership within the Corps and other institutions, as well as the operational and war-fighting aspects of the current environment. The MCU has several component parts designed to meet the needs of Marines who come to Quantico at various stages in their professional careers needing new skills and educational opportunities. The University also hosts a fascinating Marine Corps Center on Small Wars, which ponders lessons learned about the evolving world in which the United States seeks security.

National Defense University
Website: www.ndu.edu

Predated by several of its component parts, the National Defense University (NDU) began during the Gerald R. Ford administration (1974–1977) as the umbrella organization for the National War College and the Industrial College of the Armed Forces. Today, the NDU also includes the Institute for National Strategic Studies, the Information Resource Management College, the Center for Technology and National Security Strategy, the North

Atlantic Treaty Organization Staff College, the School of National Security Executive Education, and several other smaller parts. NDU is in the process of transitioning from teaching, researching, and providing outreach in the field of national defense to doing the same in the area of national security under provisions being discussed in 2007. Headed by a three-star officer with a State Department ambassador as the senior vice president, the NDU has become an integral part of the professional military education system and a crucial aspect of U.S. engagement with other militaries and civilian security officials globally. The NDU Press publishes the chairman of the Joint Chief of Staff's journal, *Joint Force Quarterly*, which ponders readiness, jointness, and the evolution of the world around us.

National War College
Website: www.ndu.edu/nwc

Created at the behest of generals Dwight D. Eisenhower and George C. Marshall, among others, the National War College (NWC) educates the future leaders of national security—policymakers, civilians, and military—of the United States and invited states abroad. The institution began in 1946 as the national military leadership evaluated the lessons of World War II. Marshall and Eisenhower, among others, hoped that the nation would enhance national security by promoting better discussion across the military community and between civilians and armed forces personnel, foretelling the advent of the term "jointness" enshrined in the Goldwater-Nichols Military Reorganization Act forty years later. The NWC encompasses relatively equal portions of the Sea Services (Navy, Marine Corps, and Coast Guard), Air Force, and Army, and a quarter of the students and faculty are from the civilian parts of the U.S. government that have a national security focus. From the beginning, the State Department has also been a partner in the enterprise. The NWC offers a ten-month master's degree in national security strategy and teaches students to analyze and prepare national security strategy. Students take a common core curriculum constituting 70 percent of their experience, then select a region to study for the entire year and four elective courses. Students at the NWC take oral examinations twice a year. Graduates of the NWC include former chairman of the Joint Chiefs of Staff General and Secretary of State Colin L. Powell; former Ambassador J. Stapleton Roy; Admiral William "Fox"

Fallen, combatant commander of the Central Command; General Michael "Buzz" Moseley, Air Force chief of staff; lieutenant generals Peter W. Chiarelli, USA, and Martin Dempsey, USA, both important figures in post-Saddam Iraq; and Marine Corps general and recent chairman of the Joint Chiefs of Staff Peter Pace. Its purpose is to educate leaders but it also studies and critiques the current national security strategy, trends at work in the global arena, and obstacles to conducting an integrated approach to providing security to the nation. Roughly three dozen international officers attend each annual class for a year. The NWC offers students the opportunity to learn how to think but is careful not to push any particular idea of what to think.

Naval War College
Website: www.nwc.navy.mil

The Naval War College (NWC), located in Newport, Rhode Island, has a distinguished history as an institution of vision for the Navy. Founded in the 1880s, the NWC has had one extraordinarily famous faculty member, Arthur Thayer Mahan, who remains the most famous naval strategist in U.S. history. The NWC is proud of its war-gaming capability, which prepared the Navy for the arduous campaign against the Japanese in the Pacific theater during World War II. The NWC hosts its students, heavily Marine and Navy in composition, for a ten-month master's degree program. It also has an extensive research facility and world-class faculty studying maritime issues, including potential threats from maritime forces such as the Chinese or Russians.

U.S. Army War College
Website: www.carlisle.army.mil

The U.S. Army War College (USAWC) started in the first decade of the twentieth century as part of the reforms set into motion by War Secretary Elihu Root, who saw changes in the international system and the U.S. role in that system because of its growing power. The USAWC originally operated in Washington DC but moved to Carlisle Barracks during World War II. The USAWC focus is on ground forces and ground power for the U.S. national security establishment. It offers a ten-month master's degree program as well as a number of highly regarded activities, such as the Peacekeeping Institute, which studies the lessons learned from various peacekeeping operations where the United States has operated in the past twenty years. The Strategic Studies Institute at the USAWC was also fundamental in creating new strategies and reconsidering current strategies of how to fight wars in the post-9/11 environment, specifically in Iraq. The Strategic Studies Institute publishes a wealth of short papers under different series, such as the *LaTort Papers*, on military issues ranging beyond just those of the ground forces. It also publishes the highly prized *Parameters*, a quarterly journal. USAWC graduates include generals Barry McCaffrey and Norman Schwarzkopf, key commanders of the first Gulf War.

8

Resources

I n many ways, this is the most challenging chapter in this volume because it ranges so broadly across literature, media, and new formats for exchanging information and opinion. Not only do these media proliferate almost daily but the output of various sources appears on topics and up-to-date publications. The creativity allowed by the emerging personal technologies is making resources available almost instantaneously. Examples of this since the first edition of *U. S. National Security* in 2001 include weblogs ("blogs"), podcasts, and webcasts, among other media.

At the same time, the resources cannot be simply thrown open for each and every thing to be listed. The chapter lists the major works in the fields of research and reporting about national security. It also explores the new media that are making an impact on public policy discussion and creating impressions. Government reports appear as a sample because the federal government issues innumerable studies almost daily. Finally, in the section on broadcast media, the list gives the names of various websites of major organizations covered in this volume.

One of the most important aspects of understanding national security is to have access to a range of materials that I prefer labeling "resources." Traditionally, the majority of items would have been listed under "Articles and Chapters," which I list together because of their length, and monographs or edited volumes (again, length leads to grouping together). This topic has a wealth of offerings in these areas, as would be expected.

Resources available electronically—whether through broadcast media or on the World Wide Web—are increasingly central to our research and reference concerns. As has been true for a decade, radio and television outlets have proliferated with the rise of cable systems around the country. An effect is that the researcher may find these resources through multiple entry points for the same material. One might use the organization's website for the overall work of the institution or one might look through a search engine such as www.google.com. In using the engine, the researcher may look for a broad category, a specific term, or the type of work the organization engages in, just to name a few methods. The effect on this chapter is an imprecise categorization of material when they are electronic. Some may appear as reports or through the particular website but this is to show the various options as much as for any other reason.

Added to this volume has been the new category "weblog," Internet-based publications on a website created by an author to proliferate his or her views while also providing an interactive method by which the reader can respond on a topic. While blogs are highly subjective and have little, if any, editorial intervention on content, they are increasingly important mechanisms for sharing views across the world, outside of the traditional methods such as voting or polling. Blogs based on field experiences, such as those of soldiers or sailors who have been deployed in a particular theater in a conflict, provide important personal insights. Finally, I have also included professional reading lists of several major institutions and individuals in the national security field.

Books that are aimed at a large commercial audience are often also available in audio format, albeit usually somewhat abridged in length and content. While I do not highlight that aspect in a separate category, I recommend that individuals interested in finding commercially successful titles look at commercial book sites such as amazon.com or bn.com for the availability of audio copies of these titles. The category of audio books is growing rapidly.

I have selected materials with a humble grasp of the enormous volume of the materials on U.S. national security. I have chosen those focused as directly as possible on national security, not on the broad issues of foreign policy.

Print Resources

Articles and Special Issues of a Single Journal

Aylwyn-Foster, Nigel. "Changing the Army for Counter-Insurgency Operations." *Military Review*, November-December 2005: 2–15.

In this startlingly candid article, a senior British Army officer reflects upon what he saw in the initial months of coalition operations in Iraq. It illustrates the U.S. military's long-term need to learn counterinsurgency techniques in the face of more likely scenarios.

Bacevich, Andrew. "Warrior Politics." *The Atlantic*, May 2007: 25–26.

This short but pointed piece argues that the recent turn of events that has a small portion of the military advocating against the war in Iraq is not a good turn because it moves away from the traditional nonpartisanship of the armed forces.

Barno, David. "Challenges in Fighting a Global Insurgency." *Parameters*, 36, No. 2 (2006): 15–29.

Insurgency has appeared again in the studies of the U.S. armed forces as the wars in Iraq and Afghanistan prove that military superiority does not guarantee easy victory.

Cook, Martin. "The Proper Role of Professional Military Advice in Contemporary Uses of Force." *Parameters*, 32, No. 4 (2002): 21–33.

One portion of national security for the United States is the civil-military balance that Cook addresses.

Dowd, Alan. "A Different Course? The United States and Europe in the 21st Century." *Parameters*, 34, No. 3 (2004): 61–74.

It has long been assumed that the United States will stay in step with its major partners in Europe, but Dowd casts doubts on this premise because of shifting interests on both sides of the Atlantic.

Flavin, William. "Planning for Conflict Termination and Post-Conflict Success." *Parameters*, 33, No. 3 (2003): 95–112.

With an increasing emphasis on interventions in conflicts in poorly governed environments, understanding how to terminate a war in a place far away becomes more important to avoid replicating the problems of Vietnam.

Gray, Colin. "How Has War Changed since the End of the Cold War?" *Parameters*, 35, No. 1 (2005): 14–26.

Gray is one of the foremost scholars on the theory and conduct of national security today. This is his assessment of the past generation of changes.

Gray, Colin. "Thinking Asymmetrically in Times of Terror." *Parameters*, 32, No. 1 (2002): 5–14.

Gray, one of the great contemporary strategists in the West, ponders what options are available to a state in the post-9/11 environment.

Henry, Ryan. "Defense Transformation and the 2005 Quadrennial Defense Review." *Parameters*, 35, No. 4 (2005): 5–15.

A senior Pentagon official comments on the role of transformation some four years into the global war on terrorism.

Hooker, R. D. "Beyond *Vom Kriege*: The Character and Conduct of Modern War." *Parameters*, 35, No. 2 (2005): 4–17.

Baron Karl von Clausewitz's work remains one of few strategic assessments of what a state faces in waging warfare, even two centuries after he wrote it.

Kibble, David. "The Attacks of 9/11: Evidence of a Clash of Religions?" *Parameters*, 32, No. 3 (2002): 34–45.

Samuel Huntington's "clash of civilizations" argument in the 1990s led some in 2001 to wonder if the true clash was between religions.

Lewis, Anthony. "Bush and the Lesser Evil." *New York Review of Books*, May 27, 2004.

Lewis, a columnist for the *New York Times*, questions the balance between national security and civil rights and liberties. This theme has arisen repeatedly in the post-9/11 era as the Bush administration has found it necessary to curtail basic rights to protect against terrorism.

"The Long War: A Dedicated Issue." Special Issue. *Third World Quarterly*, **Winter 2007.**

This dedicated issue has about two dozen assessments of the problem of the long war against terrorism, subversion, and challenges to world stability, especially for the United States.

Maloney, Sean. "Afghanistan Four Years On: An Assessment." *Parameters*, **35, No. 3 (2005): 21–32.**

The almost uniform view in the United States that Afghanistan's Taliban regime allowed terrorism to flourish makes it crucial to evaluate how this state is progressing.

O'Hanlon, Michael. "The Need to Increase the Size of the Deployable Army." *Parameters*, **34, No. 3 (2004): 4–17.**

O'Hanlon of the Brookings Institution considers the need to have a greater number of troops to meet the requirements the new warfare is imposing.

Pratt, Robert. "Invasive Threats to the American Homeland." *Parameters*, **34, No. 1 (2004): 44–61.**

Even after the 2001 attacks, some people prefer to believe in the inviolability of the homeland, which Pratt thinks is a bad analysis.

Record, Jeffrey. "The Bush Doctrine and War with Iraq." *Parameters*, **33, No. 1 (2003): 4–21.**

The question of whether Iraq fits into the ideas President George W. Bush set forth in his 2002 speech at West Point requires a reconsideration of the positive and negative aspects of going to war in this manner.

Record, Jeffrey. "Why the Strong Lose." *Parameters*, **35, No. 4 (2005): 16–31.**

Record is a professor at the Air War College, where he has often raised questions that made people uncomfortable as he does here. His questions include why the United States has done poorly in counterinsurgency operations while being more successful against larger adversaries such as the Soviet Union, as well as questioning the role of political will in these conflicts.

Schnaubelt, Christopher. "After the Fight: Interagency Operations." *Parameters*, 35, No. 4 (2005): 47–61.

One of the hardest lessons of the Iraq experience has been the reality that the interagency battles for rebuilding, governance building, and stability requirements are often as difficult as the actual conflict.

Skelton, Ike. "The Constitutional Role of Congress: Lessons in Unpreparedness." *Military Review*, July-August 1997: 1–15.

The Missouri congressman comments on congressional responsibilities and rights in national security operations.

Skelton, Ike, and Jim Cooper. "You're Not from Here, Are You?" *Joint Force Quarterly*, Spring 2004: 12–16.

One of the most common criticisms of U.S. forces in Iraq and Afghanistan has been that the troops in theater have inadequate cultural awareness. The Missouri congressman and his coauthor argue that this military preparedness—in education, situational awareness, and Middle Eastern culture, as examples—must be systematically improved upon.

Smith, Paul. "Transnational Terrorism and the Al Qaeda Model: Confronting New Realities." *Parameters*, 32, No. 2 (2002): 33–46.

In the months after the 9/11 attacks, many different views of what the al Qaeda model told us about world terrorism appeared, such as Smith's.

Snider, Don. "Jointness, Defense Transformation, and the Need for a New Joint Warfare Profession." *Parameters*, 33, No. 3 (2003): 17–30.

Much of the discussion after 9/11 has centered on the type of profession the armed forces should be along with its educational requirements. Snider, a retired Army officer, has long studied the effects of poor "jointness" as it affects things like professional military education and military professionalism.

Tomes, Robert. "Relearning Counterinsurgency Warfare." *Parameters*, **34, No. 1 (2004): 16–28.**

Some argue that the Army tried to forget counterinsurgency after the end of the war in Southeast Asia in the 1970s. Tomes discusses the lessons and overall analysis that must be reconsidered from that earlier conflict.

Wester, Franklin Eric. "Preemption and Just War: Considering the Case of Iraq." *Parameters*, **34, No. 4 (2004): 20–39.**

The Bush doctrine of "preemption" remains a major aspect of studying the war on terrorism and the new millennium. The military has always been aware of the importance of a "just war" tradition as this article explains.

Books and Monographs

Ballard, John. *Fighting for Fallujah.* **Westport, CT: Praeger Security International, 2006.**

The Marines had a tough battle in Fallujah, which Ballard recounts in detail. The book describes the challenges and overarching concerns many see in Iraq and speculates about future nontraditional conflicts for the post-9/11, globalized world.

Bamford, James. *Body of Secrets: Anatomy of the Ultra-Secret National Security Agency.* **New York: Anchor, 2002.**

Perhaps the least known of the major intelligence agencies, the National Security Agency concerns itself with signals intelligence. Bamford has written extensively about its role in protecting national security.

Boot, Max. *The Savage Wars of Peace: Small Wars and the Rise of American Power.* **New York: Basic Books, 2003.**

Boot is a scholar at the Council on Foreign Relations, where he strongly advocates the use of U.S. military power for appropriate missions, dispelling traditional arguments that the United States is isolationist in nature and prefers to project its power to protect its security.

Brzezinski, Zbigniew. *Second Chance: Three Presidents and the Crisis of American Superpower.* **New York: Basic Books, 2007.**

President Jimmy Carter's national security adviser argues forcefully against the George W. Bush administration's moves in most of the world. He is less critical of other administrations but not entirely. He believes the situation can be turned around but cannot continue as is.

Cohen, Eliot A. *Supreme Command: Soldiers, Statesmen, and Leadership in Wartime.* **New York: Anchor, 2003.**

Cohen is a scholar at the Johns Hopkins University Foreign Policy Institute in Washington DC, but his respect within the fields of practitioners and scholars ranges far beyond the nation's capital. Cohen is a strategist and high-level thinker who applies his analysis to national security leadership. In this volume he looks at how statesmen Abraham Lincoln, Georges Clemenceau, Winston Churchill, and David Ben-Gurion interacted with their military in times of war.

Cordesman, Anthony. *Salvaging American Defense: The Challenge of Strategic Overreach.* **Westport, CT: Praeger Security International, 2007.**

One of the most respected analysts of national security affairs considers what the options will be for the national security community in light of the Iraq experience.

Darmer, M. Katherine, Robert Baird, and Stuart Rosenbaum. *Civil Rights versus National Security in a Post-9/11 World.* **Amherst, NY: Prometheus Books, 2004.**

The growing discussion of whether national security is more important than civil rights and liberties is the focus of this book, coming in the aftermath of 9/11 and the global war on terrorism.

DeYoung, Karen. *Soldier: The Life of Colin Powell.* **New York: Knopf, 2006.**

A *Washington Post* reporter studies Powell's life before and during public service with heavy emphasis on his service as chairman of the Joint Chiefs of Staff (1989–1993) and as secretary of state at the beginning of the war against Iraq.

Durch, William J. *Twenty-First Century Peace Operations.* **Washington DC: U.S. Institute for Peace, 2006.**

The U.S. Institute for Peace, in conjunction with the Henry Stimson Center, discusses the experiences of peace operators in trying to establish national security around the world, specifically in Afghanistan, Bosnia and Herzegovina, East Timor, Sierra Leone, the Democratic Republic of the Congo, and Kosovo.

Dycus, Stephen, Arthur Berney, William Banks, and Peter Raven-Hansen. *National Security Law.* **New York: Aspen, 2006.**

This book takes a standard legal approach, including case studies, to various U.S. national security involvements in places like Colombia and Afghanistan.

Fair, C. Christine, and Peter Chalk. *Fortifying Pakistan: The Role of U.S. Internal Security Assistance.* **Washington DC: U.S. Institute for Peace, 2006.**

Few, if any, states are more important than Pakistan in trying to implement national security for the United States. President Musharraf's need for foreign help is emblematic of the danger posed by fragile states, especially with volatile fractures in their societies, but the United States will provide it willingly and repeatedly.

Fallows, James. *Blind into Bughdad: America's War in Iraq.* **New York: Random House, 2006.**

Fallows, the national correspondent for the *Atlantic Monthly,* wrote several extensive essays in his magazine in the months preceding and during the war's unfolding in Iraq. They pull together in a haunting manner to show that the United States had evidence available of many of the problems that have subsequently appeared in country.

Fisher, Louis. *In the Name of National Security: Unchecked Presidential Power and the Reynolds Case.* **Lawrence: University of Kansas Press, 2006.**

Fisher is a long-time scholar at the Congressional Research Service. He goes back to the 1953 *U.S. v. Reynolds* case about presidential power to ignore the separation of powers in considering President Bush's approach to the post-9/11 world.

Fisk, William. *The Great War for Civilisation: The Conquest for the Middle East.* **New York: Vintage, 2006.**

Fisk, who has been writing about Middle Eastern affairs for British publications for more than thirty years, offers a scathing critique of why U.S. desires to enhance national security in the region are futile and counterproductive. Painful to read at times, it offers a more comprehensive view of the region than is provided by many U.S. sources over the same period instead of focusing on a series of isolated events.

Flynn, Stephen. *The Edge of Disaster: Rebuilding a Resilient Nation.* **New York: Random House, 2007.**

Flynn, a former Coast Guard officer with extensive interagency experience, argues that our focus on the national security threat is not properly placed on situations outside the United States, and that we need focus on domestic threats, such as natural disasters or an avian flu outbreak. Flynn is one of a number of specialists fearing that domestic concerns have disproportionately taken a back seat to our homeland security threats from overseas.

Fouskas, Vassilis, and Błent Gökay, *The New American Imperalism: Bush's War on Terror and Blood for Oil.* **Westport, CT: Praeger Security International, 2005.**

A review of the effects on the international system by having a single superpower—the United States—and how it affects the way the United States approaches the global war on terrorism in the Middle East.

Franks, Tommy R. *American Soldier.* **New York: HarperCollins, 2004.**

The autobiography of the commanding general at Central Command through the invasions of Afghanistan and Iraq illustrates the wide array of national security conditions that have changed since the end of the Cold War in 1989.

Garrett, Laurie. *The Coming Plague: Newly Emerging Diseases in a World Out of Balance.* **London: Penguin, 1995.**

This most respected author on health threats around the world wades into the national security implications of disease in the globalized world.

George, Roger, and Robert D. Kline, eds. *Intelligence and the National Security Strategist: Enduring Issues and Challenges.* **London: Rowman & Littleman, 2005.**

This long-term analyst and former professor at the National War College offers a solid set of essays on the bureaucratic and operational issues confronting the intelligence community as the complications of national security expand.

Gerstein, Daniel. *Securing America's Future: National Security in the Information Age.* **Westport, CT: Praeger Security International, 2005.**

Gerstein, an Army officer, discusses the importance of the information tools available to the United States in the current national security environment. Many scholars believe the truly greatest threat to the United States is the ubiquitous nature of information in the current world. Examples include taking steps to protect the computer systems of the military and remainder of the government as well as ensuring the fidelity of the banking system.

Gordon, Michael, and Bernard Trainor. *Cobra II: The Inside Story of the Invasion and Occupation of Iraq.* **New York: Pantheon, 2006.**

Gordon is the foremost *New York Times* reporter on national security and military affairs, and his coauthor is a retired Marine Corps lieutenant general. Their work illustrates the many risks and adverse events that can occur when a superpower invades another state.

Kagan, Robert. *Dangerous Nation.* **New York: Knopf, 2006.**

Kagan is a scholar at the Carnegie Endowment for International Peace and is often touted, by both his critics and supporters, as a major architect of the decision to remold the Middle East through Saddam Hussein's ouster. This book is a critique of how

U.S. interests changed along with the nation's growing prowess and capacity of the past 200 years. An advocate of U.S. leadership in the world, Kagan offers a sobering view of the effects of that power.

LeMay, Michael. *Immigration and National Security*. **Westport, CT: Praeger Security International, 2006.**

The debate about immigration is taking a more central role in public policy over this decade. Its role in national security is the focus of this volume's appraisal of current and future developments.

Lord, Carnes. *Losing Hearts and Minds: Public Diplomacy and Strategic Influence in the Age of Terror*. **Westport, CT: Praeger Security International, 2006.**

A long-term analyst at the Naval War College considers how U.S. approaches to potential allies or adversaries around the world affect our security.

Mueller, John. *Overblown: How Politicians and the Terrorism Industry Inflate National Security Threats, and Why We Believe Them*. **New York: Free Press, 2006.**

As the initial shock of the September 11 terrorist attacks has worn off, a small number of books such as Mueller's have appeared questioning how widespread and real the threat is versus the costs the nation is asked to bear in combating such a threat.

Murtha, John. *From Vietnam to Iraq: On the Front Lines of National Security*. **2nd ed. State College: Pennsylvania State University Press, 2006.**

Congressman Murtha's strong criticism of President Bush's Iraq policy ignited a firestorm in 2005 and may have contributed to the Democrats' victory in the 2006 congressional elections. His own experience as a Marine in Vietnam helped form his views. He recounts that experience and the more than thirty years he spent in Congress.

Perry, John. *Torture: Religious Ethics and National Security*. **Boston: Novalis, 2005.**

The revelations about Abu Ghraib and questions about other interrogation facilities during the global war on terrorism have raised considerable debate about the ethics and morality of using torture, even for the sake of national security. Perry explores this overwhelming concern.

Powell, Colin L., with Joseph Persico. *My American Journey.* **New York: Ballantine Books, 2003.**

Written after he retired as chairman of the Joint Chiefs of Staff and as he was pondering a presidential run, General Colin Powell describes the national security challenges he faced in a variety of positions over his military career.

Priest, Dana. *The Mission: Waging War and Keeping Peace with America's Military.* **New York: W. W. Norton, 2004.**

Priest writes for the *Washington Post,* where she has covered a number of major security stories. This appraisal of the role of the military in missions beyond traditional warfare shows the methods the United States takes to achieve security.

Raddatz, Martha. *The Long Road Home: A Story of War and Family.* **New York: Putnam, 2007.**

The White House correspondent for ABC News also spends much time reporting on the war in Iraq. This recounting and consideration of the Sadr City campaigns in Baghdad tries to get at the personal experience for the Army men and women waging war there.

Ricks, Thomas. *Fiasco: The American Military Adventure in Iraq.* **New York: Penguin Press, 2006.**

Long a nationally respected military correspondent, Ricks considered the lessons, mistakes, and misassumptions about the Iraq campaign in its initial stages and the activities of the first three years. It is a powerful criticism of the war in Iraq.

Schlesinger, James, and John Deutch. *National Security Consequences of Oil Dependency: Report of an Independent Task Force.* **New York: Council on Foreign Relations, 2007.**

This special report on oil dependency, a topic President Bush recognized in his 2006 State of the Union message, has become one of the most worrisome for many in the national security community.

Snow, Donald. *National Security for a New Era*. 2nd ed. London: Longman, 2006.

The author, long a scholar of national security affairs, contemplates the role that globalization plays in the approach to national security today, especially after the 2001 attacks and years' involvement in Iraq and Afghanistan.

Tenet, George. *At the Center of the Storm: My Years at the CIA*. New York: HarperCollins, 2007.

Released to significant controversy over its timing and contents, the former CIA director makes serious charges about the process the George W. Bush administration followed in deciding to go to war in Iraq in 2003. Tenet won the National Medal of Freedom but believes himself the victim of political retribution as the war drags into its fourth year.

Watson, Cynthia. *U.S. Military Service*. Santa Barbara, CA: ABC-CLIO, 2007.

This book discusses the role of national service, especially military service, in national security and national life. It emphasizes the current climate in the aftermath of greater U.S. involvement around the world after 9/11.

Watson, Cynthia. *National Security*. Santa Barbara, CA: ABC-CLIO, 2002.

Written prior to 9/11, the first edition of this volume shows a considerably different interpretation of the world, as views of national security have changed significantly in the last six years since its publication. The first was mainly concerned with the challenges of the post–Cold War world as states and organizations sought to regain their understanding of the global system, in contrast to the current edition, which focuses on the period where Iraq and global terrorism are paramount.

Watson, Cynthia. *Stability, Security, Reconstruction and Transition Operations*. Westport, CT: Praeger Security International, 2007.

The issues facing the national security community increasingly include things beyond traditional conflict. This makes preparation much harder than before.

Wright, Lawrence. *The Looming Tower: Al-Qaeda and the Road to 9/11.* New York: Knopf, 2006.

A carefully detailed discussion of the trends that led to the individuals who became the heart of the mujahideen in Afghanistan, then al Qaeda. It has a superb explanation of the environment in which the members operate as well as a portion on the bureaucratic limits on U.S. responses to the threats.

Zinni, Tony. *The Battle for Peace.* London: Palgrave McMillan, 2006.

The former Central Command leader and long-serving Marine comments on the ways he would enhance national security in a way that is quite different from the current administration's choices.

Reports

Human Security Centre. *Human Security Report 2005 War and Peace in the Twenty-First Century.* New York: Oxford University Press, 2005.

The beginning page of the report, commissioned for Canadian and European scholars, notes that the "traditional goal of 'national security' has been defending the state against foreign threats while human security defends the individual." This is a different view but has the possibility of taking the field into another direction.

National Security Council. *The National Security Strategy of the United States of America.* Washington DC: U.S. Government Printing Office, 2002. 35 pp. (available online at www.whitehouse.gov/nsc/nss.html).

This strategy was the initial one following the 9/11 attacks, thus has a substantially greater sense of urgency and concern about addressing the terrorist threat than had been seen earlier.

National Security Council. *The National Security Strategy of the United States of America.* Washington DC: U.S. Government Printing Office, 2006. 54 pp. (available at www.whitehouse.gov/nsc/nss/2006).

Five years into the global war on terrorism, this strategy is more refined in its assessment of the threats but more detailed in the steps necessary to accomplish it.

U.S. Government Accountability Office. "Stabilizing Iraq: Preliminary Observations on Budget and Management Challenges of Iraq's Security Ministries." Washington DC: U.S. Government Printing Office, 2007.

This is one of a series of many U.S. government analyses of the evolving situation in Iraq. This particular report contains testimony before Congress on the needs of Iraq's crucial public security areas.

In addition to the specific reports above, *The Council on Foreign Relations*, being one of the most prolific and well-staffed research institutions in the nation, publishes a range of reports at its website, www.cfr.org. Some examples include the following:

Hills, Carla, and Dennis C. Blair. *U.S.-China Relations: An Affirmative Agenda, A Responsible Course.* Task Force Report No. 59, April 2007 (also available in hard copy from Council on Foreign Relations Press).
Larson, Alan, and David Marchick. "Foreign Investment and National Security: Getting the Balance Right." July 25, 2006.
Levi, Michael, and Charles Ferguson. "U.S.-India Nuclear Cooperation." Special Report, June 20, 2006.

Nonprint Resources

Think-Tank Websites and Products

Think-tank publications are crucial to the resource base on national security. This section highlights the websites for these groups and highlights the subject matter they publish.

Such resources are virtually unlimited because some organizations, such as the **American Enterprise Institute** (www.aie.org) or the **Project for the New American Century** (www.newamericancentury.org/), hold multiple events daily, a significant portion of which are national security events. This listing offers a sample of the events one can find, increasingly available as webcasts online.

The organization **GlobalSecurity.org** (www.globalsecurity.org) operates primarily on the Internet and through public appearances, providing one of the strongest databases and explanatory websites on various national security topics. It is run by John Pike, a long-time public-sector monitor of national military technologies in space, and it offers a wide range of considerations, including the technological challenges offered by other states around the world such as the People's Republic of China or India.

Similarly, the **Federation of American Scientists**, a not-for-profit of scientists interested in security issues, maintains an active database on its website at www.fas.org.

The **Global Chicago Center of the Chicago Council on Global Affairs** maintains a detailed website (www.globalchicago .org/about/website.asp) with hyperlinks to organizations associated with national security across the nation.

The **Heritage Foundation** maintains a website at www .NationalSecurity.org that offers blogs, studies, opinions, and policy statements. The regular Heritage website is www.heritage.org; it too has links to many national security thoughts, studies, and reports.

The **Atlantic Council** (www.acus.org) has a range of policy briefs on questions of pressing interest to those studying national security, including such studies as "Russia's Shrinking Population and the Russian Military's HIV/AIDS Problem," "China's Rise and U.S. Influence in Asia: A Report form the Region," and "Whither the European Union?"

The **Center for Defense Information** (www.cdi.org) publishes a raft of topics in a variety of formats. Perhaps its most venerable work is *The Defense Monitor*, which considers about two dozen broad topics in national security. The Center also puts out a range of reports and maintains blogs.

One of the more innovative sets of views appears from **Foreign Policy in Focus** (www.fpif.org), a website produced through the International Relations Center in conjunction with the Institute for Policy Studies. Some of the more recent publications on its site include "Reconstructing Iraq," "Anti-Americanism or Strategic Communication," "China: What's the Big Mystery?" and "Wrangling over Arms Sales to China."

Timely reports on topics of interest to U.S. national security students include the **International Crisis Group**, whose work appears at www.icg.org. The organization produces a weekly report, *Crisis Watch*, which maintains an ongoing assessment of the state of affairs in the places of turmoil around the world. The Center's website also indicates special concerns about known conflict zones including Darfur, Iran and its nuclear program, the Congo conflict, Zimbabwe, Afghanistan, and the role of Islam and violence. Finally, the website also publishes more immediate assessments on military coups or other key changes in a nation, as occurred with the September 2006 coup ousting Thai Prime Minister Thaksin. With its truly global ties, many of the assessments offer a completely different view than that on a topic held in the United States.

The New America Foundation maintains an extensive website at www.naf.org with a range of domestic and foreign issues.

Blogs

The most significant change to the public debate over the past five years has been the proliferation of blogs, a site maintained by an author or "blogger" who posts on a subject of interest to him or her. The website may contain text, pictures, or other material available to anyone who accesses that particular URL but also offers the opportunity for readers to respond to the views or material posted by the blogger. There is absolutely no control over the quality or accuracy of the material on any blog.

Blogs are so common that maintaining an up-to-date listing is almost impossible but the **Internet Public Library** site (www .ipl.org), maintained at Drexel University, is a good starting point . Additionally, http://About.com, Wikipedia.com, and Deepblog .com are useful starting points.

Many think tanks maintain blogs for their scholars as exemplified at a couple of organizations. **The Heritage Foundation** (www.heritage.org) maintains an active blog on national security as do a number of other organizations and individuals.

The Center for Defense Information (www.cdi.org) has links to blogs on several topics in the national security field. These include a range of opinions in various regional programs the Center follows, such as the Middle East. Blog entries on the Middle East include "UN Security Council Responds Again to Iranian Nuclear Crisis" (March 30, 2007), "East of the Middle East: The Shanghai Cooperative Organization and Security Implications" (December 21, 2006), and "The Perfect Storm: International Reaction to the Bush National Space Policy" (March 27, 2007). The blogs appear in a range of more than thirty programs.

Many blogs advocate extending the commitment of U.S. forces abroad (in Iraq and elsewhere) while many others push to withdraw U.S. forces. The number of examples are almost limitless because the process of creating blogs is open to virtually anyone with an Internet connection. The blog American Ranger discusses the downside of war but notes that leaving the United

States vulnerable to terrorists in Iraq would be worse, shown at http://americanranger.blogspot.com . The blog at http://alternet .org is a liberal blog advocating movement out of Iraq and criticizing the Congress for not doing so.

Blogs will be especially prominent in the 2008 general election, as they offer an opportunity to access an exceptional number of people with no intervening voices.

Blogs can address the broadest national security concerns within a single site such as **Blogs of War** (http://blogsofwar.com), which has hyperlinks to opinions on several topics such as Afghanistan, China, Europe, intelligence, Iran, Iraq, Islam, Israel, Lebanon, the military, North Korea, Syria, terrorism, and Venezuela.

Some of the most frequently visited types of blogs are those that discuss the experiences U.S. forces face in their deployments around the world. The blog **AmericanSoldier.com** (www .soldierlife.com) is an example, as is **Army Girl** (www.desert phoenix.blogspot.com); and another (http://bootsinbaghdad .blogspot.com) discusses deployments in Iraq while offering a wide set of hyperlinks to other websites and blogs.

Radio and Television

Literally thousands of outlets cover the national security field in the broadcast media on national security but several outlets specialize in a relatively systematic study of national security issues. Another innovation available from virtually all media today is the podcast, digitized files that maintain transcripts from media that can be replayed. Http://www.podcast.net is a relatively accessible source of podcasts that appear in radio, television, or through a think tank or another organization. The best method of tracking down podcasts, however, is to check the individual website of an organization to see about podcast availability.

The television and radio outlets below merit emphasis in the national security field and have exposure to audiences around the nation, not isolated to single cities or markets. Included in this chapter are programs that offer at least a modicum of both conservative and liberal views either in a particular show or in a pro and con format on a topic over a period of time.

Conservative Talk Radio: Rush Limbaugh
Over the past twenty years, "talk radio" has been called the purview of those advertising conservative political positions.

Probably best known has been Rush Limbaugh, who appears in markets across the country on radio. Limbaugh's prior shows up to four weeks earlier, including stories on national security concerns, are available at http://www.rushlimbaugh.com/archives. Limbaugh has had shows on terrorism, national security strategy, and al Qaeda. Limbaugh often examines security from a liberal-conservative axis.

Other commentators and hosts air in local markets across the nation.

C-Span

This is an amazing effort that began nearly three decades ago and runs 24 hours daily year round on public policy issues. Much of the C-Span programming is national security in nature, a portion of which can be purchased at the C-Span store on the website. Http://inside.C-spanarchives.org gives an archival listing of various C-Span programming, including national security.

"Brian Lamb interviews Eliot Cohen on Iraq," originally aired July 21, 2005.
"Foreign Policy Realists and Idealists with former Secretary of State James A. Baker," originally aired February 27, 2007.
Stephen Flynn, "The Edge of Disaster: Rebuilding a Resilient Nation," aired April 8, 2007.
"Bomb Scare with Joseph Cirincione and Dafna Linzer," originally aired March 9, 2007.
"U.S.–Latin American Relations with Peter Hakim and Roger Noriega," March 11, 2007.

Five services that C-Span provides—"Booknotes" (and "Booknotes Encore"), "After Words," "In Depth," "History," and "Public Lives"—are shows surveying new books and earlier books where an interviewer has an extended conversation with the author on his or her topic or philosophy, or interviews prominent figures who are at the center of public attention at the time.

Grandin, Greg, "Empire's Workshop: Latin America, the United States, and the New Imperialism," aired on March 10, 2007.
Lance, Peter, "Triple Cross: How Bin Laden's Master Spy Penetrated the CIA, the Green Berets, and the FBI—and How Patrick Fitzgerald Failed to Stop Him," aired on March 11, 2007.

"Bernard Lewis delivering the AEI Irving Kristol Lecture 2007," aired March 10, 2007.

Padma Desai, *Conversations on Russia: Reform from Yeltsin to Putin*, aired February 17, 2007.

The NewsHour with Jim Lehrer

The *NewsHour with Jim Lehrer* has been a staple on the Corporation of Public Broadcasting's Public Broadcasting System for decades. Originally a two-man effort under Robin McNeill and Jim Lehrer, the latter inherited the effort upon McNeill's retirement. It brings interviews and special reports on topics of interest from at home and abroad and covers national security issues on an almost daily basis. The NewsHour also maintains reports online (www.pbs.org/newshour), and is updated quickly to achieve relevance.

The website has a marvelous range of national security topics. One can browse based on the region or topic of interest. Along with an extensive archive access back to 1996, the site features podcasts and RSS feeds. This list is only a small number of items that the NewsHour has covered in recent years. Some are in-depth reports available online while others are reports aired on television.

"Climate Change Report," April 6, 2007.
"Tracking Nuclear Proliferation," March 26, 2007.
"President Bush Seeks Patience as Iraq War Enters 5th Year," March 20, 2007.
"Verifying and Monitoring States," May 5, 2006.
"Heart of Darkness," May 11, 2004.
"Missile Defense," December 16, 2003.
"Dangerous Cargo," December 11, 2002.
"Fighting War," November 25, 2002.
"Deadly Incident," July 2, 2002.
"Artillery Battle," June 19, 2002.
"Photo Fallout," May 5, 2002.
"Newsmaker: Condoleezza Rice," March 11, 2002.
"Prisoners of War," January 22, 2002.

Network News

The three major U.S. networks also maintain news commitments to national security. The networks multiply their output of news by loading many reports on their websites. These are available at

www.ABCNews.com, www.CBSnews.com, and www.NBCnews
.com. Many of their stories focus on national security.

British Broadcasting Corporation
The BBC has the most wide-ranging foreign reporting in the world,
in the majority of cases reporters speak the languages of the region,
including obscure languages such as Pashtun or various dialects
in Arabic. This gives them a wealth of information about parts of
the world that far too few in the United States ever consider yet
U.S. national security may depend on. Two premier BBC radio
broadcasts available from many stations are "BBC Newshour"
and "World Update," which cover many U.S. national security
topics. Similarly, the BBC also has extensive television coverage
that appears in the United States on "BBC America," which is
available in many cable outlets across the nation.

The BBC has an active website that covers many national
security concerns. It is accessible in English, Spanish, Arabic, and
other languages at www.bbcnews.org. There is also an amazing
array of resources available on radio on national security. These
are live broadcasts that can be "streamed" online on computer or
heard on traditional radio formats.

National Public Radio
National Public Radio (NPR) stations transmit to local networks
from sites across the nation, although some major markets such
as Los Angeles or New York have multiple NPR affiliates. Many
of these affiliates use only National Public Radio–created stories
for the national market but some of the affiliates broadcast their
own shows through a franchising system across the nation. Several of the shows have considerable national security content and
are highlighted below.

"To the Point" appears from KCRW Public Radio in Los
Angeles and Public Radio International with Warren Olney as
the show's host. The show's website is www.kcrw.com/news/
programs/tp, which includes descriptions of various shows as well
as the ability to hear them online. A sample of its national security
shows, shown on the www.kcrw.com/archive website, include

"Diplomacy and the Promises of Democracy in the Middle East,"
      March 28, 2007.
"New Controversy over the So-Called Israel Lobby," March 26,
      2007.

"All Eyes on Congress as House Votes on War Funding Bill,"
March 23, 2007.
"The U.S. and India: Nuclear Power and Atomic Weapons,"
December 13, 2006.
"When is National Security News Unfit to Print?," June 30, 2006.
"Civil Liberties, National Security, and Domestic Surveillance,"
December 19, 2005.
"John Bolton, Politics, and Iraq Intel," May 11, 2005.
"America and Islam, Four Years Later," March 19, 2007.
"9/11 Commission Report Urgent Action Needed," July 22,
2004.
"The CIA, the White House, and American Security," November
16, 2004.
"American Preparations for Shock and Awe in Iraq," March 18,
2003.
"Missile Defense," May 2, 2001.

"On Point with Tom Ashbrook" broadcasts from WGBH in
Boston to discuss current activities in a range of fields, including
national security. Its website is www.onpointradio.org and several of its relevant programs include

"Tom Ricks on How Progress is Going in Iraq Several Months
after Publishing *Fiasco*," aired update April 2, 2007.
"Showdown between Presidents Chávez Frías and Bush," aired
March 8, 2007.
"Terror Threat Overblown," aired March 5, 2007.
"North Korea's Nuclear Test," aired October 10, 2006.
"'Islamo-Fascism'," aired September 6, 2006.
"*The Looming Tower* with Lawrence Wright," aired September 5,
2006.
"Strategizing a Solution in the Middle East," aired August 31,
2006.
"Sarah Chayes on Afghanistan," aired August 26, 2006.
"Russia and the United States," aired July 17, 2006.
"The *Pentagon Papers* Thirty-Five Years Later," aired June 13,
2006.
"Seymour Hersh and Target Iran," aired April 11, 2006.
"Solutions to Global Warming Crisis," aired March 30, 2006.

"The Diane Rehm Show" is from WAMU in Washington DC.
The complete archive of the show is available on the station's

website at www.wamu.org/programs/dr. A partial listing of topics she has covered in recent years includes

"Climate Change and Security," March 21, 2007.
"President Bush in Latin America," March 8, 2007.
"U.S. Policy on Iraq," February 29, 2007.
"U.S.-Russia," February 22, 2007.
"U.S. Role in Security in the Middle East," February 19, 2007.
"North Korea and diplomacy," February 15, 2007.
"Presidential Powers in Time of War," February 1, 2007.
"Congressional Oversight on Iraq," January 9, 2007.
"Guantánamo Bay Interrogations," January 18, 2007.
"Iraq Study Group," December 7, 2006.
"Dialogue with Syria and Iran," November 21, 2006.
"North Korea and Nuclear Weapons," October 18, 2006.
"National Intelligence Estimate on Iraq," September 28, 2006.
"Military Commissions," September 14, 2006.
"September 11th Five Years Later," September 11, 2006.
"Middle East and U.N. diplomacy," August 14, 2006.
"Cuba," originally aired August 2, 2006.
"Lebanon," July 26, 2006.
"Middle East Crisis," July 20, 2006.
"Global War on Terrorism and External Power," July 12, 2006.
"Israel's Influence," June 21, 2006.
"Global Politics of Oil," June 15, 2006.
"Africa," June 20, 2006
"National Investigations of Haditha Deaths," June 1, 2006.
"National Security Agency and Domestic Phone Records," May 17, 2006.
"Hu Jintao's Visit," April 20, 2006.
"Iran and Nuclear Weapons," April 13, 2006.
"General James Jones and NATO," March 20, 2006.
"U.S. Strategy in Iraq," March 14, 2006.
"Congressman John Murtha and War Debate," February 13, 2006.
"Palestinian elections," January 26, 2006.
"Iran," January 19, 2006.
"Canada's Elections," January 24, 2006.
"Weapons of Mass Destruction in Iraq," June 27, 2004.

DVD, Video, Film, and Other Visual Media

"Letter to America; How Arabs View the United States," (2001) 45 minutes. An orginial BBC broadcast, available in DVD and VHS from Films for Humanities & Sciences. Phone: 800/257-5126 or www.films.com ($129.95).

"NAFTA and the New Economic Frontier: Life Along the U.S./ Mexico Border," (2001) 23 minutes. Available in DVD and VHS from Films for Humanities & Sciences. Phone: 800/257-5126 or www.films.com ($89.95).

"9/11 through Saudi Eyes," (2002) 53 minutes. Available in DVD and VHS from Films for Humanities & Sciences. Phone: 800/257-5126 or www.films.com ($149.95).

"Powerplay: End of an Empire," (no date) 50 minutes. Available in DVD and VHS from Films for Humanities & Sciences. Phone: 800/257-5126 or www.films.com ($149.95).

"The Battle for Islam," an original BBCW production. (2005) 63 minutes. Available in DVD and VHS from Films for Humanities & Sciences. Phone: 800/257-5126 or www.films.com ($149.95).

"Thomas L. Friedman Reporting: Does Europe Hate Us?," A Discovery Channel Production (2005) 45 minutes. Available in DVD and VHS from Films for Humanities & Sciences. Phone: 800/257-5126 or www.films.com ($149.95).

"Waging War against the New Terrorism," (2002) 23 minutes. Available in DVD and VHS from Films for Humanities & Sciences. Phone: 800/257-5126 or www.films.com ($89.95).

"Why the Hate? America, from a Muslim Point of View," (2001) 44 minutes. Available in DVD and VHS from Films for Humanities & Sciences. Phone: 800/257-5126 or www.films.com ($149.95).

"China on the Rise: Paul Solman Reports," (2007) 77 minutes. Item 35882 available in VHS, DVD and DVD/Computer Rom from Films for Humanities & Sciences. Phone: 800/257-5126 or www.films.com ($159.95).

"Frontline: Return of the Taliban," (2006) 60 minutes. Available for online viewing at www.pbs.org/wgbh//pages/frontline/ taliban/view or available for purchase at www.shoppbs.org/ product/index.jsp?productID=2477755 for $29.95 in VHS or DVD.

Reading Lists

The national security reading lists here are highly visible within the government professional organizations. Any university course on national security would have a reading list for a particular semester or year but the lists here are often provided to civilian agency personnel or uniformed military as they ponder their work in national security. The authors regularly update their lists.

Congressman Ike Skelton, Democrat, 4th District, Missouri, Professional Reading List

www.house.gov/skelton/book_list.pdf
Congressman Skelton has had a keen interest in national security issues for virtually his entire career. His is an influential voice in national security and military affairs.

Chairman of the Joint Chiefs of Staff Reading List

www.au.af.mil/au/awc/awcgate/jcs/reading-list.htm
The chairman of the Joint Chiefs of Staff is the highest statutory officer in the chain of command from the lowest enlistee to the president of the United States. His views can be highly influential in national security affairs.

National Defense University President's Reading List

www.ndu.edu/Library/ReadingList/NDUPReading.pdf
The National Defense University (NDU) prides itself on being the chairman of the Joint Chiefs of Staff's personal school for advancing professional military education. The readings cited by any NDU president are bound to become considered classics.

U.S. Army Chief of Staff's Professional Reading List

www.army.mil/cmh-pg/reference/CSAList/CSAList.htm
The chief of staff of the Army is the senior Army officer. As such, he guides the future of the ground forces and their concerns. His orientation has a greater emphasis on ground operations by nature of the threat posed to his forces.

U.S. Navy Professional Reading List

www.navyreading.navy.mil
The Navy as a service often accentuates the importance of being "at sea with the fleet," which is a hands-on orientation, but the

chief of naval operations and Navy bureaucracy increasingly also appreciate "book learning" in their efforts to modernize into the new millennium. Topics emphasize maritime operations, new technologies at sea, and other sea issues.

U.S. Marine Corps Reading List
https://www.marcent.usmc.mil/nipr/NIPR_Web_Reading_List.xls
The Marine Corps highly values education of its Corps. The readings noted here will be discussed and remembered by the finest of Marine Corps officers. The Marine emphasis is on amphibious operations and its links to the sea services.

Chief of Staff of the Air Force Reading List
www.af.mil/library/csafreading
This list offers an overall approach to air operations, missile concerns, and anti-missile works. The Air Force also puts a high premium on the use of technology in its education as do the other services.

U.S. Coast Guard Commandant's Reading List
http://www.uscg.mil/LEADERSHIP/lead/reading.htm
The Coast Guard is now part of the Department of Homeland Security and is an increasingly important part of the nation's national security community. The Coast Guard concentrates on border issues, coastal defense, and ties with other Coast Guard equivalent agencies around the world.

Industrial College of the Armed Forces Reading List
www.ndu.edu/info/icaf_reading_list.cfm
The Industrial College of the Armed Forces is the premier institution for considering the resource requirements to wage war and provide for peace. Their readings concentrate on acquisition, strategic resources, strategic leadership, and the links between military and civilian defense contractors.

Joint Forces Staff College Reading List
www.jfsc.ndu.edu/current_students/documents_policies/documents/ reading_list/default.asp
The Joint Forces Staff College studies the operational aspects of jointness within the United States. Its mission includes preparing junior officers for operating at the theater level and to work in Joint assignments at the operational level.

Glossary

In addition to the terms listed in the text, this glossary includes a number of terms crucial to understanding national security.

Africa Command The newest unified geographic command to operate for U.S. interests in Africa

AIDS acquired immunodeficiency syndrome

AQI al Qaeda in Iraq, the term for al Qaeda groups operating specifically in Iraq

AWOL Absent without leave

baathists Members of the Baath Party who were arguably strongly behind the anti-U.S. insurgency in post–Saddam Hussein Iraq in hopes of regaining political power

bird flu avian influenza

C3I Command, Control, Communications and Intelligence

C4ISR Command, Control, Communications, Computers, Intelligence, Surveillance, and Reconnaisance

CentCom U.S. Central Command, headquartered in Tampa; it is responsibile for the U.S. interests in the theater from Kazakhstan and Pakistan westward to Kenya and Somalia

CJCS chairman of the Joint Chiefs of Staff

combatant command A joint military command composed of two or more services

counterinsurgency operations Activities falling into the categories of civil-military operations, combat operations, and information operations that are aimed at thwarting all aspects of rebels' moves to weaken a national regime

crystal meth   A form of methamphetamines

cyberterrorism   Terrorism that occurs online or across the Internet

deployable army   The portion of the armed forces available to be sent for a task away from their bases of operations

deployments   Assignments, generally away from their bases or posts, that military officers take when assigned a certain ordered task

DHS   Department of Homeland Security

DNI   Director of National Intelligence

DoD   Department of Defense

DoS   Department of State

ECP   entry control point, a checkpoint for a closed area in a military theater

EFPs   explosive force penetrators; weapons being used in Iraq that the Bush administration believes are being supplied by Iran to further confound the conditions in Iraq

EUCOM   U.S. European Command, the theater charged with interests in Europe

exceptionalism   The idea that the United States operates with different values or mores in its interactions with other states or as a comment on its historic experience

Four Modernizations   The modernization priorities set forth by the Communist Party of China, initially by Zhou Enlai in 1973 but also by Deng Xiaoping in 1978, to lead China toward the major modernization and economic growth characterizing emergent China today; these modernizations, in order of priority, are agriculture, industry, science and technology, and the military

Geneva Conventions   Four conventions and three protocols forming the basis of international humanitarian law through their widely respected use since the 1860s, although they were substantially rewritten in 1949

glasnost   The term Soviet President Mikhail Gorbachev used for his gradual opening of the political and economic system

globalization   A historical process that has led to a much greater integration of economies and states around world, with much more immediate effects on all economies involved

Golden Triangle   The region of northern Burma, Thailand, and Laos that supplies much of the heroin in the world

governance building   The moves to help a state strengthen its capability to govern effectively

global war on terrorism   President Bush's term for the fight against al Qaeda and associated groups in the international system

H1N1 virus   The current strain of avian influenza making its way around the globe, arousing fears of a pandemic flu

Hamas   The largest and arguably most significant political movement in the Palestinian territories; it won a significant portion of the 2006 election but the United States, Israel, and the European Union see it as a violent organization; thus, it is not a negotiating partner

HIV   human immunodeficiency virus

IEDs   improvised explosive devices, roadside bombs; these have been particularly devastating in Iraq

insurgency   An organized action using subversion and antigovernment armed conflict to undermine a regime

Islamists   The term for those Islamic adherents who want to return to a much more traditional, orthodox Islam of the prior millennium, often associated with Wahhabism of Saudi Arabia

ISR   intelligence, surveillance, and reconnaissance

JCS   Joint Chiefs of Staff

jihadists   Those fighting against non-Islamic civilizations as they find advocated in the Koran

just war theory   A long-standing philosophical test, dating to St. Thomas Aquinas, of how, when, and why states wage war

Kurds   A Sunni Islamic population that is stateless and spread across Iraq, Turkey, Syria, Iran, and a few other states; the Kurds do not want to be part of the post–Saddam Hussein Iraq

LOC   lines of communication in a military threater

long war   The term for the prolonged anticipated conflict in the Middle East and elsewhere against terrorism and in trying to provide democratic stability in Iraq

Manhattan Project The Roosevelt administration's effort to win the race to build an atomic weapon. Named after the borough of Manhattan, it operated in many laboratories across the nation but the final stages were concentrated in a secret compound in New Mexico. The Project's work culminated in the first atomic blast on July 16, 1945

methamphetamines Highly addictive, artificially created drugs that have resulted in a national epidemic; also called meth

MFN most favored nation, a trading condition granted between partners

MNF multinational forces, the coalitions formed as in Iraq to address a broad-ranging threat around the world

mujahideen The Islamic fighters in Afghanistan who waged an insurgency against Soviet invaders in the 1980s, receiving help from the Central Intelligence Agency and Osama bin Laden in their efforts

NAFTA The North American Free Trade Agreement, signed by Mexico, the United States, and Canada, went into effect in 1994; it promotes free trade between the partners

nation building The activities, conducted by militaries or civilians, intended to create a stronger state, including humanitarian assistance, conflict resolution, peacekeeping, and institution building

National Guard The men and women who sign up on behalf of defending their states as generations past signed up for their state militias, which the Guard replaced in 1903 under the Dick Act

National Reserve The men and women who sign up to be a "waiting" force for deployment in a national security scenario, as is occurring regularly to the Guard and Reserve officers in today's force with multiple deployments to Iraq and Afghanistan

neoconservatives People who often were former leftists (including former Communists), who have moved to the political right, often advocating stronger defense spending; this group is believed to be the prime movers toward war against Iraq, such as former Department of Defense officials Paul Wolfowitz, Douglas Feith, and Richard Perle, as well as writers William Kristol and Robert Kagan.

NGO nongovernmental organization

NorthCom U.S. Northern Command, which encompasses U.S. national interests in the homeland and Canada

NSA National Security Agency, which monitors signals intelligence for the United States

NSS The National Security Strategy of the United States

PACOM U.S. Pacific Command, which is responsible for the U.S. national security issues of the Pacific basin westward to India

perestroika The term President Mikhail Gorbachev used for the restructuring of Soviet society, working hand in hand with glasnost

PLA People's Liberation Army of China

PLO Palestine Liberation Organization

POTUS president of the United States

PRC People's Republic of China

preemption The doctrine stressed, if not introduced, by President George W. Bush to authorize the United States to attack possible adversaries before attacks on the United States or its assets

ROE rules of engagement, the rules governing the military's use of force

RPG rocket-propelled grenade

SARS severe acute respiratory syndrome

SecDef Secretary of Defense

SecState Secretary of State

sharia Islamic law, based on the Koran, that Islamic believers would have govern human behavior

Shiites The minority sect of Islam that is largely associated with Iran, Iraq, and eastern Saudi Arabia; this sect believes Mohammed's son-in-law, Ali, was the legitimate inheritor of the power of Islam

SOCOM U.S. Special Operations Command

SOUTHCOM U.S. Southern Command, responsible for Latin American interests of the United States

Sunnis The larger branch of Islam, which is spread throughout the world except for Iran, Iraq, and small pockets around the world

splittism   The Chinese term for independence advocacy in Taiwan

surge   President George W. Bush's strategy to send a higher concentration of troops into Baghdad for a brief period to stabilize the situation and give time to the Iraqi government to gain credibility

UAV   unmanned aerial vehicle

Vietnam syndrome   The fear that the U.S. military will be drawn into another unwinnable conflict overseas

weapons of mass destruction   (WMD) weapons that can kill large numbers of people in a single strike; these generally include weapons from nuclear, radiological, biological, or chemical sources

Index

About the Author

Cynthia Watson is chair of the department of Security Studies and has taught at the National War College since 1992, having also been associate dean and director of the Electives Program. Currently, Dr. Watson teaches courses on China, east Asia, and the politics of humiliation. Her previous works include *National Security* (2002), *Nation-Building* (2004), and *U.S. Military Service* (2006), all published by ABC-CLIO. She has also published *Military Education* (2006) under the Praeger Security International Series. Dr. Watson is a popular speaker and serves on the boards of a number of professional societies.